HOMOSEXUALITY IN HISTORY AND THE SCRIPTURES

Some Historical and Biblical Perspectives on Homosexuality

Ronald M. Springett

Biblical Research Institute
General Conference of Seventh-day Adventists
Washington, DC 20012

Copyright © 1988 by the
Biblical Research Institute
6840 Eastern Avenue, NW
Washington, DC 20012

Printed in the U.S.A. by the
Review and Herald
Hagerstown, MD

Acknowledgements

Texts credited to NEB are taken from the New English Bible (©) The Delegates of the Oxford University Press and the Syndics of the Cambridge University Press, 1961, 1970. Used by permission.
Texts credited to NIV are from The New International Version. Copyright (©) 1978 by New York International Bible Society. Used by permission of Zondervan Publishing House.
The Scripture quotations marked RSV are from the Revised Standard Version Bible, copyright 1946, 1952, 1971 by the Division of Christian Education of the National Council of the Churches of Christ in the USA, and are used by permission.

Abbreviations

AB	*Anchor Bible*
ANET	*Ancient Near Eastern Texts*
Ant.	*Antiquities*
ATR	*Anglican Theological Review*
BSac	*Bibliotheca*
BTB	*Biblical Theology Bulletin*
CBQ	*Catholic Biblical Quarterly*
EncJud	*Encyclopedia judaica*
HTR	*Harvard Theological Review*
IB	*Interpreter's Bible*
IDB	*Interpreter's Dictionary of the Bible*
IDB Supp.	*Interpreter's Dictionary of the Bible, Supplement*
JAAR	*Journal of the American Academy of Religion*
JAOS	*Journal of the American Oriental Society*
BJL	*Journal of Biblical Literature*
JEA	*Journal of Egyptian Archaeology*
JHS	*Journal of Hellenic Studies*
NASB	*New American Standard Bible*

Transliteration of Hebrew and Greek Alphabets

1. Hebrew Alphabet

Consonants

א = ʼ	ו = w	כ = k	ע = ʻ	ר = r
ב = b	ז = z	ל = l	פ = p	שׁ = sh
ג = g	ח = ch	מ = m	פ = ph	שׂ = ś
ד = d	ט = ṭ	נ = n	צ = ṣ	ת = t
ה = h	י = y	ס = s	ק = q	ת = th

Masoretic Vowel Pointings

$n = \text{ָ}$
$o = \text{ֹ}$ ֺ
$i = \text{ִ}$ ֑ ֵ
$ə = \text{ְ}$ ֱ ֲ ֳ ֻ
$a = \text{ַ}$ ֶ ֵ

2. Greek Alphabet

α = a	ζ = z	λ = l	π = p	φ = ph
β = b	η = ē	μ = m	ρ = r	χ = ch
γ = g	θ = th	ν = n	σ = s	ψ = ps
δ = d	ι = i	ξ = x	τ = t	ω = ō
ε = e	κ = k	ο = o	υ = u	ʻ = h

Contents

Acknowledgements iii
Abbreviations iii
Transliteration of Hebrew and Greek Alphabets iv
Preface vii

Chapter 1
What Is Homosexuality? 1
   Definitions of Homosexuality 1
   The Condition Separated From the Act 4
   Homosexuality As Natural 5
   The Psychological Thesis 8
   Homosexuality As a Chosen Sin 10
   What Causes Homosexuality? 13
   The Genetic Thesis 13
   Hormonal Factors 14
   The Prenatal Thesis 15
   Psychosocial Factors 20
   What Do Homosexuals Do? 25

Chapter 2
Old Testament Historical Background 33
   Egypt 34
   Babylon and Assyria 40
   Cult Prostitute 41
   Canaanite and Hittite 46
   Canaanite Practice 47

Chapter 3
The Texts of the Old Testament 49
   The Use of Scripture 49
   The Bible As Opposed to Homosexuality 50
   The Bible As Condoning Homosexuality 51
   Old Testament Texts Cited With Reference to Homosexuality . . . 52
   The Case of Sodom 55

The Mosaic Laws 58
The Idolatry Thesis 60
The Outrage in Gibeah 65
Secondary Old Testament Texts Cited With Reference to
    Homosexuality 69
The Case of Jonathan and David 70
Noah and Ham 74
Ruth and Naomi 78

Chapter 4
New Testament Historical Background—The Classical Setting 83
  Homosexuality in Classical Greece 83
  Lesbianism in Greece 83
  The Development of Pederasty in Classical Greece 87
  Charges of Homosexuality As Political Handicap 89
  Plato and Pederasty 90
  Plato's Defense of Pederasty Versus Sensualism and
    Licentiousness 94
  The Androgynous Myth 97
  Homosexuality in Greek Drama 98

Chapter 5
New Testament Historical Background—The Hellenistic World .. 103
  Pederasty and Prostitution in Later Greek Practice 103
  The Reaction of Hellenistic Judaism 110

Chapter 6
The New Testament and Homosexuality 115
  The Social Background of Early Christianity: Form and
    Context of Anti-homosexual References 115
  Christians and Social Structure 116
  New Testament Vice Lists: Christian and Non-Christian 118
  Primary New Testament Texts Cited With Reference to
    Homosexuality 120
  Natural Versus Unnatural 126
  Meeting the Gnostic Approach 137
  Secondary New Testament Texts and Homosexuality 142

Chapter 7
Conclusions 153
Index of References 165
Index 168

Preface

Many Christians may wonder why a book needs to be written about homosexuality. For years the church considered itself more or less immune from many of the problems experienced in the world outside. As the church grows in numbers, however, these problems begin to appear within.

Increasingly the consciousness of society is being raised concerning social-ethical issues, such as women's rights, battered children, single-parent families, teenage pregnancy, wife beating, and of course, homosexuality. In turn, this frequently causes a corresponding rise of consciousness about these things. At such times they become widely discussed in the church.

Such has been the case with homosexuality. In recent years the church has discovered that among its members are a good number who claim a homosexual orientation. Parents find themselves confronted by a child who says he is homosexual. Children may learn that their father has declared himself homosexual. Sometimes a wife learns that her husband's preference is for another man, and the family is broken up. Great anguish, turmoil and soul searching follow. Some seek to lay blame. Others simply want answers to this seeming riddle.

As "gays" seek in sophisticated ways to justify the homosexual lifestyle, questions naturally arise in the church. Church members, particularly those who have come in contact with homosexuals, look for information and clarification about the subject. Questions rise about the origins of homosexuality, its historical background, and its causes. There is also a keen interest in an understanding of what the Bible has to say on the subject. Recently some, including certain scholars, have claimed that the Scriptures condone a loving homosexual relationship and homosexual marriage. It is not surprising, therefore, that many church members wish to know what the Scriptures have to say on the subject.

This book, we hope, begins to answer some of these questions. It surveys the definitions and causes of homosexuality and traces some of its history in both East and West. It looks briefly at the biblical texts that refer to or are thought to refer to homosexuality and examines the claims made in much of the "gay" literature with reference to these texts. However, not all the texts examined are used to defend prohomophile positions: we look also at others used by overzealous Christians bent on finding condemnation of homosexuality throughout Scripture.

Those who have read much about homosexuality already know that it is a subject plagued by lack of clarity and wide differences of opinion.[1] There is disagreement not merely about what sort of condition it might be but whether it is a pathological, biological, or even a psychological condition at all. Therefore if the church is to gain a clear picture of homosexuals within its organization and how to relate to them, much consideration remains to be done beyond this preliminary study in theology, ethics, psychology, and sociology.

Psychological theories alone pertaining to the etiology of homosexuality fill many volumes. In addition to this, biological arguments concerning genes and hormones are brought to bear on the issue as well as sociological considerations. The vast majority of this material approaches the question of homosexuality from an amoral stance, concerning itself strictly with pathology. Although such literature provides no answers about the morality or immorality of homosexuality, it is an indispensable part of the study. In it we discover that the term "homosexual" covers a number of conditions, situations, and activities that are not morally equivalent. What is referred to as the actual "condition" of homosexuality, sometimes known as inversion, accounts for a small portion of homosexual activity. Some authors suggest that the condition characterized by a desire for same-sex love need not be eroticized at all.

This raises questions about the appropriateness of the term "homosexuality" which, in turn, throws a shadow over the entire debate under the rubric of sex. Even if the subject is to be discussed in such terms, this particular book is written in somewhat of a vacuum since Seventh-day Adventists, in common with many churches, have not developed a theology of sex. A beginning has been made in this direction, however.[2]

Against these uncertainties, however, stand a number of certainties. Among them is the fact that traditionally the Judeo-Christian Scriptures have been interpreted consistently as opposed to homosexual practices until very recent times. At present homosexuality is no longer something hidden from society to be discussed in privacy and never mentioned in polite company. Today it is openly discussed on radio, television, and in

---

1   A useful, though now outdated, bibliography is found in W. B. Parker, *Homosexuality: A Selective Bibliography of Over 3000 Items* (Metuchen, NJ: Scarecrow Press, 1971); see also V. L. Bullough, et al., *An Annotated Bibliography of Homosexuality,* 2 vols. (New York: Garland Publishing, 1976), vol. 22: *Garland Reference Library of Social Science.*
2   See R. Dederen, "Homosexuality: A Biblical Perspective," *Ministry* (September 1981), pp. 14-16; also see S. Kubo, *Theology and Ethics of Sex* (Washington, DC: Review & Herald Publishing Assn., 1980).

literature. In many cases it is advocated as a way of life fully as acceptable as heterosexuality and perhaps superior to it. Homosexual groups often are militant and ally themselves with other social activist groups such as civil rights and women's rights movements. Some see themselves as a political force, and the gay community is subject to ideological pressure as are other minorities in the United States.[3]

Much literature about homosexuality is written along biblical or theological lines. It attempts to reconcile the irreconcilable differences between the Judeo-Christian view and those of the gay liberation groups. Some gays attempt to parallel the Scriptures with suggestions from modern science as various gay rights groups understand them. Some Christians reply by invoking the authority of the Scriptures above all scientific discoveries which seek to define homosexuality. The former view asserts that homosexual acts are legitimate, the latter that they are not. Both views tend to oversimplify homosexuality. To complicate matters further, various views of biblical authority are coupled with varying hermeneutical approaches.

The authors who produce this literature see homosexuality in Scripture from an existentialist point of view, through process theology, biblical liberalism, or biblical conservatism. It also is approached by way of classical Lutheran concepts of original sin and justification, Calvinism, Methodism, Catholicism, and varying combinations of these and other hermeneutical and traditional approaches. Beyond these, other authors present a unique exegesis that distorts both the sense and context of Scripture.

This book, commissioned by the Biblical Research Institute of the General Conference of Seventh-day Adventists, will attempt to look at the question from an Adventist point of view. The Adventist view of biblical authority is set forth briefly in the *Yearbook*. It states:

> The Holy Scriptures, Old and New Testaments, are the written Word of God, given by divine inspiration through holy men of God who spoke and wrote as they were moved by the Holy Spirit. In this Word, God has committed to man the knowledge necessary for salvation. The Holy Scriptures are the infallible revelation of His will. They are the standard of character, the test of experience, the authoritative revealer of doctrines, and the trustworthy record of God's acts in history.[4]

---

3 B. McCubbin, *The Gay Question: A Marxist Appraisal* (New York: World View Publications, 1976).
4 *Seventh-day Adventist Yearbook: 1987* (Hagerstown, MD: Review & Herald Publishing Assn., 1987), p. 5.

Adventists have developed no universally consistent system of interpretation of Scripture. Although Adventist theologians and exegetes have begun to write in this area, no definitive work has yet appeared.[5] It is clear, however, that certain principles of interpretation of the Scriptures are widely held in both conservative Protestant and Adventist circles. Among these are:

1. The Bible is given by divine inspiration and, therefore, has divine authority.
2. The Bible is the foundation for exegesis and hermeneutics.
3. There is a unity throughout the Scriptures.
4. Scripture interprets Scripture.[6]

This study will proceed along these lines in its approach to the Scriptures. Scriptural references will be taken from the Revised Standard Version unless otherwise identified.

While preparing this book, the writer has come in contact with numerous works which appear to attempt a revision of biblical and classical history, ostensibly in defense of gay liberation. The legal rights of gays, however, would be better served if biblical and classical history are left intact.

This study is not intended as a polemic, but a look at some of the claims put forward in prohomophile literature of the last decade or so. These claims are analyzed against the background of the history of homosexuality and a conservative approach to Scripture.

In researching and producing this book, I owe much gratitude to those who have helped me. I am particularly grateful to the interlibrary loan staff of McKee Library at Southern College, Collegedale, Tennessee, and to the library staffs at the National Library of Medicine and the Medical Library at the National Institutes of Health at Bethesda, Maryland, for their courteous and professional assistance. Also, I wish to express a special thank you to Rubye Sue, Carol Smith, Brigitte DiMemmo, Weslynne Sahly, and Melanie Boyd who labored long and patiently with the word processing.

Ronald M. Springett
January 1988

---

5 G. F. Hasel, *Biblical Interpretation Today* (Washington, DC: Biblical Research Institute, 1985).
6 A well-known non-Adventist source is B. Ramm, *Protestant Biblical Interpretation: A Textbook of Hermeneutics for Conservative Protestants* (Boston: W. A. Wilde Co., 1956).

Chapter 1
What Is Homosexuality?

Definitions of Homosexuality

The term "homosexuality" can be used for a wide variety of human experiences. Simple definitions have the disadvantage of distorting the concept by lumping all of them together. The dilemma of producing a concise definition which is not misleading is illustrated by an entry in a current college textbook. Initially a wide definition is given: "Homosexuality refers to sexual activity between same-sex partners."[1] At the end of the paragraph, however, it is followed up by a lengthy qualification.

> Some sexologists regard the homosexual experience as being so diverse, and the psychological, social, and sexual aspects so varied, that to use the words *homosexual* or *homosexuality* to describe anything more than the individual's sexual choice at a particular time is misleading and inexact.[2]

The language in the above quotation is a loose paraphrase of A. Bell from his book, *Homosexualities: A Study of Diversity Among Men and Women*. Bell, a researcher at the Kinsey Institute, would juxtapose the term "homosexualities" over against "heterosexualities" suggesting, it seems, that just as there are various kinds of heterosexuals, so there are various kinds of homosexuals. Malloy maintains that Bell's use of this terminology suggests that only a small proportion of homosexuals are mentally ill, just as a small proportion of heterosexuals are mentally ill. Consequently, most homosexuals, apart from their sexuality, are normal.

Malloy's caveat is well taken. However, he himself admits, "The word 'homosexual' will necessarily refer to a particular person only at some highly generalized level of their existence."[3] Malloy's definition of a

---

1 S. P. McCary, J. L. McCary, *Human Sexuality,* 3rd brief ed. (Belmont, CA: Wadsworth Publishing Co., 1984), p. 246.
2 Ibid.; see also E. Hooker, "Homosexuality," *National Institute of Mental Health Task Force On Homosexuality: Final Report and Background Papers,* ed. J. M. Livingood (Rockville, MD: National Institute of Mental Health, 1972), p. 11.
3 E. A. Malloy, *Homosexuality and the Christian Way of Life* (Lanham, MD: University Press of

homosexual is "person, male or female, who experiences in adult life a steady and nearly exclusive erotic attraction to members of the same sex, and who is indifferent to sexual relations with the opposite sex."[4]

It will be useful here to examine Malloy's definition. It is a more specific and carefully worded definition, of interest as much for what it excludes as for what it includes. First, for Malloy, true homosexuality is limited to "adult life" and to an adult who experiences "a steady and nearly exclusive erotic attraction to members of the same sex." This eliminates homosexuality as a spasmodic phase during adolescence from Malloy's genuine homosexual category. These teenage tendencies may be outgrown in adulthood where heterosexual attraction and activity are pursued exclusively. As Harvey states, "In some instances it may be uncertain whether an adolescent is homosexual, and diagnosis cannot be made before the mid-20s."[5] To label every youth homosexual who has experienced some homosexual activity or who expresses ambiguous homosexual feelings, without further comment, is a drastic mistake. It may accomplish the thing most feared, that is, it may drive them into the homosexual subculture for support, sympathy, and direction.

Another class excluded from genuine homosexuality by Malloy's definition are those who do not experience "a steady and nearly exclusive erotic attraction to members of the same sex." Individuals in this class of homosexuals are those referred to as "contingent homosexuals." They may include teenagers who experiment with homosexuality and outgrow it. Contingent homosexuals may also include adult heterosexuals who become bored with conventional sexual taboos and, seeking variety, go out for a fling in the gay world hoping to accomplish their purpose without fear of scandal.

By far the most numerous in this category, however, are those designated "situational homosexuals."[6] These are men who are thrown together by circumstances and situations who, having no other sexual outlet, resort to homosexual outlets. Men in prisons, military camps, boarding schools, seminaries, and other single-sex environments are most often involved in situational homosexuality. Men in such situations would not consider themselves homosexuals, and they return to heterosexual patterns once they are removed from the restrictive environment. Forced

---

    America, 1981), p. 11.
4 Ibid., pp. 11-12.
5 J. F. Harvey, "Counseling the Apparent Adolescent Homosexual," *Bulletin of the Guild of Catholic Psychiatrists*, vol. 10, No. 4, pp. 204-5; also, J. R. Cavanagh and J. F. Harvey, *Counseling the Homosexual*, (Huntington, IN: Our Sunday Visitor, 1977), p. 188.
6 H. K. Jones, *A Christian Understanding of the Homosexual* (New York: Association Press, 1966), pp. 20-23.

homosexual rape in prisons is more often the expression of a power relationship than sexual identity. It becomes an instrument "for establishing rank and status, validating masculinity, and creating protective-dependent relationships."[7]

The remaining individuals involved in homosexual acts, those who do fit Malloy's precise definition, are frequently referred to in literature as "constitutional homosexuals" or "inverts." Invert is a common term in current parlance. It originally referred to the true homosexual disposition of Malloy's definition, that is, an invert is a person whose sexual feelings are reversed or turned inside out. D. S. Bailey used the word over against "pervert" and thus gave it a moral, ethical significance which it did not have before. A pervert, by his definition, is not a true homosexual but a heterosexual who engages in homosexual practices. An invert, however, is a true homosexual, a constitutional homosexual, someone whose homosexuality is a permanent part of his very constitution and not a transitory phase of life or merely an accommodation to situational pressure. Bailey introduces morality into the picture by claiming that the true invert is not responsible for his/her condition.

> The genuine homosexual condition—or inversion, as it is often termed—is something for which the subject can in no way be held responsible. In itself it is morally neutral.... The pervert is not a genuine homosexual; rather, he is a heterosexual who engages in homosexual practices, or a homosexual who engages in heterosexual practices.[8]

Bailey's theologizing about homosexuality is based upon this distinction. He is followed by numerous authors who presuppose the moral neutrality of the homosexual "condition" as it is sometimes called. Some authors make a distinction between the condition and the practice of homosexuality—the former being morally neutral while the latter is culpable.[9] This distinction seems to be the crux of the whole issue.

---

7 A. Karlen, *Sexuality and Homosexuality: A New View* (New York: W. W. Norton and Co., 1971), pp. 187-88; see also D. J. West, *Homosexuality* (Chicago: Aldine Publishing Co., 1967), pp. 126-27.
8 D. S. Bailey, *Homosexuality and the Western Christian Tradition* (Hamden, CT: Shoe String Press, 1975), p. 38. "Pervert" is a rather harsh term to apply to all non-constitutional homosexuals. To speak of an adolescent who experiments once with homosexuality as a "pervert" is unduly pejorative and not helpful.
9 L. R. Buzzard, "How Gray is Gay?" in *Homosexuality and the Christian Faith: A Symposium*, ed. H. L. Twiss (Valley Forge, PA: Judson Press, 1978), p. 49.

The Condition Separated From the Act

The drawing of a line between the "condition," for which the individual is not responsible, and the homosexual "acts," for which one is responsible, is basically the position adopted by Kubo who makes the distinction between inversion and perversion. He sees the New Testament as dealing with the latter, not with inverts "who do not participate in homosexual practices."[10] Kubo does not see homosexual acts practiced by the invert as morally neutral. Such a person's condition "does not give license to practice homosexual acts, which violate Christian moral standards."[11] Kubo concludes, "The homosexual may not be able to do anything about his attraction for his own sex, but by God's grace he can control his impulses."[12]

Although approaching the subject in a more equivocal manner, Thielicke takes essentially the same position.[13] This view, in which the condition is neutral but the acts are not, gives the homosexual the benefit of the doubt, as it were. The homosexual condition is explained theologically as part of the post-Fall evil of which mankind is heir and which causes numerous physical and mental aberrations for which individual victims are not directly responsible.

In the present situation where certainty about the cause of homosexuality is not possible, this view presumes that the homosexual was not responsible for his condition. That is, he/she did not make a deliberate choice to become a homosexual/lesbian. It does assume however that the homosexual is responsible for any same-sex acts that he/she practices, which are therefore considered immoral. Consequently this view mandates celibacy for the confirmed or constitutional homosexual.

To a large section of the homosexual community, this is rejected as a grossly unfair consequence of their condition. Hatterer sums up the attitude of the homosexual community:

> The majority believe either that they were born as homosexuals or that familial factors operating very early in their lives determined the outcome. In any case, homosexuality is believed

---

10 S. Kubo, *Theology and Ethics of Sex* (Nashville: Southern Publishing Assoc., 1980), p. 75.
11 Ibid., p. 83.
12 Ibid.
13 H. Thielicke, *The Ethics of Sex*, tr. J. W. Doberstein (Greenwood, SC: Attic Press, 1978), pp. 282-83. Thielicke seems to allow that the homosexual who cannot practice abstinence may structure the man-man relationship in an ethically responsible way. But since so many factors work against this, it might be wiser for pastors to counsel sublimation (pp. 284-87). H. K. Jones takes a similarly ambiguous stance which results in the church accepting homosexual acts, though not sanctioning them. Thus homosexuals operate under a different ethic than the church at large and become second class Christians, it seems. (See Jones, pp. 108-10.)

to be a fate over which they have no control and in which they have no choice.[14]

Homosexuality As Natural

The implication is that if the condition is inherent to a certain extent it must be natural to him. Therefore, to fight against the same-sex drive he/she experiences is to fight against nature. Perry expresses himself along these lines, "I'm sure that homosexuality is preordained. I think a lot more work has to be done in this whole field, but I am firmly convinced that much of what we are comes to us through our genes."[15]

It is a short step from homosexuality as a part of nature's plan to homosexuality as a part of God's plan. R. Woods quotes an unnamed homosexual as follows:

> I had no choice in being born gay or hetero; rather, I was given my human nature and "beingness" from the Being of all beings! I sincerely feel that we have to accept what and who we are, and accept it with our hearts—never feeling different from others, but rather as being part of Divine Providence, the Divine Plan.[16]

N. Pittenger constructs his theology on the premise that homosexuality, as a state or habitual orientation, is fully "normal" and "natural" and is a viable moral choice for a Christian.[17] Pittenger defines the homosexual this way:

> The homosexual, then, is one who through no special choice—above all, no special fault—of his own finds that he is sexually drawn to members of his own sex. For him it is entirely "natural" thus to be drawn; that is the way he *is*. . . . If the homosexual *condition*, whatever may be its etiology, is a given fact for homosexual persons about which they can do nothing and about which most of them wish (quite rightly) to do nothing,

---

14 L. J. Hatterer, *Changing Homosexuality in the Male: Treatment for Men Troubled by Homosexuality* (New York: McGraw-Hill Book Co., 1979), p. 13.
15 T. D. Perry, *The Lord is My Shepherd and He Knows I'm Gay* (Los Angeles: Nash Publishing, 1972), p. 10. Perry states that he was introduced to homosexual experiences and culture by two Seventh-day Adventists. (See pp. 23-25, 87, 139.)
16 R. Woods, *Another Kind of Love: Homosexuality and Spirituality* (Chicago: Thomas More Press, 1977), pp. 38-39.
17 N. Pittenger, *Time for Consent: A Christian's Approach to Homosexuality* (London: SCM Press, 1976), pp. 31-32. See also, *Towards a Quaker View of Sex: An Essay by a Group of Friends,* rev. ed. (London: Friends Home Service Committee, 1966), p. 26. Where the homosexual condition is as natural as "left-handedness."

what about the overt expression of this condition in physical sexual acts? Right here there is great disagreement in Christian circles as well as among those who look sympathetically enough at the "condition" but would raise questions about the "acts."[18]

McNeill finds glaring gaps in the biblical material on homosexuality. He debunks the standard theological positions as lacking in comprehensiveness and outdated in contrast to recent scientific research. He summarizes his position:

> Given, as I believe, (1) the uncertainty of clear scriptural prohibition, (2) the questionable basis of the traditional condemnation in moral philosophy and moral theology, (3) the emergence of new data which upset many traditional assumptions and (4) controversies among psychologists and psychiatrists concerning theory, etiology, treatment, and so on, there obviously is a need to open up anew the question of the moral standing of homosexual activity and homosexual relationships for public debate . . . it would appear to follow that the same moral rules apply to homosexual as to heterosexual attitudes and behavior. Those that are responsible, respectful, loving, and truly promotive of the good of both parties are moral, those that are exploitive, irresponsible, disrespectful, or destructive of the true good of either party must be judged immoral.[19]

The underlying suggestions here are that current biblical and theological interpretations of homosexuality are inconclusive. Consequently, there is no ground for denying the basic moral and ethical equality of heterosexual and homosexual relationships. Heterosexuality and homosexuality are therefore of equal worth in the natural order.

These sentiments are echoed by Cory, who says,

> Their action is not only voluntary, but it is the natural calling of their temperaments, as these temperaments have evolved and developed as a result of various environmental conditions. In fact, no other course of action would be natural to them. Nothing would be so unnatural as to thwart and deny themselves.[20]

---

18 N. Pittenger, "The Homosexual Expression of Love," in *Is Gay Good? Ethics, Theology and Homosexuality*, ed. W. D. Oberholtzer (Philadelphia: Westminster Press, 1971), p. 227.
19 J. McNeill, *The Church and the Homosexual* (Kansas City, MO: Sheed, Andrews & McMeel, 1976), pp. 20-21.
20 D. W. Cory, *The Homosexual in America: A Subjective Approach* (New York: Greenberg Publishing, 1951), p. 29; see also, J. Babuscio, *We Speak for Ourselves* (London: SPCK, 1975), pp. 5, 10.

Of course these arguments fly in the face of the conservative Christian view of Scripture. Invoking the authority of Scripture, conservatives view the schema of Genesis as normative for all mankind, with anything contrary to it as "unnatural." Cory himself begs this question with his remark, "However, is it not, many will ask, contrary to nature? It would require a supernatural force to state what nature intended."[21] Of course this is precisely what conservative Christians claim to have in the Bible. They believe that it states what "nature," that is, God, intended.

The views of Buzzard, Kubo, and Thielicke mentioned above are representative of those prevailing in several major church bodies today. But this position is severely criticized again by Nelson on the basis of the naturalness of the homosexual's disposition.

> It holds that while homosexuality as an *orientation* is contrary to God's created intention, the homosexual *person* ought not to be adversely judged or rejected by the church. Often this position carries the acknowledgement that sexual orientation is seldom if ever the result of voluntary choice and that constitutional homosexuality appears largely unsusceptible to psychotherapeutic reorientation. While some people see this as a more tolerant and compassionate view than outright condemnation, it places gay men and lesbians in at least two impossible binds.
>
> One, of course, is the individual's recognition that her or his own sexual orientation is as natural and as fundamental to identity as is the color of the skin. It is both naive and cruel to tell a lesbian or gay man, "Your sexual orientation is still unnatural and a perversion, but this is no judgment upon you as a person." The individual knows otherwise.
>
> The other bind concerns churchly pressure toward celibacy. When the church presumes to be non-judgmental toward orientation but then draws the line against genital expression, it is difficult to understand how the sense of guilt—even in the celibate—will be significantly alleviated.[22]

Nelson finds both intellectual and psychological contradictions in any position which is based on what he refers to as an "outmoded version of natural law" or which seeks to make fine distinctions between orientation and genital expression.[23] Plainly speaking, the nub of the entire debate

---

21 Ibid.
22 J. B. Nelson, "Religious and Moral Issues in Working with Homosexual Clients," in *Homosexuality and Psycho-therapy, a Practitioner's Handbook of Affirmative Models. Journal of Homosexuality* 7, Nos. 2-3, ed. J. C. Gonsiorek, (New York: Haworth Press, 1982): 168-69.
23 Ibid., p. 169.

between homosexuals and conservative churches hangs on this point.

Thought leaders in most churches are willing to concede that some individuals involved in homosexual acts act from a condition. These individuals who are not sexually attracted to females, but who for as long as they can remember have been attracted to males, are inverts through no fault of their own. Many churches, including the Seventh-day Adventist Church, insist however, that homosexual acts are condemned as immoral in Scripture. Therefore, they conclude that the homosexual condition is an aberration due to the Fall of man and not something intended by God, and is to be counteracted and eliminated if at all possible. If this is not possible, the church still finds itself unable to condone homosexual acts because this would countermand the authority of Scripture which condemns them as sin, no matter how strong the temptation might be to participate in them.

Homosexuals reply that Scripture does not condemn loving, wholesome, homosexual relations, but only rape, lust, exploitation, and idolatry—whether heterosexual or homosexual. The homosexual condition and the acts, therefore, are seen by them as natural, even as God given.

So far two definitions of homosexuality have been surveyed. First, that which looks upon the condition as part of the post-Fall evil which is the lot of man and for which he may not be directly responsible. In this view, homosexuality is like diabetes or asthma or allergies, that is, not a part of God's plan for the world. It should be removed if possible; but if not, the people involved are not responsible unless they aggravate the condition.

The second definition states that homosexuality is natural (God given). In this view, it is not like an ailment. Rather, it is suggested, God's plan for sexuality is individualized; some prefer opposite-sex partners, some same-sex partners; both are equally natural and moral.

The Psychological Thesis

In concluding this section, two other definitions must be looked at briefly. The first proposes that homosexuality is a psychosocial maladaptation—a failure in some sense or other to reach psychological maturity. Finally, it is suggested by some that homosexuality is neither a pathological nor a psychological condition, but a series of sinful acts to which a person becomes habituated and of which they need to repent.

The most straightforward spokesman for the thesis that homosexuality is a psychological condition is Bergler. To him it is only "a therapeutically changeable subdivision of neuroses."[24] There is no healthy homosexual:

---

24 E. Bergler, *Homosexuality: Disease or Way of Life?* (New York: Macmillan Publishing Co., 1967), p. 9.

The entire personality structure of the homosexual is pervaded by the unconscious wish to suffer; this wish is gratified by self-created troublemaking. This "injustice-collecting" (technically called psychic masochism) is conveniently deposited in the external difficulties confronting the homosexual.[25]

Homosexuals take flight to men because they fear and hate women, Bergler theorizes.[26] His view of homosexuals is largely negative. By his account they are very sick people trying to claim that they are well.

For Marmor the homosexual is not necessarily neurotic. He sets forth a psychodynamic definition of homosexuality that includes motivational and operational aspects of behavior. He defines the clinical homosexual as "one who is motivated, in adult life, by a definite preferential erotic attraction to members of the same sex and who usually (but not necessarily) engages in overt sexual relations with them."[27] Marmor limits his definition, much as does Malloy, to same-sex desires which grow out of personality needs, not mere situational necessity. The homosexual is the person who preferentially seeks same-sex partners even when alternatives are present. Only these represent genuine homosexuality in motivational terms. Marmor summarizes:

> The clinicians represented in this volume present convincing evidence that homosexuality is a potentially reversible condition. There is little doubt that much of the recent success in the treatment of homosexuals stems from the growing recognition among psychoanalysts that homosexuality is a disorder of adaptation.[28]

Bieber characterizes homosexuality as a disorder of adaptation, the result of hidden but incapacitating fears of the opposite sex. Since the condition is basically an accommodation to unrealistic fears, it is necessarily pathological.[29]

Barnhouse offers a definition much like that of Marmor, "I use the word homosexuality to refer to an adult adaptation characterized by preferential sexual behavior between members of the same sex."[30] The word

---

25 Ibid.
26 Ibid., p. 16.
27 J. Marmor, "Introduction," in *Sexual Inversion: The Multiple Roots of Homosexuality*, ed. J. Marmor (New York: Basic Books, 1965), p. 4. Among the factors leading to the condition Marmor also sees fear of intimate contact with opposite sex (p. 5).
28 Ibid., p. 21.
29 I. Bieber, et. al., *Homosexuality: A Psychoanalytic Study* (New York: Basic Books, 1962), pp. 303-4.
30 R. T. Barnhouse, *Homosexuality: A Symbolic Confusion* (New York: Seabury Press, 1977), p. 22.

"preferential" or even "choice" is used in this school of thought to describe homosexual behavior. Buzzard defines homosexuality as "including both personal choice and psychological damage because of conditions in the home."[31]

Woods concludes, "Sexual orientation is not, however, a function of physiology, gender identification or role characteristics. Sexual preference is learned."[32] Moberly prefers to see homosexuality best defined as one of ambivalence to the same sex. Having assessed the same evidence as Bieber, she concludes that it is hostility to the father that defines the true homosexual, not hatred of the mother or the opposite sex.[33] Her definition is based on this insight:

> From amidst a welter of details, one constant underlying principle suggests itself: that the homosexual—whether man or woman—has suffered from some deficit in the relationship with the parent *of the same sex;* and that there is a corresponding drive to make good this deficit—through the medium of same-sex or "homosexual," relationships.

Moberly continues,

> An attachment to the same sex is not wrong, indeed it is precisely the right thing for meeting same-sex deficits. What is improper is the eroticization of the friendship. Such eroticization is secondary, and not essential to the relationship as such.[34]

Those who see homosexuality as some kind of psychosocial maladaptation usually suggest that it is susceptible to treatment of some kind.

Homosexuality As a Chosen Sin

The final definition to be considered is that homosexuality is simply a sin. Adams claims, "Homosexuality is the way in which some clients have attempted to solve the sexual difficulties of adolescence and later life."[35]

---

31 Buzzard, p. 48.
32 R. Woods, p. 23.
33 E. R. Moberly, *Psychogenesis: The Early Development of Gender Identity* (London: Routledge & Kegan Paul, Ltd., 1983), pp. 39, 44.
34 E. R. Moberly, *Homosexuality: A New Christian Ethic* (Cambridge, MA: James Clarke, 1983), pp. 2, 20.
35 J. E. Adams, *Competent to Counsel* (Phillipsburg, NJ: Presbyterian and Reformed Publishing Co., 1970), p. 36; also, K. Philpott, *The Gay Theology* (Plainfield, NJ: Logos International, 1977), pp. 94-96, 106; ns. P. Boone, *Joy* (Carol Stream, IL: Creation House, 1973), pp. 136-37. A detailed discussion of this view is found in H. Taylor, *The New Legality (PA: Crais Press, 1967), pp. 36-46.*

He perceives such a person as generally having a grossly disturbed view of sex and other interpersonal relations. Since homosexuals have to lead a double life, they carry a heavy load of fear and guilt.[36] Adams claims that his rationale is strictly biblical:

> To call homosexuality a sickness, for example, does not raise the client's hope. But to call homosexuality sin, as the Bible does, is to offer hope. Probably there is no more important factor in the work of helping homosexual sinners. Hope is desperately needed by them as much as anything else. It is essential to counteract every aspect of the hope-destroying medical and/or genetic models of homosexuality.[37]

Adams does not believe that one is a homosexual constitutionally any more than one is an adulterer constitutionally. Therefore, he views homosexuality not as a condition but an act, a sinful practice which has become a way of life. This has important ramifications. The homosexual act is the reason for calling one a homosexual just as the act of adultery is the reason for calling one an adulterer. The homosexual may commit homosexual sins of the heart just as one may commit adultery in his heart. The homosexual may lust after another man as the adulterer lusts after another woman. For Adams the key point is that precisely because homosexuality, like adultery, is an act, it is learned behavior into which men with sinful natures are prone to wander. Homosexuality is a sin that can be forgiven by Christ.[38]

In brief, we have dealt with four definitions of homosexuality:

1. Homosexual inverts or those called conditional, constitutional, essential, or genuine homosexuals have a condition natural to them. This condition or desire for same-sex genital relations is not an aberration due to the Fall of man. It is a variation in sexual preference which is part of nature. Many good, talented, spiritual, and benevolent people share this preference and homosexuals are biologically different. Since the condition is natural to so many, it must be a created variation, that is, God given, God intended.

It is malicious in the extreme to allow heterosexuals to express their natural sexual preferences freely but to forbid homosexuals the right to express their natural preferences freely by involvement in sexual activity. Therefore, the church must be mistaken in its interpretation of Scripture which says that all homosexual acts are sin. What the Scriptures condemn are prostitution, idolatry, exploitation, and violence, whether heterosexual

---

36 Ibid.
37 Ibid., p. 139.
38 Ibid., p. 139, n. 2.

or homosexual; but loving homosexual relationships are not condemned. They are natural to the individuals concerned, a gift from God.

2. Homosexuals are sick. The homosexual condition is a psychosocial maladaptation of some sort. The exact dynamics of the process are not known. It may be due to a deficit in same-sex relations or opposite-sex relations. The motivational factors producing the condition may in fact be subconscious to the individual homosexual, and the tendency for same-sex preference may have begun so early that the homosexual is not aware of having been any different.

No matter how early it ocurred, however, the condition is a learned response and constitutes learned behavior. The behavior and responses can be unlearned; that is, they are susceptible to psychotherapy and other clinical methods of psychiatry. Some homosexuals, particularly those who are unhappy with their sexual orientation, can be "cured."

3. Homosexual acts define a person as a homosexual. There is no such thing as a pathological condition of homosexuality. Homosexual acts are sin no matter how the individual wandered into the habit pattern. It is the act which defines one as a homosexual and which constitutes sin in Scripture. Lustful thoughts or sins of the heart may be heterosexually or homosexually oriented. But, as the adulterer is one who commits adultery, so the homosexual is one who commits homosexual acts. To make it sound as if homosexual acts are inevitable because of some supposed medical condition is to destroy all hope for the homosexual. The only hope is for the homosexual to realize that his acts are sin of which he needs to repent and be forgiven.

4. There may be such a phenomenon as the homosexual condition. That is to say that certain individuals, due to a biological predisposition and/or other psychosocial factors, may be erotically aroused by the same sex rather than the opposite sex. This condition is not "natural" in the sense that it is a part of God's intention for the sexes. Rather, it is an aberration of normal sexuality due to the Fall. Consequently, Scripture condemns all homosexual acts as immoral and unethical behavior. The Christian who is striving to reach the goal set by the new Adam and to restore his life to God's original intent for man cannot accept a homosexual lifestyle as part of that plan. The Bible views such acts as sin.

Of these four definitions, the last comes closest to the thinking of the Seventh-day Adventist Church. The church affirms the heterosexual creation plan for the sexes set forth in Scripture. Yet it realizes that some individuals have unusual difficulties in this area. These individuals are part of God's church and share in His love and concern. The church cares for the individuals although it cannot condone the acts which might arise from their particular type of temptation.

What Causes Homosexuality?

Without advancing claims as a medical authority we review current medical and scientific opinion on the subject to inform the reader about modern theories. Much research on this topic presently is in progress and the views expressed here are subject to revision.

What is the etiology of homosexuality, that is, what causes it? This has been debated for many years without resolution. The great number of etiologies suggested for homosexuality is the best clue to the inconclusive nature of the debate. Hatterer lists about 70 etiological factors for male homosexuality alone.[39] Bieber devotes an entire chapter to a review of possible etiologies.[40] We will not discuss all the possible etiologies of homosexuality here. A very brief survey of salient reports must suffice.

The etiology of homosexuality is divided into three categories in recent literature, namely, genetic factors, hormonal or endocrine influences, and psychosocial elements.

The Genetic Thesis

The theory that hereditary—genetic or chromosomal factors—cause homosexuality has been proposed by some researchers. It has been suggested that Klinefelters syndrome, characterized by possession of an additional female chromosome, may predispose some individuals to homosexuality. Based on this assumption some have argued that homosexuals are females in male bodies.[41] Lang's research has come under considerable scrutiny and been found inconclusive. West surveys the material and summarizes, "One may safely conclude that the presently recognized sex chromosome and endocrine anomalies do not play a significant part in the cause of homosexuality."[42] Likewise, Kallmann's studies with monozygotic (identical) homosexual twins, have not been verified by further studies.[43] Not all pairs of identical twins are both homosexual as would be expected if it were a genetic condition. Genetic studies in general have not thrown much light on the causes of the homosexual phenomenon.[44]

---

39 Hatterer, pp. 34-42.
40 Bieber, pp. 3-18; see also West, pp. 261-66.
41 T. Lang, "Studies in the Genetic Determination of Homosexuality," *Journal of Nervous and Mental Disease* 92 (1940): 55-64. A History of biological explanations and etiologies for homosexuality is found in C. W. Socarides, *The Overt Homosexual* (New York: Grune & Stratton, 1968), pp. 9ff. Socarides himself flatly states that homosexuality is not innate (p. 5).
42 West, p. 166.
43 F. J. Kallmann, "Comparative Twin Study of the Genetic Aspects of Male Homosexuality," *Journal of Nervous and Mental Disease* 115 (1952): 283-98; also, F. J. Kallmann, "Twin Sibships and the Study of Male Homosexuality," *American Journal of Human Genetics* 4 (1952): 136-46.
44 G. K. Klintworth, "A Pair of Male Monozygotic Twins Discordant for Homosexuality," *Journal of*

Hormonal Factors

Another influence on sex determination proposed as a cause of homosexuality involves hormone concentrations. During maturation the quality and concentration of hormones in the circulating blood has great influence on the growth and function of sex organs. Even persons with normal chromosomes rely upon the endocrine glands maturing at the right time and secreting into the blood the required amount of the right chemicals to promote normal sexual development. A number of experiments have shown, however, that increase of testosterone for male homosexuals, far from producing a curative effect, simply increases desire for their accustomed sexual object.[45]

Perloff reaches the same conclusions:

> In our experience, no patient, either male or female, has shown any consistent reversal of endocrine pattern to explain homosexual tendencies. We have never observed any correlation between the choice of sex object and the level of hormonal excretion.[46]

Some people, especially homosexuals themselves, find the biological theory appealing. In many cases it appears no less for genuinely scientific reasons than for the implication that sexually deviant individuals bear no personal responsibility for their condition and consequent acts, for they are biologically determined. Nevertheless, although there is a constant refrain in literature from Kinsey to Secor that we need a better knowledge of homosexuality, there is also a general consensus of opinion that the cause is not wholly biological. The Wolfenden Report states, "Biochemical and endocrine studies so far carried out in the field have, it appears, proved negative."[47] Speaking to Goldschmidt's theory of a biologically determined intersex, Kinsey remarks,

> Those who have accepted this interpretation have assumed without asking for specific evidence that an individual's choice of a sexual partner is affected by some basic biological capacity.

Nervous and Mental Disease 135 (1962): 113-25; see also C.M.B. Pare, "Etiology of Homosexuality: Genetic and Chromosomal Aspects," in Marmor, pp. 70-80, and J. Money, "Sexual Dimorphism and Homosexual Gender Identity," *National Institute of Mental Health Task Force on Homosexuality Final Report and Background Papers,* pp. 42-54, and Appendix B, pp. 73-77.

45 H. S. Barahal, "Testosterone in Psychotic Male Homosexuals," *Psychiatric Quarterly* 14 (1940): 319-29.

46 W. H. Perloff, "Hormones and Homosexuality," in Marmor, p. 57.

47 *The Wolfenden Report: Report of the Committee on Homosexual Offense and Prostitution,* Authorized American Edition (New York: Stein & Day, 1963), p. 32.

No work that has been done on hormones or any other physiologic capacities of the human animal justifies such a conclusion (Kinsey 1941).[48]

The committee responsible for the Presbyterian *Blue Book* reached the same conclusion after their study, writing, "However, psychosocial factors rather than biological factors appear to be primarily determinative."[49] Many scientists involved in the study of homosexuality claim that sexual orientation arises from psychosocial factors related to the development of gender identity and role with postnatal biological and endocrinological factors having perhaps some mediating influence in certain cases.

The general consensus is that transmission studies in single families have failed to indicate a clear genetic basis for homosexual preference. Likewise, postnatal endocrine studies have, for the most part, failed to establish a physiological basis for sexual behavior. In particular, they have failed to shed light on homosexuality and choice of sexual object in humans.

The Prenatal Thesis

During the past decade the major focus of psycho-endocrine theories of sexual orientation has shifted from the hormone situation in adulthood to the role of prenatal hormones. As early as 1971 Feldman and Macculloch theorized that primary male homosexuals had sexually undifferentiated brains of a female pattern due to a lack of hypothalamic exposure to androgens during intrauterine life.[50]

In humans the embryonic process leads automatically to the production of females unless something is added to produce a male. In the absence of gonads or hormones, the fetus differentiates autonomously as a female; it can only differentiate as male if something is added, that is, the secretions of the fetal testes. External morphologic sex changes which produce male physical characteristics are the final step in the embryonic development of sexual morphology. Organization of the brain as male or female occurs at about the same time in human fetal development that the hormones from the testes begin the development of male sexual morphology. In animals

---

48 A. C. Kinsey, W. B. Pomeroy, C. E. Martin, *Sexual Behavior in the Human Male* (Philadelphia: W. B. Saunders, Co., 1965), pp. 658-59.
49 B. E. Shafer, ed., *Blue Book* I (The Church and Homosexuality), 190th General Assembly (1978) of the United Presbyterian Church in the United States of America (San Diego, May 16-24, 1978), p. D14. Ollendorff finds homosexuality more prevalent in sex-negating societies. Where heterosexual outlets are frowned upon, group masturbation may be an early homosexual activity. R.H.V. Ollendorff, *The Juvenile Homosexual Experience and Its Effect on Adult Sexuality* (New York: Julian Press, 1966), pp. 63, 115-16.
50 M. P. Feldman and M. J. Macculloch, *Homosexual Behavior: Therapy and Assessment* (Oxford: Pergamon Press, 1971).

masculinization of brain cells seems to occur in the small part of the brain called the hypothalamus. This segment of the brain is most immediately involved in the regulation of sexual activity and most sensitive to sex hormones. It serves as a gate or funnel for eroticism and mating behavior.[51] All later behavior as male or female is determined by the presence or absence of male hormone during a brief critical period of prenatal life. The exact mechanism is not known, but it seems to be the removal of chemical blocks that allow transmission of impulses from one cell to another.[52]

The prenatal hormone theory was developed to explain the puzzling observations of male (human) homosexuals. Its pursuit in the laboratory naturally is heavily dependent on extensive animal studies on sexual dimorphism. The theory states that a hormone (androgen) deficiency during a critical period of prenatal life, that is, when sex differentiation occurs, results in an otherwise normal male developing a female differentiated brain. Dörner states the theory in terse language:

> An absolute or relative androgen deficiency in the first hypothalamic organization phase, that is intra-uterine, leydig cell degeneration, results in a predominantly female brain differentiation. A normal or at least approximately normal androgen level during the second phase, that is post-pubertal leydig cell generation, then exerts a sex non-specific activating effect on the predominantly female differentiated brain. Thus a genetic and somatic phenotypic male with a predominantly female differentiated brain is primarily sexually excited by another male.[53]

This theory suggested that a positive estrogen feedback effect, characteristic of normal females, should be present in primary (constitutional) homosexuals. Dörner's experiments demonstrated that in 13 out of 21 homosexuals this was the case. In contrast, only two out of 25 secondary (non-constitutional) homosexuals showed this response.[54] This suggests

---

51 J. Money, A. A. Ehrhardt, *Man and Woman, Boy and Girl* (Baltimore: Johns Hopkins Univ. Press, 1972), p. 238.
52 F. A. Beach, "Experimental Studies of Mating Behavior in Animals" in *Sex Research: New Developments*, ed. J. Money (New York: Holt, Rinehart & Winston, 1965), p. 127. Stoller found no histological evidence, i.e., no tissue difference in male and female brains, although the experiments seem to demand that there should be. R. Stoller, *Sex and Gender: On the Development of Masculinity and Femininity* (New York: Science House, 1968), p. 6. On the other hand G. Raisman and P. M. Field present an anatomical demonstration of sexual dimorphism in the nerve connections of the preoptic area of rats. They also point out however, that anatomical sexual dimorphism in one part of the brain, is not proof of a direct relationship to sexually differentiated functions in sexual behavior.
53 G. Dörner, W. Rhode, et al., "A Neuroendocrine Predisposition For Homosexuality In Man," Archives of Sexual Behavior 4 (1975): 2.
54 Ibid., pp. 4-5. A more recent study shows that the concentration of luteinizing hormone in

that secondary homosexuality may rise from psychosocial influences acting in accordance with learning theory.

Experimentation with animals has produced discordance between chromosomal sex and genital structure and also has distorted those parts of the central nervous system that mediate sex-related behavior.[55]

I. L. Ward has shown that prenatal stress on rats feminizes and demasculinizes the behavior of male offspring.

> The prenatally stressed males showed low levels of male copulatory behavior and high rates of lordic female responding. Postnatal stress had no effect. The modifications are attributed to stress-mediated alterations in the ratio of adrenal to gonadal androgens during critical stages of sexual differentiation.[56]

Harvey and Chevins achieved similar results in England. Pregnant mice were placed in overcrowded conditions during days 12-17 of pregnancy. Males from crowded mothers displayed poorer copulation than control mice as well as fewer mounts and intromissions, and no ejaculations.[57] On the basis of the evidence Young and his colleagues suggest the possibility of predetermined psychosexuality at birth as opposed to a psychosexual neutrality filled in later by experience. They conclude that "typical and deviant behaviors have a physiologic as well as a psychologic basis."[58]

The immediate question here, of course, is that of homology (sameness) between rats and human beings. The basic assumption underlying Dörner's theory is of homology between the homosexuality of lower mammals and human homosexual orientation. Meyer-Bahlberg has questioned at several points validity of the presumption that the homosexuality of lower mammals is sufficiently like that of human beings to allow a definite

---

homosexuals was intermediate between that of heterosexual men and women. B. A. Gladue, R. Green, R. E. Hellman, "Neuroendocrine Response to Estrogen and Sexual Orientation," *Science* 225 (1984): 1496-98.

55 V. E. Headings, "Etiology of Homosexuality," *Southern Medical Journal* 73, No. 8 (1980): 1025.

56 I. L. Ward, "Prenatal Stress Feminizes and Demasculinizes the Behavior of Males," *Science* 175 (1972): 82. Dr. Ward speculates that stress due to overcrowding might trigger this mechanism which then serves as a form of population control. Also I. L. Ward, "Female Sexual Behavior in Male Rats Treated Perinatally With an Anti-Androgen," *Physiology and Behavior* 8 (1972): 53-56; I. L. Ward, "Effects of Perinatal Androstenedione on Sexual Behavior Differentiation in Male Rats," *Behavioral Biology* 23 (1978): 243-48; I. L. Ward, "Effects of Maternal Stress on the Sexual Behavior of Male Offspring," *Monographs in Neural Sciences* 9 (1983): 169-75; I. L. Ward, F. S. Renz, "Consequences of Perinatal Hormone Manipulation on the Adult Sexual Behavior of Female Rats," *The Journal of Comparative and Physiological Psychology* 78 (1972): 349-55. Anti-androgen treatment had no effect on female rats.

57 P. W. Harvey, P.F.D. Chevins, "Crowding or ACTH Treatment of Pregnant Mice Affects Adult Copulatory Behavior of Male Offspring," *Hormones and Behavior* 18 (1984): 101.

58 W. C. Young, R. W. Goy, C. H. Phoenix, "Hormones and Sexual Behavior," *Science* 143 (1964): 216-17.

correlation.[59] He points out that in rats homosexuality is applied to female-typical reflexive mating behavior of a genetic male in the presence of another male. In contrast, human homosexual orientation refers to the degree of sexual responsiveness to the same sex but as expressed in erotic attractions, and sexual fantasies, not necessarily actual sexual experiences. In addition, homosexual behavior in humans is defined as any overt sexual behavior with the same sex regardless of orientation.

Homology of rats and humans in this respect is further complicated by the fact that mating behavior in rats is stereotyped and reflexive. Human sexual behavior, on the other hand, is highly variable and to a considerable degree non-reflexive, making the establishment of homologies, even with respect to overt sexual behavior, very difficult. In short, we speak of animals as only male and female but of men and women as masculine and feminine as well as male and female.

The second problem with animal models pointed out by Meyer-Bahlberg is that they are not in full agreement with the prenatal hormone theory.[60] Although the male rat fulfills the theoretical prediction that prenatal androgen deficiency in males leads to feminine sexual behavior, the same is not true concerning predictions about female rat homosexuality. This is true with females among primates also. Consequently, none of these findings to date constitutes unequivocal support for the prenatal hormone theory of sexual orientation.

The third difficulty cited by Meyer-Bahlberg is the fact that in animal studies systematic manipulation of sex hormones in the pre- or perinatal stage of development results not only in shifts of sexual dimorphic behavior and in structural changes in (some) of the underlying brain systems, but also in corresponding alterations of the genitalia.[61] Human homosexuals, however, have normal genitalia.

The prenatal hormone theory also is subject to test by study of human individuals with prenatal hormonal abnormalities such as prenatally hypoandrogenized males and hyperandrogenized females. In these cases the individuals are found to be heterosexual to the sex of assignment and rearing.[62] Homosexuals did not predominate among even the most extreme cases of women whose treatment did not start till adolescence or adulthood and who experienced pre- and postnatal virilization.[63]

---

59 H.F.L. Meyer-Bahlberg, "Psycho-endocrine Research on Sexual Orientation, Current Status and Future Options," *Progress in Brain Research* 61 (1984): 375-76.
60 Ibid., p. 381.
61 Ibid.
62 Ibid., p. 382; see also, A. A. Ehrhardt and H.F.L. Meyer-Bahlberg, "Effects of Prenatal Sex Hormones on Gender-Related Behavior," *Science* 211 (1981): 1315. The possibility of factors other than hormones cannot be excluded.
63 Meyer-Bahlberg, p. 382.

This evidence from offspring of hormone treated pregnancies of human beings shows that prenatal hormones may contribute to but do not actually determine the development of sexual orientation. None of the studies done so far allow one to exclude completely the fact that there may be a confounding of prenatal hormone influence with putative social factors.[64]

Dörner's theory suggested also that a positive estrogen feedback (luteinizing hormone feedback, L.H.) would be present in homosexuals as in females. Meyer-Bahlberg[65] suggests two major problems with the research approach however. One is that it is unlikely that L.H. dynamics are necessarily correlated with sexual orientation. He points to two studies of gonadally intact genetic males with a complete syndrome of androgen insensitivity who have an L.H. response that is typically masculine—this despite the fact that these patients have a female gender identity and feminine heterosexual orientation toward males in direct contrast to their L.H. dynamics.[66]

Despite these difficulties, the prenatal hormone theory is currently the dominant biological hypothesis. This is due to the fact that the anatomical structure of genitals and sex-behavior-related areas of the brain as well as the role of sex hormones are similar throughout the mammalian class. In addition, available information on patients with prenatal hormone abnormalities appears to implicate prenatal hormones as a contributing factor, although the exact mechanisms are not known. But as Meyer-Bahlberg observes, "The large number of hypothetical neuroendocrine mechanisms that must be considered in the search for an explanation of homosexuality makes it unlikely that a single mechanism underlies all forms of homosexuality."[67] He suggests the intersex rationale applies at best only to a

---

64 Ibid. p. 386. Also the study by I. L. Ward and J. Reed, "Prenatal Stress and Prepuberal Social Rearing Conditions Interact to Determine Sexual Behavior in Male Rats," *Behavioral Neuro-Science* 99 (1985): 307, where it is reported, "the present data suggest that the amount and type of sexual behavior displayed by an adult male depend not only on the hormonal milieu that persisted during fetal ontogeny but also on the quality of the social environment experienced during prepuberal development. Both factors exerted independent effects on sexual behavior potentials and interacted to produce consequences different from what either treatment would have if acting alone." In humans one study shows that of 44 children showing cross-gender identity in childhood (prepuberal) 30 were bisexual or homosexual in adulthood as opposed to none of the control group. See R. Green, "Gender Identity in Childhood and Later Sexual Orientation: Follow-up of 78 Males," *American Journal of Psychiatry* 142 (1985): 339-41.
65 Meyer-Bahlberg, p. 389. West finds that the theory has not always been replicated in the lab and therefore still remains highly speculative. D. J. West, "Homosexuality and Lesbianism," *British Journal of Psychiatry* 143 (1983): 223; also R. M. Rose, and E. Sachan, "Psychoendocrinology," *Textbook of Endocrinology,* ed. R. Williams (Philadelphia: Saunders, 1981), p. 651.
66 Meyer-Bahlberg, pp. 389-90; also J. K. Meyer, "Ego-Dystonic Homosexuality," *Comprehensive Textbook of Psychiatry,* ed. H. Kaplan, B. Sadock (Baltimore: Williams and Wilkins Co., 1984), p. 1058.
67 Meyer-Bahlberg, p. 392.

subgroup of homosexuals and that if valid for this subgroup, it is likely to be multifactorial in itself.[68]

Ward finds the theory unassailable as far as male rats are concerned, but she also suggests, "Whether or not this model holds as one moves up the philogenetic scale remains to be determined. The optimistic conclusions of Dörner, and others, that this syndrome provides a direct explanation of homosexuality in human males (Dörner, 1980; 1981) should be greeted with some caution."[69]

The consensus appears to be that prenatal hormone conditions alone do not rigidly determine homosexuality. However, prenatal hormone influences have to be considered along with other factors as contributing to sex-dimorphic behavior. Evidence concerning the exact role of prenatal hormones and how they exert their influence is inconclusive at the present time.

Psychosocial Factors

Leaving biological factors aside, we turn our attention to researchers who focus on the psychosocial evidence that may provide clues to the etiology of homosexuality. In the nature versus nurture debate over the origin of homosexuality, these investigators show a decided preference for the nurture theory. Because no consensus has been reached about what psychosocial factors are determinative or how they are determinative, this does not mean that every theory mutually excludes the others.

We can agree with Secor that far too few data cards appear on the table of honest investigation. Secor's statement epitomizes the views of this group. "The only fact that appears with some certainty is that homosexual identification and practice are learned in the human growth process, much the same way as are all personality identifications and practices."[70]

Money, one of the foremost experts in the field, agrees. Although Money's clinical studies were used to support experimental evidence linking prenatal hormonal influences on the fetal brain to subsequent masculine-feminine behavior, Money and his coworkers, the Hampsons, emerge as the chief proponents of the *nurture* theory. Money concludes "that erotic outlook and orientation is an autonomous psychologic phe-

---

68 Ibid., p. 393.
69 I. L. Ward, "The Prenatal Stress Syndrome: Current Status," *Psychoneuroendocrinology* 9 (1984): 9. The consensus of a MIT group on this subject was that more evidence was needed. See R. W. Goy, B. S. McEwen, *Sexual Differentiation of the Brain: Based on a Work Session of the Neuroscience Research Program* (Cambridge, MA: MIT Press, 1980), p. 73.
70 N. A. Secor, "A Brief for a New Homosexual Ethic," *The Same Sex: An Appraisal of Homosexuality*, ed. R. W. Weltge (Philadelphia/Boston: Pilgrim Press, 1969), p. 77.

nomenon independent of genes and hormones and, moreover, a permanent and ineradicable one as well."[71] The Hampsons agree with him:

> The evidence militates too strongly against a theory of innate, preformed, and inherited behavioral imperatives, hormonal or otherwise. . . . Instead the evidence supports the view that psychologic sex is undifferentiated at birth, a sexual neutrality in the place of the Freudian bisexuality, and that the individual becomes differentiated as masculine or feminine, psychologically, in the course of the many experiences of growing up.[72]

If the nature versus nurture debate appears inconclusive, an even more difficult feat is to determine the amount of conscious participation the person exerts in becoming homosexual. Some suggest that a person is not conscious of the psychosocial factors which shape his or her sexual orientation. These processes, it is claimed, begin at such an early age that in essence sexual orientation cannot be said to be chosen.[73] Oberholtzer, however, presents the opposite view in a forceful manner and suggests that homosexuals are responsible for their lifestyle.

> It is bad faith to pretend that homosexuality is necessary when it is in fact partly conscious and voluntary. Gay attractions are not sneakily created while Jack is out of the room. He becomes gay with his consent, although not without the consent of others. . . . Gay persons remember only what happened. They forget what *might have happened.* Thus, instead of remembering the choice among possibilities that was actually experienced in the past, they fasten upon the single action chosen and baptize it as inevitable—an exercise in bad faith.[74]

Weltge has commented also on the ambiguous stance taken by a number

---

[71] J. Money, "Sex Hormones and Other Variables in Human Eroticism," *Sex and Internal Secretions,* ed. W. C. Young (Baltimore: Williams & Wilkins Co., 1961), 2:1397.

[72] John Hampson, Jean Hampson, "The Ontogenesir of Sexual Behavior in Man," *Sex and Internal Secretions,* ed. W. C. Young (Baltimore: Williams & Wilkins Co., 1961), 2:1413, 1428. Other researchers believe that as the child discovers his/her own body and reacts to it he or she is influenced by it. That is to say there is a high correlation between biology and experience. Biology sets limits on what much of one's experience will be. See W. J. Gadpaille, *The Cycles of Sex,* ed. L. Freeman (New York: Charles Scribner's Sons, 1975), esp. chap. 2.

[73] See Shafer, The difficulty arises when the results are designated as "natural" to the person concerned. See Cory, Harvey comments in this respect, "It is difficult to see how one can call an inclination 'natural' which originates in a series of psychological privations." J. F. Harvey, "Pastoral Responses to Gay World Questions," *Is Gay Good? Ethics, Ethology and Homosexuality,* p. 125.

[74] W. D. Oberholtzer, "Introduction: Subduing the Cyclops--A Giant Step Towards Ethics," *Is Gay Good? Ethics, Theology and Homosexuality,* p. 28.

of homosexuals who claim that the condition is the result of a blind determinism ensuing in practices of a compulsive nature, in all of which they are innocent and powerless. At the same time they claim homosexuality is a responsible, morally good *choice* biologically and psychologically natural and normal. Weltge points out that these self-deceptions become noticeable when the ideology transforms the homosexual into a veritable saint and claims fellatio as a sexual sacrament. He continues, "What reason is there to believe that homosexuals are necessarily more honest about themselves, or less prone to self-justification, than other men?"[75]

Other researchers do not see homosexuality as either a grim determinism or a deliberate conscious choice. This mediating position interprets the condition as a subconscious decision or maladaptation taking place during childhood. Harvey, discussing the guilt that many homosexuals experience, sees it as more than the guilt placed on the homosexual by the heterosexual society. He detects a deeper disorientation going back to the early years of life that may be the result of a skein of factors which is difficult to disentangle. "But no matter which factor is stressed, it is a disorder in the due psychological relationship of the child to some significant person or group."[76] Others agree that this is the most likely origin of homosexuality. Among them, Barnhouse, Moberly, Bieber, Joner, Marmor, von Rohr, Shafer, and others who believe that early psychosocial factors are predominant in the formation of homosexual orientation.

Kinsey's challenge to psychologists who posit a psychosocial origin still stands in many respects, for in his view it must account not merely for an all-or-none condition, as homosexuality once was thought to be, but for the continuum found, ranging from those exclusively homosexual to those who are exclusively heterosexual. Said Kinsey,

> Whatever factors are considered, it must not be forgotten that the basic phenomenon to be explained is an individual's preference for a partner of one sex, or for a partner of the other sex, or his acceptance of a partner of either sex. This problem is, after all, part of the broader problem of choices in general: the choice of the road that one takes, of the clothes that one wears, of the food that one eats, of the place in which one sleeps, and of the endless other things that one is constantly choosing.[77]

---

75 R. W. Weltge, "The Paradox of Man and Woman," *The Same Sex: An Appraisal of Homosexuality*, p. 64.
76 J. F. Harvey, "Pastoral Responses to Gay World Questions," *Is Gay Good? Ethics, Theology and Homosexuality*, p. 124.
77 Kinsey, Pomeroy, Martin, p. 661.

From a layman's perspective, it seems that Moberly's work is doing much to answer these questions as she pulls together the various theories and observations into a more coherent picture.[78]

Finally, if homosexuality is experientially determined, hence consists of learned behavior, what chances are there of reversing the experience and unlearning the behavior? According to most experts, the prognosis is not good for the essential adult homosexual with a great deal of homosexual experience. Bieber reports on 72 exclusively homosexual patients who had undergone psychotherapy, and only 14 (19.44 percent) had become exclusively heterosexual.[79] It was also reported that 42 (58.33 percent) had remained exclusively homosexual. Hatterer followed up 143 patients who had undergone psychotherapy. Of this number, 49 (34.27 percent) were said to have "recovered" and 76 (53.15 percent) to have remained homosexual.[80] The Wolfenden report, however, concludes that the outlook for adolescent and transitional homosexuals often is very good; and complete pessimism in all regards is justified only for long-term homosexuals.[81]

In order to make ethical or moral judgments on homosexuality, one would have to prove the existence of a man whose sexual condition or orientation is homosexual. At that point such a person would be in himself a deviation from the normal heterosexuality of most men, that is, to that extent abnormal. The questions are: (1) Do such people really exist? (2) If so, is their condition morally reprehensible or is homosexuality of such a nature to be beyond the conscious control of the person so afflicted?

The answers seem to be: (1) In a minority of homosexuals, sometimes referred to as essential homosexuals or inverts, the factors that make them homosexually orientated are subconscious and may be influenced by some biological factor. Their homosexuality is caused by early environmental factors and influences outside the scope of conscious memory. (2) Such persons cannot be held morally responsible for the condition, although they are accountable for their acts. Some who are unhappy with their orientation may be helped by psychotherapy.

Other homosexuals, called perverts, acquired, or situational homosexuals, are those in whom the tendency to commit homosexual acts is predominantly determined by new factors arising later in life, that is, later childhood, adolescence, or manhood. Their homosexual acts are not motivated so much by deep, subconscious personal needs. Some individuals in this category are not essential homosexuals in any sense of the word.

---

78 Moberly, *Psychogenesis*.
79 Bieber, p. 276.
80 Hatterer, pp. 465-83.
81 The Wolfenden Report, p. 124.

Buckley points out that at times it is extremely difficult to distinguish the "essential" from the "acquired."[82] A man in middle life who commits a homosexual offense for the first time initially might be thought to belong to the acquired group. Further investigation might show that he is actually an essential homosexual whose resistance and self-discipline only recently weakened. On the other hand, acquired or situational homosexuals with incidental homosexual experience frequently are simply labeled homosexuals.

Giving someone a negative identity like "homosexual" usually prepares him/her in our society for a destiny of dehumanization. As we said at the beginning of the section on definitions, the word "homosexual" covers a wide variety of experiences. We need to be extremely careful that we define just what we mean by it. Are we speaking of disposition or the act?

The explanations most often cited to explain the homosexual condition or predisposition to prefer the same sex are as follows:

1. The homosexual condition is caused by a genetic abnormality of some kind. Evidence for genetic abnormality as the direct cause of the homosexual condition has not been found. Neither have abnormal hormone levels in the blood been tied directly to the homosexual condition. Whether the abnormal hormone levels themselves are caused by congenital defect or some later malfunction, they do not determine choice of sex partner. They simply increase or decrease, as the case may be, desire for the sex object of preference.

2. The homosexual condition is caused by prenatal hormonal influences. Research with rats shows that at least rats stressed during vital phases of pregnancy produce male offspring that exhibit feminized or demasculinized behavior. The theory proposes that male rats from stressed mothers have a female differentiated brain although they are otherwise normal males. This is caused by a hormone deficiency (androgen) during a critical period of prenatal life. This theory also faces many difficulties, not the least of which are the substantial differences between rats and human beings. Furthermore, the experiments do not work with female rats from stressed mothers. Human studies suggest that while this may be a contributing factor to the homosexual condition, other factors are operational as well.

3. The homosexual condition is caused predominantly by psychosocial factors. The exact dynamics of the process are not known, but it is probably due to an undefined same-sex relationship deficiency or, some would argue, an opposite sex relationship deficiency. The process may be sub-

---

82 M. J. Buckley, *Morality and the Homosexual: A Catholic Approach to a Moral Problem* (Westminster, MD: Newman Press, 1959), p. 17.

conscious to the individual, having taken place for the most part in early childhood. Some experts suggest that conscious decisions play a large part in the process. Although there is general agreement that the psychosocial factor plays a large part in causing the homosexual condition, there is wide disagreement as to just how this occurs. Many homosexuals object to this theory since it suggests that the condition is an illness or psychological abnormality capable of being treated.

What actually causes homosexual orientation of an individual remains something of a mystery. Often more than one factor is no doubt at work, defining the condition, therefore, as one of multiple etiology. One person may have more of this or that factor while another person would have other factors weighing more heavily in the balance. There is no way at present to measure the relative inputs of the different variables.

From the Christian point of view as well, human sexuality consists of more than genes, genitals, and hormones. Although the body clearly is necessary to our sexuality, human sexuality cannot be adequately described without including the mind and the freedom to think and choose characteristic of humans. The large part played by learning in the development and expression of human sexuality as opposed to the instinctive reflexive mating of animals means that human beings can control and are, therefore, responsible for their sexual expression.

The point we wish to stress here is that even if such a homosexual condition were thoroughly diagnosed and its dynamics completely known, this would not render it "natural" in any biblical sense of the word. Since same-sex acts are condemned in the Scriptures, conservative Christians would see this condition as further evidence of the Fall. The condition itself would be simply another example of how the evil consequences of the Fall alienate man from God. Therefore, unless a person were somehow subhuman, he/she still would be responsible for sexual expression.

What Do Homosexuals Do?

The sociological aspect of homosexuality is surrounded by considerable mythology. Ignorance, fear, and guilt play a large part in forming popular opinion. Lack of proper and accurate information and a vast collection of misinformation propagated in popular culture prevail. Not all homosexuals seduce boys or can be easily detected by their feminine features, gait, and gestures.

Due to social and legal pressures, most homosexuals who have not "come out" are forced to lead a type of Jekyll-and-Hyde existence, posing among their work-mates as "normal," perhaps dating girls for the sake of appearance, while at other times losing themselves in the various haunts of the gay subculture. The writings of Cory, Bengis, and Clark portray vividly the difficulties and discomforts of the homosexual way of life as well as its high points.[83] According to these and other authors, the pleasure that can be experienced and sustained in homosexual relations seems to equal anything that heterosexuals can achieve in their sexual bonding. In this discussion we are not addressing the essential or constitutional homosexual alone, but all homosexual behavior. Kinsey's statistics give some idea of how wide a cross section of the population this includes,

> 37 percent of the total male population has at least some overt homosexual experience to the point of orgasm between adolescence and old age. This accounts for nearly 2 males out of every 5 that one may meet.
>
> 50 percent of the males who remain single until age 35 have had overt homosexual experience to the point of orgasm, since the onset of adolescence.
>
> 58 percent of the males who belong to the group that goes into high school but not beyond, 50 per cent of the grade school level, and 47 per cent of the college level have had homosexual experience to the point of orgasm if they remain single to the age of 35.
>
> 63 percent of all males never have overt homosexual experience to the point of orgasm after the onset of adolescence.
>
> 50 percent of all males (approximately) have neither overt nor psychic experience in the homosexual after the onset of adolescence.
>
> 13 percent of the males (approximately) react erotically to males without having overt homosexual contacts after the onset of adolescence.
>
> 30 percent of all males have at least incidental homosexual experience or reactions (i.e., rate to 6) over at least a three-year period between the ages of 16 to 55. This accounts for one male out of every three in the population who is past the early years of adolescence.
>
> 25 percent of the male population has more than incidental

---

83 Cory, I. Bengis, *Combat in the Erogenous Zone* (New York: A. A. Knopf, 1973). The Life Story of a Lesbian; D. Clark, *Loving Someone Gay* (Millbrae, CA: Celestial Arts Publishing Co., 1977). Clark documents the extreme trauma of some gays in society whose failure at attempts to conform may lead to suicide (p. 26). Problems of sexual adjustment in early adolescence may lead to alcoholism or even more serious problems for gays. Some 20 to 30 percent of the homosexual population is alcoholic. See T. O. Ziebold, J. E. Mongeon, "Introduction: Alcoholism and the Homosexual Community," *Alcoholism and Homosexuality, Journal of Homosexuality* 7, No. 4, ed. T. O. Ziebold, J. E. Mongeon (New York: Haworth Press, 1982): 5.

homosexual experience or reactions (i.e., rates 2-6) for at least three years between the ages of 16 and 55. In terms of averages, one male out of approximately every four has had or will have such distinct and continued homosexual experience.

18 percent of the males have at least as much of the homosexual as the heterosexual in their histories (i.e., rate 3-6) for at least three years between the ages of 16 and 55. This is more than one in six of the white male population.

13 percent of the population has more of the homosexual than the heterosexual (i.e., rates 4-6) for at least three years between the ages of 16 and 55. This is one in eight of the white male population.

10 percent of the males are more or less exclusively homosexual (i.e., rate 5 or 6) for at least three years between the ages of 16 and 55. This is one male in ten in the white male population.

8 percent of the males are exclusively homosexual (i.e. rate 6) for at least three years between the ages of 16 and 55. This is one male in every 13.

4 percent of the white males are exclusively homosexual throughout their lives, after the onset of adolescence.[84]

Kinsey's figures do not take into account psychological or other factors which might induce homosexual behavior; they are merely a record of such behavior for whatever reasons. An essential or constitutional homosexual could fit in any category depending on the circumstances. In the same way a situational homosexual could fit almost any category with possible exception of the very last one.

The homosexual act and the factors which predispose an individual to perform the act are two very different considerations. This fact gives rise to a number of legal and ethical dilemmas. Any person who commits a homosexual act, which currently is illegal by general United States standards, tries to hide behind the claim that he is an invert. Since at the present time it is impossible to tell who is and who is not an invert, it is doubtful that the law will recognize this distinction.

The church faces an ethical dilemma for the same reason. The church cannot overlook all homosexual acts among its members on the supposition that they are inverts. The statistics show that the majority of those indulging in such acts probably are not inverts. Not only would the church face the problem of trying to determine who is and who isn't, it would also

---

84 Kinsey, pp. 650-51.

have to accept the doubtful assumption that such inversion is a natural God-ordained condition to begin with. Then it would need to reinterpret scriptural statements which condemn homosexual acts as referring in reality to something else, a task which some, regrettably, have begun already.

The main question here is how do these statistics translate into social activity? According to Malloy, solitary masturbation with male objects of fantasy is the most common form of homosexual activity.[85] The Hite report catalogs a variety of sexual activities under the title homosexual.[86] Today's homosexuals are not exclusively active or passive but frequently mixed, playing both roles, perhaps even with the same partner.

Hooker has done extensive research on homosexual social patterns. She discovered that more than two-thirds of the male homosexuals in a San Francisco study visited gay bars to seek out a sexual partner or partners. The most common form of social activity among homosexuals is "cruising," that is, visiting bars, baths, the street or the public toilet in search of a "one night stand." This is a strictly formal arrangement for sexual gratification with the least possible risk. The two people involved may be strangers who probably will not see each other again for an extended time. The casual noncommittal nature of these relations is a noted feature. Hooker characterizes the essential feature of such activity as "the standardized expectation that sex can be had without obligation or commitment."[87] Recently the threat of AIDS has disrupted established practices, notably by bringing an end to the popularity of gay bathhouses and imposing limits on the widespread promiscuity characteristic of homosexual activity.

Gay bars also serve as social centers where gossip and the latest news and views are exchanged not unlike any other bar in that sense. According to Hooker, bars also serve as induction, training, and integration centers for the community. Very often a new homosexual will declare himself as such, that is, "come out" by visiting a gay bar. Hooker describes the process of integration which follows:

> Once he has "come out"—that is, identified himself as a homosexual to himself and to some others—the process of education proceeds with rapid pace. Eager and willing tutors—especially if he is young and attractive—teach him the special language, ways of recognizing vice-squad officers, varieties of sexual acts and social types. They also assist him in providing

---

85 Malloy, p. 55; also Harvey, "Homosexuality," *New Catholic Encyclopedia*, p. 118.
86 S. Hite, *The Hite Report on Male Sexuality* (New York: Alfred A. Knopf, 1981), pp. 793-848.
87 E. Hooker, "The Homosexual Community" in *The Same Sex: An Appraisal of Homosexuality*, p. 32.

justifications for the homosexual way of life as legitimate, and help to reduce his feeling of guilt by providing him with new norms of sexual behavior in which monogamous fidelity to the sexual partner is rare.[88]

Not all homosexuals are to be seen in public, however. Hooker likens the homosexual world to an iceberg—only a small part of it is visible on the surface. Many come to dislike the bar activities or fear them because they pose a threat to established relationships. Others of high occupational or socioeconomic status may restrict their community life to private social cliques because of the fear of exposure or arrest. These communities Hooker describes as a "loosely knit extended series of overlapping networks of friends."[89] The homosexual subculture has its own system of beliefs by which it justifies its homosexual way of life. The central point is the explanation of why they are homosexual.

Humphreys' observations on the impersonal sexual liaisons that take place in public bathrooms led him to conclude that only a small percentage of the gay bar crowd visits park rest rooms. He concurs with Hooker that the gay bar clientele is not all of the homosexual subculture:

> But this more overt, gay bar clientele constitutes a minor part of those in any American city who follow a predominantly homosexual pattern. The so-called closet queens and other types of covert deviants make up the vast majority of those who engage in homosexual acts—and these are the persons most attracted to tearoom encounters.[90]

Park rest rooms, known as tearooms in homosexual subculture jargon, are frequented by homosexuals, only a minority of whom are active in the homosexual subculture. A large group of these people have no homosexual self-identity; they do not want to be seen or identified with homosexuals on a social basis. These are "nice people" who might be one's next-door neighbors. Humphreys points out that, surprisingly, most of these men are married.[91] The type of homosexual encounter is usually fellatio, usually a service performed by an older man upon a younger, by far the greater proportion of insertees being the younger man of the duo.

Humphreys divides the clientele at the park bathrooms into four

---

88 Ibid., p. 34; also, West, pp. 107-112.
89 Ibid., p. 36.
90 L. Humphreys, "The Tearoom Trade, Impersonal Sex in Public Places," *Transaction* 7, No. 3, (January 1970): 13. The sociological aspects of the English homosexual scene are outlined in detail in, R. Hauser, *The Homosexual Society* (London: Bodley Head, 1962), pp. 26-81.
91 Ibid., p. 14.

categories. First of all a category called "Trade." This usually consists of married men with dependent occupations. Typical of this group is George, a truck driver. His wife of Roman Catholic persuasion bore him seven children, wants no more, yet objects to any other method of contraception outside of the rhythm method. George finds his sexual outlet in the tearooms.[92]

A second type to frequent the tearooms Humphreys labeled "ambisexuals." These are married men with independent occupations. They sometimes enjoy managerial status and can hire other men who share their sexual and other interests. This group expressed a liking for anal intercourse as well as fellatio and even for mild forms of sadomasochistic sex. Men in this group are not seeking out deviant sex from desperation, but more for kicks.[93] Of this group Humphreys says, "They think of themselves as bisexual or ambisexual and have intellectualized their deviant tendencies in terms of the pseudopsychology of the popular press."[94]

A third group frequenting the tearooms are the "Gay Guys." These men are usually unmarried and have independent occupations. They are a part of the homosexual subculture which provides them with knowledge about the tearooms. Typical of this group is Ricky, a 24-year-old university student who has an older "permanent" lover. Most of his friends and social contacts are connected with the homosexual subculture. He frequents tearooms because he is afraid that open cruising in the more common homosexual market places of the baths and bars might disrupt his current love affair.

Finally, a fourth group is described as "Closet Queens." These are unmarried men with dependent occupations. They are covert unmarried men, and social isolation is characteristic of this group. They seem to be afraid of becoming involved in other forms of the sexual market, preferring the sheltering silence and furtive involvement of the tearoom encounters. (In these encounters no verbal communication takes place, and the men are usually strangers to each other.) A number of these men (of the fourth group) regularly cruise the streets where boys thumb rides each afternoon after school is over. One closet queen from Humphreys' group had been arrested for luring boys in their early teens to his home.[95] It is clear from Humphreys' description that homosexuals of both the constitutional and situational types are involved in this "tearoom" activity. It is dif-

---

92 Ibid., p. 17.
93 Ibid., pp. 19-20.
94 Ibid., p. 22.
95 Ibid., p. 24. The Wolfenden Report, p. 114, notes that in a survey of 1,022 in prison for homosexual offenses in 1954, no fewer than 590 (58 percent) were involved in offenses against boys aged 15 or under. But see also West, pp. 114-24.

ficult to draw a distinction between them legally, morally, or ethically. By some present definitions George, probably a pervert, is more culpable than Rick, an apparent invert. The framers of the Wolfenden Report experienced the same difficulty in this respect and they note that,

> Some writers on the subject, and some of our witnesses, have drawn a distinction between the "invert" and the "pervert." We have not found this distinction very useful. It suggests that it is possible to distinguish between two men who commit the same offense, the one as the result of his constitution, the other from a perverse and deliberate choice, with the further suggestion that the former is in some sense less culpable than the latter. To make this distinction as a matter of definition seems to prejudge a very difficult question.[96]

Kinsey's statistics and the various forms of homosexual activity persuade us that homosexual acts are performed to fulfill needs on grounds other than inversion.

The compulsion for homosexual acts is manifested in a number of ways in society; among these being:

1. Solitary masturbation with male objects of fantasy as well as mutual masturbation among males.

2. Homosexual "marriage" where two males share the same home, domestic duties, and so forth, and the same bed. They usually enjoy a limited circle of friends and acquaintances of like mind.

3. Homosexual promiscuity, which usually takes the form of "cruising" the gay bars for one-night stands. Many of the more conservative and reserved homosexuals dislike this practice and consider this to be living life in the homosexual "fast lane."

4. Adolescent experimentation with homosexual acts. Such acts by no means indicate that the youngsters are confirmed homosexuals.

5. The tearoom "trade." Those who would not class themselves as homosexuals but seek safe sexual outlets out of desperation or for kicks.

6. Closet Queens, who tend to get involved with minors rather than adults or other homosexuals.

It is clear that a variety of motives, situations, and contingencies predispose these persons to homosexual activity. According to Kinsey only three or four percent of homosexuals are exclusively homosexual after adolescence. However, it is impossible to say that only this number are constitutional homosexuals. It would require a considerable detailed history of each individual to tell which were inverts and which were not, with no cer-

---

96 The Wolfenden Report, pp. 35-36.

tainty about it at that. Criteria to determine inversion or lack of it are simply unreliable or nonexistent. Therefore, to assign culpability or lack of it on the basis of this distinction for overt acts committed by either represents an unwarranted generalization.

Chapter 2
Old Testament Historical Background

In the literature assessing the biblical attitude toward homosexuality we find differing estimates of its prevalence in ancient times. If it is difficult to determine the nature and extent of homosexuality at the present time, it is even more so in ancient times. Most of the surviving literature comes from professional literary hands and does not address homosexuality per se. Although incidental mention is not without historical value (some think it presents a less-biased picture), it limits the amount of material to work with and presents difficulties for interpretation. Therefore a survey of the historical background is helpful prior to interpreting the relevant OT texts.

Leviticus 18:1-3, 24-30; 20:23-25 give the impression that the practices forbidden in the book of Leviticus also were known among the Egyptians and Canaanites, perhaps being customary or prevalent among these peoples. Some scholars agree with this estimate, stating that "male homosexuality was rampant in biblical times and has so remained in the Middle East down to the present day."[1] It is possible the mores of Sodom and Gibeah were not greatly different from those of other Canaanite and Israelite towns and villages.[2] Harrison agrees with this estimate also, writing, "Homosexuality was known and practiced in the Near East as a form of carnal indulgence from very early times."[3] Moreover, he suggests that homosexual activity within the cultus predated the Israelite arrival in Canaan. "Sacro-homosexual practices and female prostitution within the context of the cultus was probably well established throughout the ancient Near East long before the Israelites occupied Canaan."[4] Bailey, on the other hand, finds it impossible to confirm such a conclusion from the available evidence, he states,

---

1   R. Patai, *Sex and Family in the Bible and the Middle East* (New York: Doubleday & Co., 1959), p. 169.
2   Ibid.
3   R. K. Harrison, *Leviticus: An Introduction and Commentary* (Downers Grove, IL: Inter-Varsity Press, 1980), p. 191.
4   Ibid.

Research fails to establish any satisfactory positive support for the allegation that homosexual practices were customary among the nations surrounding the Hebrews; rather, the meager evidence suggests that such practices were variously regarded as criminal, sinful, or personally degrading.[5]

From this perspective, he treats statements in Leviticus that attribute such practices to the nations around Israel as exaggeration, "simply a piece of rhetorical denigration—or at most, a polemical exaggeration of heathen vice—designed to intensify Israel's sense of national 'holiness' or separation as a peculiar people dedicated to Yahweh."[6] Accordingly, they are disregarded as accurate indications of contemporary pagan morals, they simply express the Israelite condemnation of the ethos of heathenism which Israel must renounce just as it renounces religious and cultural syncretism with surrounding nations practicing idolatry.[7]

We will attempt to gauge the accuracy of the biblical statement as a historically valid observation describing the surrounding nations. Clearly, if the statements in Leviticus are mere rhetorical flourish, much of the content of the book becomes bombast. The great seriousness and sternness of the book verges on farce if it is in fact set against a backdrop of nonexistent internal or external dangers for Israel.

Egypt

The ideal family relationship in Egypt was for a young man to find himself a good wife and raise a fine family of children. Since inheritance was through the female line, daughters were important. The young husband stood in close relationship with his maternal grandfather. He was the natural protector of the youth after marriage more so than even his own father.[8]

Unconventional sexual practices are not well documented in ancient Egypt. Herodotus, a Greek traveler and author who visited Egypt sometime after 460 B.C., mentions bestiality and necrophilia.[9] The Talmud states that Potiphar bought Joseph for himself, suggesting a homosexual intention.[10] From earlier Egyptian sources, Pritchard cites two statements,

---

5 D. S. Bailey, *Homosexuality and the Western Christian Tradition* (Hamden, CT: Shoe String Press, 1975), p. 59.
6 Ibid.
7 Ibid., p. 60.
8 M. S. Shaw, "Family Life in Ancient Egypt," *Journal of the Manchester Egyptian and Oriental Society* 28 (1933): 37-40.
9 Herodotus 2. 46. 89.
10 Sot. 13b, see also I. Jakobovits, "Homosexuality," in *EncJud* 8 (1972): 961.

the first from the eighteenth dynasty (ca. 1550 B.C.) which he categorizes as Egyptian social law. Here a man asserts, "I have not had sexual relations with a boy." Another statement from the 125th chapter of the Book of the Dead reads, "O His Face Behind Him, who comes forth from Tep-het-djat, I have not been perverted; I have not had sexual relations with a boy."[11].

The outstanding account of homosexuality in Egyptian literature is a story about the attempt of the god Seth to violate his younger brother. The myth, which deals with conflict between the gods Horus and Seth, presents a number of settings in which the struggle takes place. One of these is the homosexual rape of Horus. The homosexual interest of Seth is seen clearly in a papyrus fragment found in Kahun, where Seth shows a decided interest in the body of Horus, "The majesty of Seth said to the Majesty of Horus: 'How beautiful are thy buttocks.' "[12]

Papyrus Chester Beatty I, dated about 1160 B.C., records the homosexual act of Seth,

> Thereupon Seth spake unto Horus: Come let us pass a happy day in my house.
> Thereupon Horus said to him: I will do so, verily I will do so. And when it was eventide the bed was spread for them, and they twain lay down. And in the night Seth caused his member to become stiff, and made it go between the loins of Horus.
> Thereupon Horus put his two hands between his loins, and he caught the seed of Seth.[13]

The conflict between Horus and Seth has been seen as having either a cosmological significance explaining the relationship of sun and moon or a political significance relating to some conquest of the past. Whatever the intent of the myth, what is the significance of the homosexuality in the two legends from Kahun and P. Chester Beatty? Griffiths finds more than the ignominy dealt by the conqueror to the conquered:

> At first sight Seth's homosexual treatment of Horus seems to fall in better with the idea of the ignominy inflicted on an enemy. But Seth is not the ultimate conqueror, although he is represented as boasting of his deeds of war. . . . It is certainly looked upon as a mark of ignominy for the sufferer; but it is abominated

---

11 J. B. Pritchard, ed., *ANET* (1950), pp. 34-35.
12 G. W. Griffith, ed., *The Petrie Papyri: Hieratic Papyri from Kahun and Gurob* (principally from the Middle Kingdom), 2nd ed. (London: B. Quaritchs, 1898), Pl. 3, VI, 12, 1-29.
13 A. H. Gardiner, tr., ed., *The Library of A. Chester Beatty: Description of a Hieratic Papyrus with a Mythological Story, Love-Songs, and Other Miscellaneous Texts--Chester Beatty Papyri, No. I* (London: Oxford Univ. Press, 1931), see Rect. 11, 2-4 and p. 21.

not as an expression of triumph by the enemy so much as for the shame attached to the act itself, just as the eating of excrement is abominated.[14]

Westendorf points out that the shame in homosexual intercourse belongs entirely to the underdog, whereas the act itself seems unimportant.[15] Seth boasts of having performed the job of a man on Horus who is insulted and spit upon by the Ennead (P. Chester Beatty I, 12, 3-4).

In Egyptian thinking the change of roles rendered the passive partner powerless. Even for the gods this was true. Westendorf observes, "Atum has no power over NN; rather NN copulates in his anus" (Coffin Texts VI, 258 f-g).[16] This seems to imply that one rendered another completely powerless by violating him sexually and lends support to the view that the Egyptians had a custom of violating defeated enemies in this way.

On this point Gardiner finds no evidence of such a practice, "Here, at all events, we have unmistakable evidence of the *belief* that such a practice existed, though of its actual performance there is no proof either in Ancient Egypt, or, as Prof. Seligman informs me, anywhere else in Africa."[17] Perhaps the significance of the homosexual act is to be found in the nature of Seth himself. Seth is scarcely a god of fertility, for in this myth his boundless energy is not productive. Isis had already warned Horus how to deal with Seth so that his seed would be wasted. In this myth his seed is feared not for its generative power, but as poison.[18] Griffiths translates the Kahun account thus:

> The Majesty of Seth said to the Majesty of Horus, How beautiful are thy buttocks! How flourishing(?) ... The majesty of Horus said, Wait that I may tell it ... to their palace. The Majesty of Horus said to his mother Isis ... Seth desires(?) to have intercourse with me. And she said to him, Take care, do not approach him for that; when he mentions it to thee a second

---

14 J. G. Griffiths, *The Conflict of Horus and Seth from Egyptian and Classical Sources* (Liverpool University Press, 1960), p. 43. Bruns finds similarities between the Seth-Horus story and the Ham-Noah account. He suggests that Ham did more than look at Noah and finds an anti-Egyptian polemic here. Homosexuality was an abomination, he claims, because it undermined patriarchal society where a man could not use a man as a woman or be used as a woman, the dignity of the male being dishonored by both. See J. E. Bruns, "Old Testament History and the Development of a Sexual Ethic," *The New Morality: Continuity and Discontinuity*, ed. W. Dunphy (New York: Herder and Herder, 1967), pp. 75-76.
15 W. Westendorf, "Homosexualität," *Lexikon der Ägyptologie* 2, ed. H. W. Helck (Wiesbaden: O. Harrassowitz, 1977): col. 1272.
16 Ibid.
17 Gardiner, p. 22, n. 2.
18 See Westendorf. The same Egyptian word serves for "semen" and "poison." Spells to protect against poisoning by semen were used in Egypt.

time, say thou to him, It is altogether too difficult for me because of (my) nature(?), since thou art too heavy for me; my strength will not be equal to thine, thou shalt say to him. Then when he shall have given thee strength, do thou place thy fingers between thy buttocks, Lo it will give... Lo, he will enjoy it exceedingly(?) ... this seed which has come forth from his generative organ without letting the sun see it ... Come thou.[19]

Seth is fooled. He does not introduce his semen (poison) into Horus. Horus catches it and throws it into the water. Isis succeeds in impregnating Seth with the seed of Horus by placing it on a lettuce leaf which Seth eats. In the context of the legend the dominance theme is unmistakably cloaked in sexual imagery.

H. Te Velde scrutinizes Seth and sees him as the symbol of abnormal or irregular sexuality, "Seth's homosexuality and the fact that he was credited with practices of abortion, demonstrate that Seth is a god of sexuality which is not canalized into fertility."[20] The sexuality of Seth is always irregular; he does not care whether women are married or not. The animal of Seth, the ass, was proverbial for its lasciviousness.

Seth is an enemy of boundaries; he does not respect the boundaries of sex and wants to have relations which are sometimes homosexual and sometimes heterosexual. He is the author of confusion, refusing to recognize the divinely ordained boundaries. "Seth does not respect existing boundaries. The frontier between the sexes, which was created by Atum, is ignored by Seth."[21]

This is significant in that Seth's immorality and homosexuality contravene the status quo created by the Egyptian god Atum. Seth would thus be considered as one not living, according to *Maat* ("Wisdom"), the social, moral, ethical, and religious regulations instituted by the gods at Creation.

Seth was regarded by the Egyptians as Lord of foreign peoples; of Libyans, Hittites, and Semites. He is given two Syrian goddesses, Anat and Astarte, as wives.[22] He rapes Anat. But in the account in P. Chester Beatty VII, she is dressed like a man. The Egyptian word used is not that for human intercourse, even when one of the partners is an animal, but for intercourse between animals.[23] Seth seems to be practicing his usual craft,

---

19 Griffiths. p. 42. Also H. Goedicke, "Seth as a Fool," *Journal of Egyptian Archeology* 47 (1961): 154. Seth is made to look a fool not only by acts like this but by the use of puns which he takes literally.
20 H. Te Velde, *Seth: God of Confusion* (Leiden: E. J. Brill, 1977), p. 55.
21 Ibid., p. 59.
22 For the background, see R. T. Rundle Clark, *Myth and Symbol in Ancient Egypt* (New York: Grove Press, 1960), p. 197ff.
23 W. R. Dawson, "Observations on Passages in Chester Beatty Papyri VII, VIII and XII," *JEA* 22

with defloration as the result. Consistency in ancient legends was not an essential element. He is described as leaping upon the goddess as a ram. He deflowers her with a chisel and rapes her with fire. Anat is taken ill after the event.

Here again the dominance-poison motif appears. Stadelmann suggests that here we have an Egyptian enactment of a Canaanite myth, that is, the rape of Anat by Baal.[24] Syncretism of Canaanite and Egyptian religion was widespread during the Ramesside period in Egypt. Albright speaks of it as the most cosmopolitan in the ancient world:

> In the capital itself the great Canaanite gods Baal and Horon, with the goddesses Anath and Astarte, were worshiped on a par with the native Egyptian deities Seth and Horus, Nephthys and Isis, with which they were identified. Egyptian adaptations of several Canaanite myths have been discovered.[25]

According to Albright, Canaanite practices shockingly immoral to the Israelites were bound up with the introduction of the myths. This included rampant prostitution of both sexes. "The cinaedus (homosexual) formed a recognized guild in Canaanite temples, and there were other groups which combined dancing and singing with divination in a peculiarly unholy union."[26]

Due to the nature of the Egyptian religion, these rites had a direct influence on the people. Among the Egyptians there were no sacred books as such. The divine life was dramatized in rites and festivals and it is through them that a man confirms his virtue and attains salvation. The acts of the gods as revealed in the cult dominated religious thought and life.[27] "Religious renewal is the magic effect of the rites performed during festivals."[28] The acts of the gods became important and the days on which they were

---

(1936): 107.
24 R. Stadelmann, *Syrisch-Palästinensische Gottheiten in Ägypten--Probleme der Ägyptologie, Bd.* 5, ed. W. Helck (Leiden: E. J. Brill Pubs., 1967), pp. 130-133.
25 W. F. Albright, *The Biblical Period from Abraham to Ezra* (New York: Harper and Row Pubs., 1963), p. 16. Van Seters suspects that the syncretism dates at least to the Hyksos period. J. Van Seters, *The Hyksos: A New Investigation* (New Haven, CT: Yale Univ. Press, 1967), pp. 175-80. See also, J. Gray, *The Canaanites* (New York: F. A. Praeger Pubs., 1964), p. 49; and E. A. Leslie, *Old Testament Religion in the Light of Its Canaanite Background* (Nashville: Abingdon-Cokesbury Press, 1936), pp. 21-22.
26 Ibid.
27 C. J. Bleeker, "Egyptian Festivals: Enactments of Religious Renewal," *Studies in the History of Religions,* XIII, Supplements to *Numen* (Leiden, 1967), p. 6. Also, C. J. Bleeker, "Religious Tradition and Sacred Books in Egypt," *Holy Book and Holy Tradition International Colloquium Held in the Faculty of Theology University of Manchester,* ed. F. F. Bruce and E. G. Rupp (Grand Rapids: Wm. B. Eerdmans Publishing Co., 1968), p. 22.
28 Ibid., p. 44.

enacted equally important and were sometimes observed as festivals. The observation of days was the culmination of the tendency to count particular days of the year as specially lucky or unlucky, depending on what the gods had accomplished on those days.[29]

The Egyptians, says Herodotus, "assign each month and each day to some god; they can tell what fortune and what end and what dispositions a man shall have according to the day of his birth."[30] Thus, although various rites were enacted in the temple out of sight of the people, the festivals and myths were open to all.[31]

Therefore, the gods set the moral tone for the people. The worshippers of Seth would imitate his deeds although these acts might be considered an abomination by those devoted to other gods. The fact that negative assertions about homosexuality were contained in the Book of the Dead could mean that it was only before the judgment of the dead that public lewdness was being denied. Public homosexual activity in connection with a festival would not render one liable to judgment. However, if all the denials of wrongdoing in the Book are to be taken seriously as representing the character of the dead, then they would not have needed the magical charms and incantations of the Book to see them through the hall of judgment.

The Book of the Dead mentions boys in both instances, which leads to the surmise that minors may have been protected but were nevertheless a source of temptation to some. Westendorf notes that Goedicke was convinced that homosexual intercourse with adults was not considered immoral in Egypt. He points to the "grave of the two friends" as perhaps a proof that an intimate relationship based on the grounds of mutual attraction could be maintained for eternity in Egyptian thinking without offense to the community.[32]

We conclude therefore that homosexual relationships were known in Egypt. Negative assertions may be simply part of a magical formula in the Book of the Dead. The common people enjoyed hearing about if not practicing homosexuality. At least the homosexual legends of Seth were written in a style for purely popular consumption, such as might be related by a village storyteller. The passive partner seems to have been the only one

---

29 G. Steindorff, *The Religion of the Ancient Egyptians* (New York: G. P. Putnam's Sons, 1905), pp. 111-13.
30 Herodotus, 2. 82.
31 C. J. Bleeker, "Hathor and Thoth: Two Key Figures of the Ancient Egyptian Religion," *Studies in the History of Religions* 26, Supplements to *Numen* (Leiden, 1973). Bleeker describes the "festival of inebriety to Hathor" in which drunkenness was considered ecstasy in honor of the goddess. See also G. A. Gaballa, K. A. Kitchen, "The Festival of Sokar," *Or* ns 38, 1969, pp. 1-76 for a detailed account of an Egyptian festival.
32 Helck, col. 1273.

scorned. Regarding homosexuality, the syncretism of West Canaanite and Egyptian religions in the delta resulted in a much more morally degrading outlook than Egyptian religion of past eras had produced.

Babylon and Assyria

Sexual potency in ancient times was regarded as a great generative force, both venerated and worshipped. If the deity worshipped was female and the attendants also female, men would visit the temple to have intercourse with the "deity," that is, the attendants. From their point of view the experience was a religious one and even homosexuality could appear in a "good" light rather than a bad one. It was seen as a natural form of indulgence for the active partner, and if condemned at all it was only in situations analogous to those in which one might condemn gluttony, drunkenness, and other excesses.

Furthermore, marriage was primarily an economic association, frequently impermanent in character and not the exclusive source of sexual gratification. Sometimes a female deity might be served by male as well as female attendants. Usually, perhaps invariably, such males wore female costume and were considered to have adopted the life of women. When men resorted to the temple to perform ritual intercourse with the deity, if the attendant was biologically a male, the intercourse was technically homosexual.

However, simply to speak of these people as prostitutes or homosexual prostitutes does not convey to the modern mind an accurate picture of the motives or practices of the people involved. Perhaps a more accurate term would be ritual intercourse. Such rites, whether heterosexual or homosexual, contravened the moral codes of Israel though not the moral practices of a large part of Israel, who repeatedly fell prey to the enticing forms of pagan worship. The Old Testament condemns this type of practice by the Israelites (Deut 23:17; 1 Kgs 14:24; 15:12; 22:46; 23:7).

Sumerian and Middle Assyrian Laws have little to say about homosexuality as such. The Laws of Hammurabi 142, allow redress to a woman whose husband is a gadabout *(wasi)*. It is possible that this implies a male prostitute or perhaps a homosexual.[33] Middle Assyrian Laws 19, 20, deal with accusations of homosexuality against a man:

> 19. If a man has secretly defamed(?) his neighbor, saying: "He is a (common) catamite," or has spoken to him in a quarrel in the presence of (other) people, saying: "Thou art being used as

---

[33] J. J. Finkelstein, "Sex Offenses in Sumerian Laws," *JAOS* 86 (1966): 366, n. 34.

a catamite" and saying: "I myself will charge thee, . . ."

20. If a man has defiled his neighbor (and) charge (and) proof have been brought against him, he shall be defiled (and) made a eunuch.[34]

Miles and Driver ask why sodomy is treated as an offense at all in Assyrian Laws. It is treated so only when the victim is the *tappau* ("equal") of the offender. They conclude that it may be that a slanderous charge of unnatural vice and the commission of the offense were only regarded as criminal when the victim stood in a specially close relationship to the offender, and were not punishable in other cases.[35]

Cult Prostitution

Sexual intercourse in the service of a god or goddess was a common practice, which was not regarded as criminal, but a sign of dedication or devotion. Priestesses who followed the custom apparently were highly respected in some manner since even kings dedicated their daughters to the temple. Money was paid into the temple treasury for the service despite the fact that it was an act of dedication in glorification of a goddess.[36] On the other hand, temple prostitutes were not recommended as wives even by Babylonian authors:

> Do not marry a prostitute (harimtu) whose husbands are legion (literally 3600), A temple harlot (istaritu) who is dedicated to a god, A courtesan (kulmasitu) whose favors are many.[37]

The males attached to the cult *(assinnu)* are sometimes considered to be eunuchs or homosexuals or both. Some argue that the strong biblical repudiation of homosexuality refers to homosexual service in a pagan temple.[38] The wages of a temple servant *(hierodule)* were not to be paid into the house of God for the payment of any vow (Deut 28:13; Judg 19:22). An argument is advanced that homosexuality is not involved at all, only male prostitution with female worshippers.[39] Others agree that homo-

---

34 G. R. Driver and J. C. Miles, *The Assyrian Laws Edited With Translation and Commentary* (Oxford: Clarendon Press, 1935), p. 391.
35 Ibid., p. 71.
36 E. M. Yamauchi, "Cultic Prostitution—A Case Study in Cultural Diffusion," *Orient and Occident: Essays presented to C. H. Gordon,* ed. H. A. Hoffner Jr., *Alter Orient und Altes Testament Veröffentlichungen zur Kultur und Geschichte des Alten Orients und des Alten Testaments* 22, ed. K. Bergerhof, et al. (Neukirchen: Butzon & Bercker, 1973): 215.
37 Ibid.
38 O. J. Baab, "Homosexuality," *IDB* 2 (1962): 639.
39 Bailey, p. 53. Homosexual relations would be meaningless in a fertility cult, he argues. But no more

sexuality was involved but hold that the Bible does not condemn the homosexuality as such, only idolatry is condemned.[40]

It is doubtful that the Israelites made the neat and rather modern distinction between sacred and secular. The cult of the covenant people and covenant morality were integrally bound together in Old Testament times. The Israelites were alone among the peoples of the ancient Near East in not separating the spheres of religion and morality. For the faithful Israelite a moral life was in itself a form of religious worship. Furthermore, Hebrews had been exposed to pagan cult and morality from the beginning of their history and had come to grips with the philosophy, theology, lifestyle, and world view involved in idolatry.

> The translation of cuneiform inscriptions throughout recent decades has confirmed in substance the statements of Herodotus (1, 182) and has made evident that the licentious rites of sympathetic magic described by various Greek historians, Strabo, Lucian, etc., were not confined to a late period in Syria, Asia Minor, or Greece, but that these ideas and practices may be found as early as the beginning of the historical period.[41]

The basic idea behind ritual intercourse was the belief that greater productivity of fields and flocks and thus prosperity for the entire community could be brought about by the propagation of human life under certain conditions. This intercourse with the representative of a god was viewed as a way of controlling the universe by sympathetic magic.

> Persons dedicated to the gods who were officials of the cult were sought, especially at festivals, by laity who sincerely believed that intercourse with these persons would cure sterility of human beings, of animals and of the land, and that by actual union with the human representatives of the deity one could assist the gods in bringing prosperity to mankind.[42]

We may safely assume that the Israelites would reject as idolatry any practice which claimed to control God automatically. No doubt some of the functionaries involved in these services were men. It is also highly prob-

---

so than the absolute chastity of the Entu in Babylonian religion and cult. See H.W.F. Saggs, *The Greatness that was Babylon* (New York: Mentor Books, 1963), p. 333.

40 J. Z. Eglinton, *Greek Love* (London: Neville Spearman Pub., 1971), p. 51.
41 B. A. Brooks, "Fertility Cult Functionaries in the Old Testament," *JBL* 60 (1941): 232.
42 Ibid., p. 243. Babylonian creation myths depicted the creation of the earth as a result of the intercourse of male and female deities. The primeval fertility of the earth was maintained by imitating and valorizing the acts of the gods. See R. Collins, "The Bible and Sexuality," *BTB* 7 (1977): 149-51.

able that a good number of them were eunuch-priests. That a eunuch-priest should have a part in religious fertility cults seems at first sight inconsistent. However, eunuch-priests are well attested in India, Egypt, the Near East, Greece, and Africa. According to the belief of the times, such persons were more fittingly prepared to represent the deity, to function in phallic worship, or to secure fertility for the fields. They were accustomed to wearing female dress.[43] Albright suggests that they wore female dress because they functioned as women.[44] Again, magical ideas were at work which suggested the apotropaeic value of disguising sex.[45] Kramer reproduces a text which suggests a similar idea.

> Babylon a ruin, he turned to Erech, "the city of hierodules, courtesans, and sacred prostitutes to whom Ishtar (the goddess of love) was husband and master," the city "of eunuchs and sodomites, the merrymakers of Eanna (Ishtar's temple), whose maleness Ishtar had turned to femaleness, in order to terrify man."[46]

In Mesopotamia as in Egypt it is the passive homosexual who is despised, especially one who is habitually passive. The Mesopotamians, however, seem to have made a virtue of necessity. The strange abnormality of the homosexual and the abhorrence felt toward the habitually passive homosexual were attributed to the power of the goddess Ishtar. It was she who had wrought this change in order to instill fear in man. Oddly enough the safest place for these individuals was under her protection.

This strange relationship is spelled out in detail by Bottéro and Petschow. They find ample evidence of homosexuality in Mesopotamia in figure drawings and treatises on divination by dreams, especially those dedicated to erotic dreams. They assume that homosexuality is normal practice without complications or condemnation.

> *Active* homosexuality, if it is performed upon an individual of the same social level, does not constitute a crime except insofar

---

43 Ibid., pp. 247-48, n. 2; also Lambert, p. 230.
44 W. F. Albright, "Historical and Mythical Elements in the Story of Joseph," *JBL* 37 (1917): 116; also, R. H. Wood, *Christ and the Homosexual* (New York: Vantage Press, 1960), p. 140; and G. R. Taylor, "Historical and Mythological Aspects of Homosexuality," *Sexual Inversion: The Multiple Rooms of Homosexuality*, ed. J. Marmor (New York: Basic Books, 1965), pp. 151-54.
45 Sir J. G. Frazer, *Adonis Attis Osiris: Studies in the History of Oriental Religion* 2 (New York: Macmillan Publishing Co., 1935): 257-64.
46 S. N. Kramer, "Mythology of Sumer and Akkad," *Mythologies of the Ancient World*, ed. S. N. Kramer (New York: Doubleday & Co., 1961), pp. 130-31. Yamauchi cautions that there is no specific evidence that the assinnu of Ishtar were eunuchs or homosexuals. Yamauchi, p. 215, n. 27. However, CAD Z 117a 2b is a mistranslation; his view seems to be based on it.

as it involves force or violence; otherwise it seems perfectly permissible and outside of all legal restraint, and as we have seen above (par. 5) on the subject of C.T. 39, 44, it is no more blamable or dishonoring than heterosexual love. On the other hand, *passive* homosexuality, whoever the "active" partners are, is degrading from the single fact that it is *habitual,* that it constitutes, after some fashion, a way of life. It will be noted in passing that the young age of the passive partners is mentioned nowhere in these texts.[47]

Those who, despite their masculine sex, behaved voluntarily and habitually as passive lovers opposite partners of the same sex and took on feminine habits and a sort of feminine nature lost status in society. They ceased to be "the equal" *(tappau)* of others and joined, whether willing or not, a group of men who may be designated professionals of passive homosexuality, the most famous of whom were the *assinnu.* For the majority of these individuals, their lives consisted of a career or an art which was the object of a contract of apprenticeship. They may have played a role in the liturgy by disguising and masking themselves and bearing the distaff. They played music and sang and danced and perhaps interpreted plays or pantomimes. Most often they were connected with ceremonies in honor of Ishtar.[48] Due to the bisexual nature of the goddess, their role was necessarily ambiguous; but certain texts allow their erotic nature to appear, and they are found more than once associated with other courtesans of high quality whose vocation as prostitutes has never been doubted. Some texts like the *Summa alu* 15-32 explicitly denote that the *assinnu* subjected himself sexually to men.[49]

Some of these prostitutes were eunuchs or castrati, but what characterized them more than real emasculation was their behavior which is designated as *sinnisanu* ("effeminate") a synonym of *ur, sal,* and *assinnu.* The sumerogram *ur. sal/mi* is significant since it adds to the name "dog" *(ur),* which is used in biblical texts (Deut 23:19), the word "woman" *(sal/mi),* and might be translated literally "female dog."[50]

As individuals, however, they were rejected and were the object of scorn because they had deviated from their fundamental destiny and norm. Ishtar transformed them from "men into women." Because of this fact, their destiny is so aberrant and exceptional that in order to gladden the heart of

---

47 J. Bottéro, H. Petschow, "Homosexualität," *RLA* 4 (1972-1975): 1-4.
48 Ibid., p. 5, see also, B. A. Brooks, *A Contribution to the Study of the Moral Practices of Certain Social Groups in Ancient Mesopotamia* (Leipzig: W. Drugulin, 1921), pp. 72-78.
49 Ibid., p. 6.
50 Ibid., p. 7; see also Brooks, "Fertility Cult Functionaries in the Old Testament," p. 250.

the goddess whom they serve, "they engage in sacrilege" *(itakkatu a-[sakka]* Erra IV 58) . . . in other words, in practices normally forbidden to others . . . because they are not like others. This is the cause of the scorn which surround them.[51] Contrary to some evaluations, Bottéro and Petschow emphasize the freedom allowed to practice homosexuality:

> In itself, homosexuality was not at all condemned as profligacy, as immorality, as social disorder, or as transgressing any human or divine law . . . : anyone could practice it freely, just as he could freely visit the (female) prostitutes, provided in both cases that it was without violence or force, and therefore preferably with "specialists" as passive partners. But the latter like the (female) prostitutes, were social outcasts and scorned (with a scorn that must of necessity have overflowed upon the "non-professionals," as seen above, par. 8f), precisely because of the fact that they were beings to some extent mutilated, fallen from their primary destiny, and a-normal, in the etymological sense of this word.[52]

Individuals of the same sex could readily experience and express the same feelings for each other as individuals of the opposite sex without the opprobrium of society. The "Almanac of Incantations" consists of a series of prayers for assistance in love. First the love of a man for a woman, second the love of a woman for a man and third the love of a man for a man. The three prayers are on the same level, with the same verb "ramu" which marks a sincere and sentimental attachment to others. Homosexuals in Mesopotamia felt free to turn to their gods for help with their homosexual love problems as heterosexuals did with theirs.[53]

While in Babylonia and Assyria homosexuality was not illegal except as accompanied by force or was perpetrated upon an equal with coercion, it may have been forbidden with relatives or close kin. Those who adopted a permanent passive homosexual role usually became *hieroduloi* in the service of Ishtar, dressing and acting as women and performing homosexual and other services in the temple. These priests may have been eunuchs. They were scorned as deviates. Ishtar had changed their sex to put fear into man. Homosexuals felt free to petition the gods for help. The Egyptian grave of the two friends and the homosexual prayers in the "Almanac of Incantations" may mean that the ancients were not totally ignorant of homosexual types approximating what modern parlance calls "inverts."

---

51 Ibid., pp. 8-9.
52 Ibid., p. 9.
53 Ibid., p. 10.

Canaanite and Hittite

The situation with respect to homosexuality in Canaanite and Hittite society does not appear to be very different from the general picture in the ancient Near East. Hittite law did not condemn homosexuality as such. The only instance of condemnation is that of a man with his own son, which is in the same law with the interdiction of heterosexual relationship between near kin.[54] In addition, among the Hittites bestiality, like homosexuality, was susceptible to regulation but not complete interdict. A man became guilty of *hurkel* ("abomination") because his partner was his son, not because they were the same sex. Homosexuality then was not outlawed among the Hittites. The main version of Hittite law comes from about 1650 B.C. In it *hurkel* refers to an offense against the culprit's city. By perpetrating such an act he brought impurity upon his fellow townsmen and made them liable to divine wrath.[55]

The regulations concerning bestiality may possibly throw light on the laws about homosexuality. Sexual intercourse with sheep and cows was forbidden in Hittite law. Infractions incurred the death penalty.[56] But intercourse with horses or mules incurred no punishment.[57] Phillips offers the suggestion that the animals in the first category were considered sacred animals and that bestiality with them was an attempt at union with the deity through the sacred animal, after which the animal was sacrificed. Intercourse with these animals was in this case strictly limited to the cult.[58] Nevertheless, even the man who coupled with a horse or mule could not come before the king or become a priest (Hittite Laws 200A), although he was not guilty of *hurkel.* The man who had committed *hurkel* was killed or banished, and the townsmen bathed themselves to remove the impurity.[59] It is possible that, although homosexuality did not incur *hurkel* it may have restricted the individual in some other way.

---

54 E. Neufeld, *The Hittite Laws Translated Into English and Hebrew With Commentary* (London: Luzac and Co., 1951), pp. 54, 188. Law 189 reads "[If a man] sins with his mother, (it is) an abomination. If a [man] sins with a daughter, (it is) an abomination. If a man sins with a son, (it is) an abomination." See also H. A. Hoffner Jr., "Some Contributions of Hittitology to Old Testament Study," *Tyndale Bulletin* 20 (1969): 41.
55 H. A. Hoffner, Jr., "Incest, Sodomy and Bestiality in the Ancient Near East," *Orient and Occident Essays Presented to Cyrus H. Gordon*, ed., H. A. Hoffner Jr., *Alter Orient und Altes Testament, Veröffentlichungen zur Kultur und Geschichte des Alten Orients und des Alten Testaments* 22, ed. K. Bergerhof, et al. (Neukirchen: Butzon & Bercker, 1973): 85.
56 Neufeld, p. 53, Laws 187, 188. Law 199 includes pigs and dogs in the interdict.
57 Ibid., p. 57.
58 A. Phillips, *Ancient Israel's Criminal Law: A New Approach to the Decalogue* (New York: Schocken Books, 1970), p. 121.
59 Hoffner, "Incest, Sodomy and Bestiality . . . ," p. 85.

Canaanite Practice

In Canaanite religion and society the same elements prevailed as in other ancient societies of the Near East. Among them were sacred prostitution, male and female as well as homosexual. Transvestite behavior for magical purposes and even bestiality were part of the cult.[60] Self-mutilation and child sacrifice also were known in the Canaanite religion.[61]

As with many other fertility cults, Canaanite ritual employed hosts of male and female prostitutes as an integral part of the temple personnel. These and other *hieroduloi* acted out the mythical stories that provided a rationale for the status quo. The cultic rites sought to maintain the status quo by seeking magically to strengthen man's relationship with nature and the spirit world.[62]

The gods and goddesses of Israel's neighbors were organically related to nature. For the most part they appear in pairs and were depicted in myths and legends as creating the world by copulation. Cole surmises that their worship consisted of an imitation of their creative acts, "Their worship apparently required a kind of imitative magic in which male and female devotees yoked their bodies sexually and spilled their seed upon the fields they desired to yield bounteous crops."[63] In the milieu of the Canaanite fertility cult, the woman became a symbol for the ground which had to be plowed and sowed, and an object of the lust and conquest of man.[64]

Like Ishtar who changes men into women, the Canaanite Anath takes away men's bows. Hillers concludes that this means the same thing, that is, changing men into women. He quotes the Ishtar episode but also a Hittite prayer, "Take from (their) men masculinity, prowess, robust health, swords(?), battle-axes, arrows, and dagger(s)! And bring them to Hatti! Place in their hand the spindle and mirror of a woman! Dress them as women!"[65] Both the bow and the spindle are mentioned in Canaanite mythological contexts. Baal's only recorded use of the bow results in an

---

60 W. F. Albright, *Yahweh and the Gods of Canaan: Historical Analysis of Two Contrasting Faiths* (Garden City, NY: Doubleday & Co., 1968), p. 128; also, W. F. Albright, *Archeology and the Religion of Israel* (Baltimore: Johns Hopkins Univ. Press, 1946), pp. 75-755; and F. D. Nichol, ed., *The SDA Bible Commentary* 2 (Washington DC: Review & Herald Publishing Assn., 1954): 40.
61 F. M. Cross, *Canaanite Myth and Hebrew Epic, Essays in the History of the Religion of Israel* (Cambridge, MA: Harvard University Press, 1973), p. 25; also, Leslie, pp. 39-50; and Gray, p. 136.
62 G. H. Livingston, *The Pentateuch in its Cultural Environment* (Grand Rapids: Baker Book House, 1974), pp. 130-31.
63 W. G. Cole, *Sex and Love in the Bible* (London: Hodder and Stoughton, 1960), p. 181.
64 T. C. DeKruijf, *The Bible on Sexuality,* tr. F. Vander Heijden (De Pere, WI: St. Norbert Abbey Press, 1966), p. 64.
65 D. R. Hillers, "The bow of Aqhat: The Meaning of a Mythological Theme," *Orient and Occident Essays Presented to Cyrus H. Gordon,* p. 74.

orgy in which he copulates with a heifer and sires a calf. Hoffner sees unmistakable marks in style and content between Hittite and Canaanite texts whose symbols for male and female are used in major rituals, especially in cases of impotency.[66]

The evidence points to the idea that symbols of masculinity and femininity, the wearing of clothes of the opposite sex and the carrying of implements associated with the opposite sex were used in Canaanite ritual, these activities again probably involving eunuch-priests clad in female garb as well as male and female prostitutes. Homosexual activity and bestiality were considered ways of having intercourse with the gods and thus affecting the course of nature.[67]

It is significant, therefore, that the Old Testament opposes all of these activities. Deuteronomy 22:5 reads, "The implement of a man shall not be borne by a woman, nor shall a man clothe himself in the attire of a woman, for whoever does this is an abomination to Yahweh your God" (Hoffner's tr.). Deuteronomy 27:21, Exodus 22:19, and Leviticus 18:23 all forbid copulation with animals by men or women, and Leviticus 18:24 states that the Canaanites did such things. In the light of the extant texts, there is no reason to doubt the biblical records on these matters.

The evidence from the extant literature of the ancient Near East does not support the thesis that homosexuality was unknown among Israel's neighbors. On the contrary, it suggests that cultic homosexual practices were entirely legal. Furthermore, private homosexual practices were not forbidden but regulated by cultic and civil laws. Consequently the practice was regarded as criminal, sinful, or personally degrading only when it contravened these specific regulations; otherwise it seems to have been practiced freely without hindrance. Israelite law is the exception in that it banned all homosexual practice and excluded anyone who practiced it from participation in the cult of Yahweh.

---

66 H. A. Hoffner Jr., "Symbols for Masculinity and Femininity: Their use in Ancient Near Eastern Sympathetic Magic Rituals," *JBL* 85 (1966): 330.
67 Ibid., pp. 332-33; Brooks, p. 250; S. H. Horn, "The Depravity of the Canaanites" *Review and Herald* (December 18, 1952), pp. 9-10; R. W. Wood, "Homosexual Behavior in the Bible," *Homophile Studies: One Institute Quarterly* (Winter, 1962), p. 11; C. H. Gordon, *Ugaritic Literature, a Comprehensive Translation of the Poetic and Prose Texts* (Rome: Pontificum Institutum Biblicum, 1949), p. 8; United Church of Christ, *Human Sexuality: A Preliminary Study* (New York: United Church Press, 1977), p. 76.

Chapter 3
The Texts of the Old Testament

The Use of Scripture

For conservative Christians the Bible is central in any formulation concerning homosexuality, whether theological or ethical. How one handles the scriptural material determines the answers received. In fact one's view of Scripture at the outset influences the questions asked. Although considerations of space require us to opt for a proof text approach in this book, the vital concerns dealt with here can be answered satisfactorily only by developing a coherent theology of sex.

Scriptures set forth certain values as an integral part of the Christian's self-understanding. Love is a central value and virtue, for example, but it must be understood in the context of biblical anthropology. That is, love is not self-authenticating; love is not allowed to discover or dictate its own standards or patterns of conduct.[1] Love, which is the fulfilling of the law, always has existed and operated in context of the revelation from God that concerns His will. Love is not its own law, nor is the renewed consciousness its own moral monitor. Homosexuality, therefore, cannot be rendered acceptable simply by labeling it "loving" any more than any other controversial activity could be condoned this way. On the other hand, the acceptance of scriptural authority on questions of ethics and morals does not mean the natural and social sciences may be ignored in favor of strict biblicism. Many specific contemporary ethical dilemmas were unknown or ignored in the ancient world. The modern phenomenon must be studied carefully before biblical principles can be applied and judgment made.

In recent years arguments have appeared attempting to negate biblical authority in the discussion of homosexuality. At times the Scriptures are looked upon merely as the word of humans, not as expressing the mind of God, and are held to be no more authoritative than anyone else's "word."[2]

---

[1] J. Murray, *Principles of Conduct: Aspects of Biblical Ethics* (Grand Rapids: Wm. B. Eerdman's Publishing Co., 1964), p. 24.
[2] R. L. Treese, "Homosexuality, A Contemporary View of the Biblical Perspective," *Loving*

Others question their relevance for today. Homosexuality, it is argued, is not condemned as such. It was condemned because of its association with idolatry. That is, it had a cultic or symbolic significance due to its use by pagans, which it does not now have.[3] Coupled with this argument, although sometimes found in isolation from it, is the contention that the Scriptures are historically conditioned, that the biblical authors knew nothing about the condition of homosexuality. They knew nothing about the modern "invert." Furthermore the contention is that in the Scriptures homosexuality is condemned as rape, perversion or exploitation. The loving relation of two constitutional homosexuals is not condemned because such was not known in biblical times or at least not understood.[4]

Two main positions are present among these views; either that the Bible opposes homosexuality or that it does not. Scroggs has given a clear outline of these positions.[5] To provide the substance of the main arguments pro and con, we give a condensation of his material.

The Bible As Opposed to Homosexuality

1. The Bible opposes homosexuality and is definitive for what the church should think and do about it. Here the Bible stands as the objective revelation of God's eternal will. God is completely opposed to homosexuality.

2. The Bible opposes homosexuality, but it is one sin among many. There is no justification for singling it out as more serious than other sins castigated in the Bible. In this case homosexuality is a sin but not a unique sin—no worse than that of liars, thieves, or drunkards.

3. The Bible opposes homosexuality, but specific injunctions must be placed in the larger biblical context of the theology of creation, sin, judgment, and grace. Here we have in essence the "analogy of faith" argument. It goes something like this. The heart of the Bible is its central message. This central message becomes a principle to evaluate other less specific or

---

Women/Loving Men: Gay Liberation and the Church, ed. and auth. S. Gearhert and W. R. Johnson (San Francisco: Glide Publications, 1974), p. 28; T. Maurer, "Toward a Theology of Homosexuality—Tried and Found Trite and Tragic," *Is Gay Good? Ethics, Theology and Homosexuality,* ed. W. D. Oberholtzer (Philadelphia: Westminster Press, 1971), pp. 98-100.

3 H. K. Jones, *Toward a Christian Understanding of the Homosexual* (New York: Association Press, 1966), p. 69.

4 R. Woods, *Another Kind of Love: Homosexuality and Spirituality* (Chicago: Thomas More Press, 1977), p. 103; J. McNeill, *The Church and the Homosexual* (Kansas City, MO: Sheed, Andrews & McMeel, 1976), p. 39; J. B. Nelson, "Religious and Moral Issues in Working With Homosexual Clients," *Homosexuality and Psychotherapy, A Practitioner's Handbook of Affirmative Models: Journal of Homosexuality* 7, Nos. 2-3, ed. J. C. Gonsiorek (New York: Haworth Press, 1982): 166-67.

5 R. Scroggs, *The New Testament and Homosexuality: Contextual Background for Contemporary Debate* (Philadelphia: Fortress Press, 1983), pp. 7-11.

less essential parts of Scripture. The actual application of this principle can take many directions since the interpreter decides what is central. Here homosexuality will be viewed in different lights depending on the central principle selected, for example, creation, love, justification, or others.

4. The Bible opposes homosexuality but is so time and culture bound that its injunctions may and should be discarded if other considerations suggest better alternatives. Here contemporary biological, psychological, theological, or sociological considerations may outweigh the biblical material as authority in forming a judgment about homosexuality.

The Bible As Condoning Homosexuality

Arguments which claim that the Bible does not oppose homosexuality are outlined by Scroggs as follows:[6]

1. The Bible does not oppose homosexuality because it does not describe true or innate homosexuality, but homosexual acts by people who are not homosexuals. This is basically the "invert" versus "pervert" argument.

2. The Bible does not oppose homosexuality because the texts do not deal with homosexuality in general. Here the key phrase is *in general.* The Bible opposes prostitution and idolatry in conjunction with homosexuality, not homosexuality, as such. Whenever the Bible appears to condemn homosexuality, related evils are really being condemned, not homosexuality.

On both sides of the issue arguments surface to cast doubt on the authority, historicity, inspiration, and relevance of the Scriptures to the homosexual question. Some propose that the time conditioned statements of Scripture deal with phenomena that no longer exist or are based on obscure and uninformed views of homosexuality. This disqualifies them from current debate.

To a great extent the way the biblical exegete relates to homosexuality depends upon how he or she relates to these arguments. The Adventist position on the inspiration and authority of Scripture would result in a position similar to the first cited in the previous section.

It might be necessary to ask, however, what is meant by "God is completely opposed to homosexuality." Is the Bible opposed to the condition, the acts, or both? Is God opposed to any individual who has a homosexual orientation? If not, under what circumstances can one say that God is "completely opposed to homosexuality?" The answers to these and other questions will emerge as we proceed to analyze our subject more fully.

---

6   Ibid., pp. 11-16.

Old Testament Texts Cited With Reference to Homosexuality

As Smedes has observed, for many thoughtful Christian believers how to feel about sexuality is part of a larger question, that is, how to feel about Creation.[7] If our sexuality is part of creation, our feelings about it can reflect God's feelings about what He made.

Writers who begin a discussion of homosexuality with Genesis 1 and 2 are not necessarily adopting the "analogy of faith" argument. These chapters are not seen as the primary revelation in Scripture by which all else is to be scrutinized, but as the essential starting point in any scriptural discussion of sex. Both Jesus and Paul discuss sexual relationships in the light of Genesis (Matt 19:7-10; Mark 10:2-9; Rom 1:18-25), making it a reference point even more critical for the Christian interpreter.

> Genesis 1:27. So God created man in his image, in the image of God he created him; male and female he created them.

Genesis asserts that God created them male and female. Therefore sexual distinction is created. As von Rad comments, "By God's will, man was not created alone but designated for the thou of the other sex."[8] The passage, when properly understood, makes each partner the complement of the other, enjoying spiritual equality.[9] There is no suggestion in Genesis of any division of a bisexual or sexually undifferentiated creature into two different sexes. Sex is not deified but neither is it denied. It is firmly rooted within the good creative purposes of God. The essential need of male and female for each other is recognized and underlined. Together they form the unity which is mankind.[10] The much debated "image of God" in this verse has been explained by Barth as consisting in man's being in fellowship.[11] Kubo also finds the male-female duality essential to a complete understanding of the image of God in man:

> What the verse primarily means is that not mankind as male but male and female together make up the image of God. It must

---

7 L. B. Smedes, *Sex for Christians, the Limits and Liberties of Sexual Living* (Grand Rapids: Wm. B. Eerdmans Publishing Co., 1977), p. 26; also, C. Wittschiebe, *God Invented Sex* (Nashville: Southern Publishing Assoc., 1974), pp. 50-51.
8 G. von Rad, *Genesis: A Commentary*, tr. J. H. Marks (Philadelphia: Westminster Press, 1961), p. 58; C. F. Keil, F. Delitzsch, *The First Book of Moses (Genesis)*, tr. J. Martin (Grand Rapids: Wm. B. Eerdman's Publishing Co., 1949), pp. 88-89.
9 D. Kidner, *Genesis: An Introduction and Commentary* (Downers Grove, IL: Inter-Varsity Press, 1973), p. 52.
10 R. Davidson, *Genesis 1-11 Commentary* (Cambridge, MA: Cambridge University Press, 1973), pp. 25-26.
11 Karl Barth, *Church Dogmatics* III, 4, tr. A. T. Mackay, et al. (Edinburgh: T. and T. Clark, 1978): 117. For a contrary argument to Barth see G. T. Sheppard, "The Use of Scripture within the Christian Ethical Debate Concerning Same-Sex Oriented Persons" *USQR* 40 (1985): 23-32.

denote more than the fact both male and female have the image of God. While that fact is true, it is also true that one sex alone does not constitute the image of God in its totality. The sexual duality of male and female is necessary for our full understanding of the image of God.[12]

To reflect fully the image of God, man and woman not only stand in relation to each other but to God. As Smedes puts it, "Personal communion is what the image of God is about."[13] The primal form of humanity is the fellowship of man and woman.[14] "To be human is to share humanity with the opposite sex."[15] But we are not necessarily speaking about marriage. The blessing of procreation is quite distinct from being made in the image of God as male and female, as our next text illustrates.

> Genesis 2:18, 24. Then the Lord God said, "It is not good that the man should be alone; I will make him a helper fit for him."... Therefore a man leaves his father and his mother and cleaves to his wife, and they become one flesh.

God made "a helper fit for him," literally "a help as opposite him," that is, corresponding to Him.[16] Mankind as male and female are not created simply for the purpose of procreation.[17] Procreative ability is carefully removed from God's image and shifted to a special word of blessing. Consequently, sexual ability is not an emanation or manifestation of the divine image as in the fertility cults.[18] Sexuality as such does not intrude into man's relationship with God.[19] Man and woman become one flesh, one personality, for flesh here means more than the physical side of life, it is the medium through which the whole personality communicates.[20] Williams sums up the Genesis material in the same way, contending that male or female alone does not adequately represent the divine image.

> Here we come to see that man is created in the image and likeness of God as male and female. Male alone does not fully

---

12 S. Kubo, *Theology and Ethics of Sex* (Washington, DC: Review & Herald Publishing Assn., 1980), p. 24.
13 Smedes, p. 33.
14 P. K. Jewett, *Man as Male and Female: A Study in Sexual Relationships from a Theological Point of View* (Grand Rapids: Wm. B. Eerdmans Publishing Co., 1975), p. 36; S. Sapp, *Sexuality, the Bible and Science* (Philadelphia: Fortress Press, 1977), pp. 9-10.
15 D. Williams, *The Bond That Breaks: Will Homosexuality Split the Church?* (BIM, 1978), p. 53.
16 Kidner, pp. 65-66.
17 McNeill, p. 60.
18 von Rad, pp. 58-59.
19 W. Eichrodt, *Theology of the Old Testament* 1 (Philadelphia: Westminster Press, 1967): 128.
20 Davidson, p. 38.

represent the divine image. Female alone does not fully represent the divine image. A community of simply one sex does not reflect God's intention for us or His character in the world.[21]

Therefore the actual manner in which man exists in the image of God is as male and female together. This line of reasoning, particularly as presented by Barth and Thielicke, has been rejected by many other scholars. Thielicke sees the differentiation of the sexes as so constitutive of humanity that it appears in Genesis as a primal order which endures as a constant despite human depravation in the Fall. Others do not believe the text teaches an ontological unity of biological sex difference and psychosexual expressions. Such unity is not inherent in Creation, they say; and therefore, does not define man as made in the image of God. This means

> male and female at birth may be no more than a physical differentiation. . . . The potentiality for sexual expression may simply be an undifferentiated potential at birth, and the direction which the sex drive takes in seeking expression—the choice of another human being to which the drive shall ultimately be attached—may be truly conditioned learning.[22]

Humanity has no choice but to be "fellow-human" in relation to "fellow-human." The question is, but must the fellow-human be in relationship to a "fellow-human" of the opposite sex?[23]

These considerations raise serious questions. What about biological sex distinction and psychological sex identity—how are they related? Can a male be a whole person without a personal relationship with a female, and vice versa? This suggestion that there is a kind of dualism between the obvious physical sex and the psychosocial expression of it emanating from the inner being needs to be measured against biblical anthropology.

Biblical anthropology tends to be holistic. It allows for a dialectic between inner and outer man but hardly a dualism between sexual morphology and sexual expression. Such a dualism may occur in Scripture as an aberration due to the Fall of man, but not as the intent of the Creator.

It would be extremely useful if the dynamics of sexuality and personality were spelled out from the biblical perspective. Such a study would supply a fitting background for these remarks and provide a necessary context for them. However the brief remarks above must suffice and we must turn now to the most discussed passage in Scripture with respect to homosexuality.

---

21 Williams, pp. 56-57.
22 Treese, p. 47.
23 Ibid., p. 48.

The Case of Sodom

> Genesis 19:4-10. But before they lay down, the men of the city, the men of Sodom, both young and old, all the people to the last man, surrounded the house; and they called to Lot, "Where are the men who came to you tonight? Bring them out to us, that we may know them." Lot went out of the door to the men, shut the door after him, and said, "I beg you, my brothers, do not act so wickedly. Behold, I have two daughters who have not known man; let me bring them out to you, and do to them as you please; only do nothing to these men, for they have come under the shelter of my roof." But they said, "Stand back!" And they said, "This fellow came to sojourn, and he would play the judge! Now we will deal worse with you than with them." Then they pressed hard against the man Lot, and drew near to break the door. But the men put forth their hands and brought Lot into the house to them, and shut the door.

Throughout the history of the church this passage has been used to show God's displeasure with homosexuals. In this instance, it was claimed, homosexuality caused the destruction of the cities in the plain.

In 1975 the first extensive and radically new interpretation of this passage was published by D. S. Bailey, whose ideas have been repeated in numerous books. Bailey is an Anglican clergyman who was a member of an informal group of Anglican clergy and physicians that produced a report called "The Problem of Homosexuality," published by the Church of England Welfare Council. Bailey, the main lecturer for the Council, later published his own book, *Homosexuality and the Western Christian Tradition*. Bailey was also instrumental in inaugurating a government committee to investigate law and practice relating to homosexual offenses. This report, The Wolfendon Report, named after the committee chairman, recommended that homosexual behavior between consenting adults in private no longer be considered a criminal offense in England. The recommendation of the Committee was adopted legally by Parliament in 1967.

Crucial to their decision was Bailey's thesis that Christian tradition has misread the account of the judgment of Sodom in Genesis 19. This undercut the notion that toleration of homosexual behavior is a sign of national decay and paved the way for relaxing legal sanctions.

Bailey, considered by many the high priest of pro-homosexual interpretation of Scripture, raises numerous questions about this passage. "What ground is there," he asks, "for the persistent belief that the inhabitants of the city were addicted to male homosexual practices, and punished accordingly?"[24] He finds little evidence. Beginning with verse 5, "Bring them out to us, that we may know them," he suggests that the word "know" *(yada^c)* occurs some 943 times in the Old Testament; but in only twelve instances, without qualification, does it mean coitus. On the basis of these statistics, he adopts Barton's[25] view that there is no actual necessity to interpret "know" in Genesis 19:5 as equivalent to "have coitus with" and that it may mean no more than "get acquainted with."

Few biblical scholars agree with this restricted interpretation of *yada^c*.[26] Many point to verse 8 which is manifestly sexual in connotation. Even McNeill, a Catholic priest who advocates responsible homosexual behavior, admits that the case has been overstated here.[27] However, many scholars who admit that this interpretation is weak still point out that it is clearly violent homosexual rape that is intended and which is being condemned here. Therefore if this text does not speak negatively about a loving homosexual relation between consenting adults, it cannot be used to condemn it, they claim.

Those who accept this new interpretation, however, have to explain why the mere request to get acquainted with the visitors is made in such a violent manner. The suggested answer proposes that Lot was a sojourner *(ger)*, and as a resident alien, he did not have the right to bring other aliens into his house, especially those whose credentials were unknown to the citizens. Furthermore, he was unpopular. The citizens of the place might be accused of boorish inhospitality, but there is no evidence that homosexual vice was prevalent there.

In trying to explain why, under these circumstances, Lot offered his virgin daughters to the citizenry to do as they pleased with them, Bailey's argument is at its weakest. He suggests, "that it was simply the most tempting bribe that Lot could offer on the spur of the moment to appease the hostile crowd."[28] This assumes that the crowd was bent on violence, perhaps rape. But Bailey has assured us already that they are just concerned citizens who want to clarify the status of Lot's visitors. If this is so, Lot's offer of his daughters is most incongruous and calculated to heighten the suspicions of the citizens about his visitors.

If "know" in verse 5 simply means "get acquainted with," Lot grossly

---

24 D. S. Bailey, *Homosexuality and the Western Christian Tradition* (Hamden, CT: Shoe String Press, 1975), p. 1.
25 G. A. Barton, "Sodomy," in *Encyclopedia of Religion and Ethics,* ed. J. Hastings (New York, 1928), p. 672.
26 J. P. Lewis, "Yadha," *Theological Wordbook of the Old Testament* 1, ed. R. L. Harris (Chicago: Moody Bible Institute, 1981): 366-67; also Kidner, p. 136, are among many who disagree with Bailey.
27 McNeill, p. 47.
28 Bailey, p. 6.

misunderstood the citizens. His best course of action would have been to acquaint them with the visitors. In addition, this interpretation finds the biblical account to be influenced by later legends dealing with punishment for inhospitality.

But this entire reconstruction throws a serious question on the justice of God, for we are presented with God destroying the cities by fire for their lack of hospitality, first and foremost, as well as undefined general wickedness. Bailey points out that no Old Testament citation of this passage explicitly identifies the sin of Sodom as homosexuality. (See Gen 13:13; 18:20; Jer 23:14; Ezek 16:49, 50.) It is only in the post-canonical literature relating to Hellenism that these passages are interpreted of homosexuality, he suggests, and in the late New Testament books influenced by Hellenistic literature and pseudepigrapha—2 Peter and Jude.

The Old Testament depicts the people of Sodom as a symbol of utter wickedness and grievous sin, who committed adultery, walked in lies, were haughty, and committed abomination. Sodom was also a symbol of complete destruction (see Isa 1:9; 13:19; Jer 49:18; 50:40; Amos 4:11; Zech 2:9). True, there is no explicit mention of homosexuality here. The further claim is made that this witness, that is, that Sodom was destroyed for inhospitality, folly, and pride, is continued in the Apocrypha. Especially quoted are Wisdom 10:8 and 19:8 and Ecclesiasticus 16:8.

In Wisdom 19:13, 14 (Bailey cites Wisdom 19:8 but quotes 19:14) neither the words "Sodom" nor "Egyptians" appear in the text, though they are implied. The Egyptians are being compared with Sodom and seem to be declared the more wicked. In Wisdom the Egyptians are accused of "hatred of strangers" *(misozenia,* vs. 13); and this is construed, along with verse 14, as a testimony to inhospitality.

This particular argument has not reckoned with the fact that in the Hellenistic world *misozenia* was a loaded word. As Radin[29] points out, it had within its broad range of meaning not only inhospitality and a social behavior but also abuse of strangers and, in extreme cases, even cannibalism.

This particular passage does not support the new thesis as thoroughly after careful inspection. We can agree with those who contend that it is nonsense to assume that Sodom and Gomorrah were destroyed solely because of homosexuality. The Old Testament clearly states that the sins of the cities were many and grievous. On the other hand, we cannot agree with attempts to exclude homosexuality as one of these sins. Therefore, we conclude that Genesis 19 is clearly a reference to an attempted homo-

---

29 M. Radin, *The Jews Among the Greeks and Romans* (Philadelphia: Jewish Publication Society of America, 1915), p. 186. Josephus describes the Egyptian army as cannibalistic in *Ant.* XIII. 340-41, Jewish women and children are the victims.

sexual rape of Lot's visitors. The question of whether this text condemns all homosexual activity does not seem to be answered here but perhaps comes within the scope of the next references.

The Mosaic Laws

> Leviticus 18:22. You shall not lie with a male as with a woman; it is an abomination.
>
> Leviticus 20:13. If a man lies with a male as with a woman, both of them have committed an abomination; they shall be put to death, their blood is upon them.

These texts unquestionably prohibit and condemn male homosexual genital activity. But a number of reasons are put forth to negate their impact. They are seen by some as part of a cultic taboo in primitive Judaism. Homosexuality is condemned, it is claimed, because of its association with the religious practices and licentious behavior of the Gentile idolaters. Others think these laws applied only to priests at any rate and none of them applies to Christians since the early church had been released from the necessity of keeping the Levitical laws.[30]

McNeill finds an interesting social reason for these laws, that is, it was necessary for Israel to increase her population, therefore homosexuality was discouraged. A more cogent reason for McNeill, however, is the connection between idolatry and homosexuality. As he states, "Whenever homosexual activity is mentioned in the Old Testament, the author usually has in mind the use male worshippers made of male prostitutes provided by the temple authorities."[31] Others find little homosexuality among Israel's neighbors and none in pagan temples. For them homosexual acts are an abomination, not because of pagan cults, but because they reverse the natural order of sexuality, which in doing they show the spirit of idolatry.[32] Homosexuality itself is a fundamental subversion of the true order of things. This is a creation order of things, as Bailey implies by following up this argument with an examination of Romans 1.

To be properly appreciated, the Levitical laws need to be seen in the context of chapters 18-20. They were not merely for the priests but for all the people of Israel (Lev 18:1). Israel was to live according to God's laws to show contemporary Near Eastern nations the true nature of holiness.

---

30 M. Olson, "Untangling the Web: A Look at What Scripture Does and Does Not Say About Homosexual Behavior," *Other Side (April 1984)*, p. 25.
31 McNeill, pp. 57-58.
32 Bailey, p. 60. This position is supported by Don Williams. See Williams, p. 65; and L. Scanzoni and V. R. Mollenkott, *Is the Homosexual My Neighbor?* (New York: Harper & Row Pubs., 1978), p. 60.

A special responsibility lay on the priests. "Not merely are the priests to observe the cultic regulations for ceremonial holiness, but they are required to live lives of moral purity and spiritual dedication, so that they will be examples to Israel of divine holiness."[33]

Chapters 18-20 deal with various laws and punishments. In 18, various sexual relationships are predominant: incest, adultery, and homosexuality, as well as child sacrifice and bestiality. Few Christians would be prepared to say that all of this is now acceptable because the early church was freed from the Levitical law, or that if it is done in loving relationship, it is not to be condemned.

But what about commands such as in Leviticus 19:19—"You shall not sow your field with two kinds of seed; nor shall there come upon you a garment of cloth made of two kinds of stuff." Surely this places these laws in the cultic taboo category. Not necessarily. As the covenant people of God, the Israelites were expected to maintain ceremonial and moral holiness. The book of Leviticus is a compendium of both ritual and moral enactments, an ideal manual for the purpose. Whether certain enactments were moral or ritual it is sometimes difficult to tell. The Presbyterian *Blue Book*[34] here relies heavily on Mary Douglas' *Purity and Danger,*[35] in which the criteria cited for holiness are: (1) Holiness is a whole body, (2) Holiness is internal peace and social order, (3) Holiness is unmixed classes and categories of creation. Homosexuality is condemned on this thesis because it violates the integrity of primary categories of creation.

As to seeds and cloth, this text is difficult to interpret at best. We do not really know what is meant here. But to throw out all of chapters 18 and 19 on the basis of one verse is surely throwing out the baby with the bath water. Leviticus 19:18 reads, "you shall love your neighbor as yourself." The application of the all or nothing principle in relation to the Levitical laws was not applied by Jesus in His ministry.

The great majority of Christians have always recognized the continual ethical significance of much of the material in Exodus 20-40 and Leviticus. The practices listed in chapter 18 have been considered particularly abhorrent to Christians throughout the ages. In addition, the New Testament reiterates the negative attitude toward homosexual acts found in Leviticus.

---

33 R. K. Harrison, *Leviticus: An Introduction and Commentary* (Downers Grove, IL: Inter-Varsity Press, 1980), p. 27. See also G. J. Wenham, *The Book of Leviticus* (Grand Rapids: Wm. B. Eerdman's Publishing Co., 1979): "Most of the laws apply to all Israel: only a few sections specifically concern the priests alone."

34 B. E. Shafer, *Blue Book I,* "The Church and Homosexuality" (San Diego: 190th General Assembly [1978] of The United Presbyterian Church in the United States of America, May 16-24, 1978), pp. D-39—D-43.

35 M. Douglas, *Purity and Danger: An Analysis of Concepts of Pollution and Taboo* (London: Routledge and Kegan, 1978).

This endorsement by the New Testament is perhaps the best criterion we have at present that any particular part of the Levitical law is still an element of God's will for His people.

The Idolatry Thesis

The most repeated argument attempting to negate the force of the Levitical statements is that homosexuality is condemned here because of its relation to idolatry. A man is condemned as an idolater, not as a homosexual. The unstated assumption implies that a homosexual who is not an idolater would not be condemned.

Dr. John Boswell, a homosexual and professor at Yale University, presents a detailed study of the Hebrew *to^cebah* and the Greek *bdelugma* and reaches this conclusion. The line of reasoning followed by Boswell is that the Hebrew word *to^cebah* ("abomination") as in Leviticus 18:22 and 20:13 does not usually signify something intrinsically evil, such as rape or theft, but something ritually unclean.[36] The point frequently is emphasized that the prohibition of homosexual acts follows immediately upon a prohibition of idolatrous sexuality. "And thou shalt not let any of thy seed pass through the fire to Molech" (Lev 18:21, KJV). The implication here is that the Molech text and the text following on homosexuality are both ritual in nature, not ethical or moral.

Although both chapters 18 and 20 contain prohibitions against incest and adultery that might stem from moral absolutes, some contend that their function in Leviticus 18 and 20 is to serve as symbols of Jewish distinctiveness. What appears to clinch this argument is the claim that the Septuagint, a Greek translation of the Hebrew Scriptures, draws the distinction between intrinsic wrong and ritual impurity by translating *to^cebah* sometimes as *anomia* (violations of law and justice) and sometimes as *bdelugma* (infringements of ritual purity or monotheistic worship). In the Septuagint homosexuality is characterized as *bdelugma* in both texts.

The conclusion drawn here, apparently, is that homosexuality was not considered a violation of law and justice, or itself intrinsically wrong, but rather was a matter of ritual purity and monotheistic worship, that is, idolatrous. It was related to Jewish cult and culture but was not something immoral or unethical. This argument is more subtle, but it contains the same kind of logic as Bailey's statistical reasoning concerning *yada^c* ("know").

It is true that in the majority of instances, *to^cebah* refers to ritual infrin-

---

36 J. Boswell, *Christianity, Social Tolerance and Homosexuality: Gay People in Western Europe From the Beginning of the Christian Era to the Fourteenth Century* (Chicago: Univ. of Chicago Press, 1981), pp. 100-101.

gements of the law. But just as *yada^c* is sometimes used in a sexual sense meaning coitus, so *to^{c}ebah* is occasionally used in an ethical sense concerning truth and justice (Deut 25:16; Prov 8:7; 16:12; 29:27; Jer 6:15).[37] Although there is a tendency in the Septuagint to ethicize *to^{c}ebah* as do the prophets and Proverbs, the Septuagint is not consistent in its treatment of *to^{c}ebah*. Deuteronomy 25:16, a clearly ethical statement, is described as *bdelugma* in the Septuagint. Fundamental to this issue is the fact that God has a contrary mind to the practice involved and rejects it.[38]

Furthermore, the ancients were not in the habit of dividing their thought and action into the neat modern categories of sacred and secular. For Jew and pagan alike the sacred covered all of life, as the books of Leviticus and Deuteronomy testify. This means that some ideas and activities of their pagan neighbors were acceptable to the Jews. In significant aspects the cult and literature of Israel and its neighbors were similar, with Israel clearly the borrower.

It is not enough, therefore, to state that homosexuality was condemned merely because it was a product of pagan society and a part of pagan cult. The reasons why Israel borrowed ideas and practices from pagan neighbors, which she did, are more complex than this simple formula suggests.[39] Consequently, when she did not borrow or even forbade the assimilation of pagan thought and practice, the reasons are likewise more complex than the abhorrence of idolatry. Idolatry, the bowing down to images or performing certain cult acts, was simply a part of an entire lifestyle, philosophy, theology, and cosmology fundamentally inimical to Israel's self-understanding as proclaimed to them by God in covenant relationship with Him.

Separation from pagans involved more than mere avoidance of idolatry. Israel mediated the presence of the divine to her neighbors.[40] Hence the outward form of Israel's life was not a matter of indifference. The visible

---

37 See F. Brown, S. R. Driver, and C. A. Briggs, *A*
38 W. Foerster, *"Bdelussomai, bdelugma, bdeluktos"* in *TDNT* 1 (1968): 598-99, also, P. M. Ukleja, "Homosexuality and the Old Testament," *BSac* 140 (1983): 262-64; Hebrew and English Lexicon of the Old Testament (Oxford: Clarendon Press, 1976), pp. 1072-73, who list Leviticus 19:22 as ethical; see also, R. F. Youngblood, *"to eba,"* *Theological Wordbook of the Old Testament* 2, ed. R. L. Harris (Chicago: Moody Bible Institute, 1981): 976-77.
39 J. Jensen, "The Relevance of the Old Testament I: A Different 'Methodological Approach,'" *Dimensions of Human Sexuality*, ed. D. Doherty (Garden City, NY: Doubleday & Co., 1979), p. 5. As Jensen notes, so frequently did Israel share with pagan neighbors that where some objection is raised to a pagan rite, "some reason other than its pagan associations must be sought."
40 Eichrodt, p. 404. Concerning the testimony of the prophets: Carol Stuhlmueller concludes that "sexual sins like adultery and prostitution, whether involving Gentile or Israelite people, are condemned as evil per se and not simply as Canaanite fertility rites which invaded Israelite sanctuaries." C. Stuhlmueller, "The Relevance of the Old Testament, II. Prophetic Ideals and Sexual Morality," *Dimension of Human Sexuality*, ed. D. Doherty (Garden City, NY: Doubleday & Co., 1979), p. 12.

community was to be clearly distinguishable from the surrounding nations, their pagan gods and immoral practices.

The fact that idolatry and homosexual practice were found together in pagan religion does not mean that they are one and the same thing. In our texts we have a simple prohibition against homosexual acts. The fact that those acts were sometimes practiced in pagan rituals also compounded the abomination rather than detracting from it. Some commentaries, however, see idolatry as the main problem.[41]

One Old Testament commentary concludes that the ban on homosexuality is merely cultic by interpreting Leviticus 18:22 in the light of the previous verse (18:21, devoting children to Molech).[42] It observes that "by fire" is not in the Hebrew text. This law then is not dealing with child sacrifice by fire to Molech, but in fact prohibits giving children to Molech as temple prostitutes. Then it interprets verses 21 and 22 both as reflecting cultic sexual violation. Therefore homosexuality is condemned because of its association with idolatry.

There are a number of problems with this interpretation. First, if any verse is out of context in chapter 18, it is verse 21 concerning Molech. All other salient verses clearly refer to sexual practices; it does not. Noth speaks of the Molech law as "striking" since it is out of context.[43] He suggests that "it was only the key word 'seed' ['children,' RSV] which brought this verse into the present context." Furthermore, giving children to Molech does not necessarily imply sexual or homosexual behavior on their part. Finally, in the light of clear biblical reference to human sacrifices to Molech (2 Kgs 23:10; 1 Chr 28:3; Jer 7:31), the observation of Noth that verse 21 is out of context is preferred. The verse does not have to mean devotion to Molech as a prostitute or as a sacrifice but may mean that the child was dedicated to the cult as Samuel was to the temple.

Sapp concludes that the laws against bestiality and homosexuality were based on three major concerns.[44] First, that such relations were "simply unnatural." "Moral law and natural law—both products of the one God—could not conflict. Thus to defy nature's law is to violate the revealed law of morality. What nature abhors the law prohibits."[45] Second, and integrally related to the first, is the concern for wasted seed. Finally, the Israelites saw a link between these types of sexual misconduct and idolatry.

---

41 S. H. Kellogg, "The Book of Leviticus," *The Expositor's Bible* 1, ed. W. R. Nicoll (Grand Rapids: Wm. B. Eerdmans Publishing Co., 1943): 334.
42 N. H. Snaith, *Leviticus and Numbers* (Greenwood, SC: Attic Press, 1977), pp. 125-26.
43 M. Noth, *Leviticus: A Commentary*, tr. J. E. Anderson (Philadelphia: Westminster Press, 1965), p. 136.
44 Sapp, p. 31.
45 Ibid.

The Texts of the Old Testament

Homosexuality was not a widespread problem in Israel and these laws were promulgated to assure that it could not be. At the very least, these laws are the best available evidence for determining the established Jewish legal position on homosexual activity between men.

Presumably the attitude of Jesus and the early church toward it was the same. Homosexuality was not a major problem among the Jews in Christ's time, and His silence on the subject can also be construed this way: it simply was not an issue.

The Talmud considered the laws prohibiting copulation with beasts and sodomy to be universal in nature and part of the seven moral laws applicable to Noahides as well as Jews. Epstein notes that "in talmudic as well as in biblical times, the heathen was held under suspicion of committing this crime when the opportunity was afforded him."[46] In addition, " 'Jews are above suspicion of committing sodomy.' If the law prohibits an unmarried man to be a teacher of boys, it is because of the visits of their mothers to the schoolhouse, not because of his association with the boys themselves."[47]

The plain meaning of Leviticus 18:22 and 20:13 is a prohibition of male genital homosexual acts. Since no provisional or exception clauses are included, as is the case with some of the laws, we can only conclude that they prohibit and condemn such acts. At least the onus or burden of proof is on those who would interpret these texts to mean something else. We cannot accept the premise that morality was not an issue here, although we recognize that other factors were linked to the prohibition.

> Deuteronomy 23:17-18. There shall be no cult prostitute of the daughters of Israel, neither shall there be a cult prostitute of the sons of Israel. You shall not bring the hire of a harlot, or the wages of a dog, into the house of the Lord your God in payment for any vow; for both of these are an abomination to the Lord your God.
>
> 1 Kings 14:23-24. For they also built for themselves high places, and pillars, and Asherim on every high hill and under every green tree; and there were also male cult prostitutes in the land. They did according to all the abominations of the nations which the Lord drove out before the people of Israel.

In the Deuteronomy passages the key phrases in these texts are, "cult prostitute of the sons of Israel," "a dog" and "male cult prostitutes." Only

---

46 L. M. Epstein, *Sex Laws and Customs in Judaism* (New York: Ktav Publishing House, 1967), pp. 134, 136, and references cited there.
47 Ibid., p. 137.

two Hebrew words are involved here, *qadesh* ("cult prostitute"; literally, "holy man") and *keleb* (a "dog"). The question is, Was the King James version correct in translating *qadesh* as "sodomite"?

Some readers claim that in 1611 "sodomy" was not restricted to sexual intercourse with the same sex and with beasts, but was applied to intercourse between unmarried human beings also.[48] The *Oxford English Dictionary*, however, clearly shows that the meaning of this word was reserved for homosexual intercourse; for example, 1601—"which if he wanted he would hire a boy sodomitically to use," 1677—"two noble youths being sodomitically abused by this infernal goat." The dictionary presents examples ranging in date from 1300 to 1705 which are references to same-sex relations.[49] The text reading "whore" in the AV for "sodomitess" in the margin is the only evidence favoring the above argument.

Others find the influence of the Vulgate at work here. Sometimes *qadesh* is translated with the Latin *scortator* ("fornicator") and sometimes *effeminatus,* a synonym of *pathicus* which denotes the male homosexual prostitute, especially one who plays the passive role in sodomy by permitting anal intromission. Such authors reject the Vulgate translation because supposedly it does not express the sense of the Hebrew.

Neither, it is claimed, do the five words used in the Septuagint (LXX) strictly translate the Hebrew. For example, in Deuteronomy 23:17 the Septuagint translates *qadesh* with a participle meaning to prostitute. First Kings 14:24 translates the Hebrew as *sundesmos,* a noun meaning to bind together. The word originally had no sexual meaning. In 1 Kings 15:12 *qadesh* is translated as *telete,* meaning an "initiate" or a *hierodulos* ("temple-servant"). In 2 Kings 23:7 the term is simply transliterated into Greek. Finally, 1 Kings 22:46 reads *endiellagmenos,* a derivate of *allasso,* meaning to alter or change. Some suggest the expression may mean one who has changed his nature by becoming a homosexual or one who has become an apostate by leaving the religion of Yahweh.[50] In fact any reading which implies homosexuality is immediately rejected by some.

Consequently, in this text certain readers find nothing but ritual prostitution between male and female. For them the "hire of a harlot" or "wages of a dog" refer to the same thing, the "harlot" (Heb., *zonah*) who cohabited with males in the temple and the "dog" (Heb., *keleb*) being those who had intercourse with women devotees. In this interpretation the term "dog"

---

48 Barton, p. 672.
49 *Oxford English Dictionary* 9 (Oxford: Clarendon Press, 1933): 366.
50 Bailey, pp. 50-51. The texts under discussion, Deuteronomy 13:17-18; 1 Kings 14:23-24 and other texts, such as 1 Kings 15:12; 22:47; 2 Kings 23:7 do not make clear that castrated sodomites are indicated. Aquila's rendering of the LXX assumes such, and they were not unknown in Israel. See J. Gray, *I and II Kings: A Commentary* (Philadelphia: Westminster Press, 1963), p. 311.

or "servant" simply refers to the male who served as a temple prostitute.

Bailey, who finds no reference to homosexuality in these texts, finally comments, "Homosexual coitus would be meaningless in the ritual of a fertility cult, with its exclusively heterosexual rationale."[51]

Although the term "dog" could be used as equivalent to the word "servant," as found in Aramaic inscriptions, "who is your servant (if not) a dog"[52] we have suggested earlier that "dog" implies more than simply a cult servant or "a cultic functionary dressed like a dog,"[53] but rather a group of eunuchs (Deut 23:17) or effeminates, who dressed like women (cf. Deut 22:5) and subjected themselves sexually to other men.

Since many gods or goddesses were considered bisexual and were involved in such activities themselves, this would not be an unusual practice in a fertility religion. These types were well known in Assyria and in Syria, as in Lucian's description of the priests of Cybele,[54] and they are not unknown in the modern world.[55]

Concerning these texts we lean to the view that homosexual activity was sometimes involved in the meaning of the words *qadesh* ("cult prostitute"), or *keleb* ("dog") and cannot be entirely ruled out as a part of their meaning.

The Outrage in Gibeah

> Judges 19:22-25. As they were making their hearts merry, behold, the men of the city, base fellows, beset the house round about, beating on the door; and they said to the old man, the master of the house, "Bring out the man who came into your house, that we may know him." And the man, the master of the house, went out to them and said to them, "No, my brethren, do not act so wickedly; seeing that this man has come into my house, do not do this vile thing. Behold, here are my virgin daughter and his concubine; let me bring them out now. Ravish them and do with them what seems good to you; but against this man do not do so vile a thing." But the men would not listen to him. So the man seized his concubine, and put her out to them; and they knew her, and abused her all night until the morning. And as the dawn began to break, they let her go.

---

51 Ibid., pp. 52-53.
52 H. Donner, W. Rollig, *Kanaanäische und Aramäische Inschriften*, Bd. I., Text. Otto Harrassowitz (Wiesbaden, 1979), pp. 190-91.
53 M. H. Pope, "Homosexuality," *IDB* Supp (1976): 417.
54 Lucian, *The Goddesses of Syria*, p. 15.
55 J. G. Frazer, Adonis, Attis, Osiris: *Studies in the History of Oriental Religion* 2 (New York: Macmillan Publishing Co., 1935): 253-64.

The story related in Judges, chapters 19-21, is from the period of the tribal leagues in Israel, that is, twelfth to eleventh century B.C. The events take place before the days of Samuel or Saul.

The story is about a Levite sojourning in the country of Ephraim. He has a concubine who becomes angry with him and leaves him, returning to her father in Bethlehem. After four months the Levite journeys to Bethlehem seeking his concubine. He is well received by his father-in-law who wines and dines him and begs him to extend his visit. The Levite finally decides to leave, taking his concubine with him. They get a late start and it begins to get dark so they look for a safe city to stay in for the night. The narrator points out that they bypass Jerusalem, which was at that time a Canaanite city, and pass on to Gibeah or Ramah, an Israelite city. Here, apparently, they expected hospitality but received none.

After sitting in the open square of the city for some time, a resident alien *(ger),* an old man from Ephraim, spots them as he is returning from a day in the fields and extends hospitality to them. While the old man is entertaining his guests, the men of the city, Benjaminites, beat on the door and demand to "know" the man. The conclusion of the story, following our text, is that the Levite's concubine dies, which becomes the immediate cause of a war between the tribes of Israel and the Benjaminites, with dire consequences for the latter. The book of Judges, as well as this episode, concludes with the line, "In these days there was no king in Israel; every man did what was right in his own eyes" (Judg 21:25).

Similarities between Genesis 19 and Judges 19 are obvious. Many commentators assume one of the authors heard about or was looking at the other author's work. The Sodom and Gomorrah story usually is considered older. In that case possibly we have a commentary on the sin of Sodom.

Looking at the text under discussion, the base fellows (literally, sons of Belial), a term for worthless scoundrels, beat upon the door. They demand to "know" the man who is the guest *(yada^c)*. But Bailey insists that even here the word *yada^c* means simply "get acquainted with," despite the fact that the text states concerning the Levite's concubine that "they knew *[yada^c]* her, and abused her all night." He says,

> As in the case of the Sodom story, the view that the Gibeathites were prone to homosexual practices and desired the Levite for the satisfaction of their unnatural lusts is nothing more than an inference from the words: "Bring forth the man ... that we may know him"—the verb yadha^c ("to know") being again construed in a coital sense.[56]

---

56 Bailey, p. 54.

Commenting on the same word in our text, *yada^c*, a recent commentator observes that *yada^c* is never used unambiguously of homosexual intercourse.[57] Here the author sees the first use of *yada^c* as deliberately ambiguous, but with the offer of the young women, the ambiguity disappears.

We may agree with the commentator that here, as in Genesis 19, the initial and determinative offense is a violation of the law of hospitality. But homosexual overtures played a clear part in it. It is scarcely possible for *yada^c* to be used twice in such close proximity in the same context and to be completely ambiguous in one instance and completely unambiguous in the next. For in this case the first use of *yada^c* never means homosexual intercourse. If it means that the second use of *yada^c* takes away the ambiguity of the first occurrence in the context, his point makes better hermeneutical sense. As it is, the comment itself is rather ambiguous and may be interpreted either way.

The host at Gibeah implores them not to do this "foolish" thing *(nebalah)*. Cundall[58] makes two pertinent comments on this situation. First he notices that no attempt was made by the rulers of Gibeah to punish the offenders or to repudiate their actions. So it appears that the men of the city generally were involved, not just a lewd minority. Second, his study of the word *nebalah* leads him to conclude that the interpretation "foolish" is not strong enough here. The word denotes "an insensibility to the claims of God or man." Better translations would be "impiety" or "wantonness." These men were not about to recognize any moral or religious claims upon them.

Bailey is aware of the thrust and import of *nebalah* but brushes it aside as an editorial addition introduced to bring this story into line with the Sodom story.[59] The word has other meanings, he suggests, such as inhospitable, churlishness, and need be seen as nothing more than "a rhetorical addition designed to emphasize the deplorable lack of courtesy shown by the Gibeathites towards the visitor." Currie, however, following Noth and von Rad, sees the word as a technical term involving a violation of covenant obligations. "But all uses thus listed clearly point at violation of covenant obligations to the LORD and especially to wanton sexual conduct out of keeping with allegiance to YHWH."[60] Collins also sees human sexuality

---

57 R. G. Boling, *Judges: Introduction, Translation and Commentary* (Garden City, NY: Doubleday & Co., 1969), p. 276.
58 A. E. Cundall, *Judges: An Introduction and Commentary* (Downers Grove, IL: Inter-Varsity Press, 1973), pp. 196-97.
59 Bailey, p. 55.
60 S. D. Currie, "Biblical Studies for a Seminar on Sexuality and the Human Community," *Austin Seminary Bulletin* 87 (1971): 19.

in the Old Testament as lying in the sphere of human responsibility, a sphere in which man has dominion but within covenant obligations to Yahweh.

> Human sexuality was indeed a dimension of human experience which fell within the parameters of Yahweh's hegemony and the covenant relationship. The presence of "Thou shalt not commit adultery" within the covenant clauses of the Decalogue (Ex. 20:14; Dt. 5:18) serve as a clear reminder that the fashion in which man lived his sexuality was not independent of his relationship to Yahweh, God of his people. Similarly, the different outcomes of the encounter between Joseph and Potiphar's wife (Gen. 39) and that between David and Bathsheba (2 Sam. 11) indicate well that human sexuality is not an awesome force over which man has no control. These stories, told so often in Jewish tradition, clearly proclaim that man is responsible for the way in which he uses his sexuality, that God given gift over which he exercises dominion in Yahweh's name and by Yahweh's power.[61]

Bailey's interpretations have been extremely influential, being repeated in much of the pro-homophile literature despite the fact that most biblical commentators do not agree with him. His interpretations do not do justice to the context and do not place the same gravity on the recorded events that the narrators themselves sense. Consequently, Bartlett's criticism seems fair when he says,

> It takes special imaginative power to believe, as Bailey does, that what the men of the city of Gibeah were after was the acquaintance of the visiting man, or that the old man of Gibeah offered his virgin daughter and the other's concubine only to protect his rights of hospitality.[62]

The idea that the accepted codes of hospitality allowed a man to sacrifice women instead of guests is far removed from modern Western concepts of behavior and ethics. But womanhood was lightly esteemed by some in the ancient world, as evidenced by the action of the Levite whose greater concern was to save his own skin.[63]

As in Genesis 19, so also in Judges 19, it would be oversimplification to

---

61 R. Collins, "The Bible and Sexuality," *BTB* 7 (1977): 158.
62 D. L. Bartlett, "A Biblical Perspective on Homosexuality," *Homosexuality and the Christian Faith: A Symposium*, ed. H. L. Twiss (Valley Forge, PA: Judson Press, 1978), p. 25.
63 Cundall, p. 197.

say that the sin of Gibeah was homosexuality alone. The wrongdoing of the Gibeathites, as with the inhabitants of Sodom, was far more than homosexuality. In our view, however, one goes too far to claim that the Sodomites and the Gibeathites had no proclivity to homosexuality. In this passage there is a clear reference to attempted homosexual rape, actual heterosexual gang rape, and murder. As in the Genesis account, so also here we cannot agree with Bailey that this is merely a gentlemanly disagreement and inhospitality. The text and context suggest far more than that. Furthermore, none of this is connected with idolatry or pagan ritual; and it took place in an Israelite city in a period of general anarchy of which it serves as an example.

Secondary Old Testament Texts Cited With Reference to Homosexuality

Other texts are cited as records of homosexual conduct in the Old Testament. All of them will not be dealt with in detail here since, in our opinion, there is insufficient evidence that they contain homosexual overtones at all. Narratives alleged to recount homosexual experiences are said to be those about David and Jonathan (1 Sam 18:1; 19:1; 20:30; 2 Sam 1:26;), Ham and Noah (Gen 9:21-27), Ishmael and Isaac (Gen 21:9), Ruth and Naomi (Ruth 1:16, 17) and Joseph and Potiphar (Gen 39).[64] Some claim that Nebuchadnezzar kept Daniel for homosexual purposes. We will consider the cases of David and Jonathan, Ham and Noah, and Ruth and Naomi.

> 1 Samuel 18:1. When he had finished speaking to Saul, the son of Jonathan was knit to the soul of David, and Jonathan loved him as his own soul.
>
> 1 Samuel 19:1. And Saul spoke to Jonathan his son and to all his servants, that they should kill David. But Jonathan, Saul's son, delighted much in David.
>
> 2 Samuel 1:26. I am distressed for you, my brother Jonathan; very pleasant have you been to me; your love to me was wonderful, passing the love of women.

---

[64] Brim claims that among the Egyptians pederasty was one of the forms of worship and the high officials in Pharaoh's court purchased good-looking boys for performing religious services, especially to the idol Baal-Peor. The most outstanding case was Joseph. Brim presents no evidence and many of his views are based on the comments of Rashi. See J. Brim, *Medicine in the Bible* (New York: Froben Press, 1936), p. 362.

The Case of Jonathan and David

The episode most frequently mentioned as a homosexual love affair in the OT is the relationship of David and Jonathan. T. M. Homer speaks of it as "the only example of an unabashed homosexual love of one well-known character for another."[65] He quotes 1 Samuel 18:1-3 where Jonathan makes a covenant with David, strips off his clothes and gives him his armor. He also makes reference to 1 Samuel 20:30 where Saul berates Jonathan for having chosen David to be his own shame and the shame of his mother's nakedness. In 1 Samuel 20:41 he points out that David and Jonathan kiss one another and weep with one another. Then in 2 Samuel 1:26 David tells how he valued the love of Jonathan. Homer concludes that they must have been bisexual since they both married and had children.[66]

Homer does not find it surprising at all that homosexuality existed in Israel, for the influence of all the nations around them, particularly the Philistines, was bound to have been felt.[67] Other factors that point to a homosexual relation are the aristocratic, heroic station of Jonathan and the later heroic stature of David himself, "the two heroes gravitated toward each other."[68] Could the two men be friends without raising the issue of homosexuality? Homer answers:

> Yes, they can. But when two men come from a society that for two hundred years had lived in the shadow of the Philistine culture, which accepted homosexuality; when they find themselves in a social context that was thoroughly military in the Eastern sense; when one of them—who was the social superior of the two—makes a public display of his love; when they meet secretly and kiss each other and shed copious tears at parting; when one of them proclaims that his love for the other surpassed his love for women—and all this is present in the David-Jonathan liaison—we have every reason to believe that a homosexual relationship existed.[69]

Dr. G. W. Henry, a psychiatrist of some 30 years' experience, examined

---

65 T. M. Homer, *Sex in the Bible* (Rutland, VT: Charles E. Tuttle Co., 1974), p. 85.
66 Ibid., p. 87.
67 T. Homer, *Jonathan Loved David: Homosexuality in Biblical Times* (Philadelphia: Westminster Press, 1978), pp. 20-21.
68 Ibid., p. 26. Kirkpatrick also sees here the first Biblical instance of romantic friendship. "Each found in each the affection that he found not in his own family." He sees analogies with the Greek heroes and comrades in arms but makes no mention of homosexuality per se. A. F. Kirkpatrick, *The First Book of Samuel: With Introduction and Notes* (Cambridge, MA: Cambridge Univ. Press, 1930), p. 152.
69 Ibid., pp. 27-28.

the story of David and Jonathan. He found that the influence of women on David seems negligible. David's name is not even associated with women until after the slaying of Goliath when Saul presents him with a wife. However, by this time he had developed a strong friendship with Jonathan. In this friendship Jonathan was the aggressor and David unreservedly responsive. David's homosexuality is looked upon as a passing phase in the young lad's experience.[70]

Quite a different interpretation emerges from the text as Johnson reads it, for he advances the theory that David was a constitutional homosexual who only consorted with women under pressure.

> King Saul persecuted his very own son, referring to Jonathan's love for David as a perversion. He screamed, "You are an intimate lover to that son of Jesse." Jonathan made a beautiful love covenant with David, promising undying devotion. In 1 Samuel 18:3 these two young men took the Bereeth love oath, used in ancient marriage vows (Malachi 2:14). These two lovers secretly met in the bushes, kissed, embraced and performed *gadal* (sexual intercourse). They were even married to each other *(laeuach,* 1 Samuel 19:2). David publicly declared: "Jonathan, beloved and lovely, very pleasant have you been to me, your love to me was wonderful, passing the love of women." (2 Samuel 1:23.) This statement is exactly the definition of a homosexual according to Sigmund Freud. David also lead [sic] the young men in dancing naked and after Jonathan's death developed a love relationship with Jonathan's only son.[71]

The key words in the story are "love" *('ahab),* "covenant" *(berith),* and "sexual intercourse[?]" *(gadal).* Of course the words cannot be taken in isolation since they are an integral part of a context. The verses cited at the beginning of this section as well as those mentioned since must also be interpreted in their respective contexts, not independently.

First Samuel 18:1 states that "the soul of Jonathan was knit to the soul of David, and Jonathan loved him as his own soul." Ihe verb "was knit" or "bound" also meaning "to league together" has no sexual connotation in the Old Testament. The verb *qashar* ("to knit" "bind") carries more the meaning of treason or conspiracy than "love affair."[72] The verb "love"

---

70 G. W. Henry, *All the Sexes: A Study of Masculinity and Femininity* (New York: Rhinehart and Co., 1955), p. 498.
71 P. Johnson, *The Gay Experience* (Lambdas, 1978), p. 7, quoted in P. R. Johnson, T. F. Eaves Sr., *Gays and the New Right* (Los Angeles: P. R. Johnson, 1982), p. 107.
72 Cf Gen 44:30-31 where Judah says to Joseph, "since [my father's] life is bound up in the [boy's] life, ... when he sees that the ... [boy] is not with us, ... he will die" (NASB); i.e., Jacob was in-

(*'ahab*) has a wide range of meanings referring to affection between members of the opposite sex (Gen 24:67), sexual intercourse (Hos 3:1), and affection between mother and child (Gen 25:28). It refers to affection between adults of the same sex (Ruth 4:15; 1 Sam 16:21), and between teacher and student (Prov 9:8), servant and master (Exod 21:5), and between a whole people and a military leader (1 Sam 18:16, 22).[73] When referring to sexual love it refers to the marital relationship as something given at Creation in a positive sense. For the act of sexual intercourse itself a different root *yada*ʿ ("to know") is used. Thus the emphasis suggested by the word 'ahab is not really on sexual love but more on experiencing and desiring love.[74]

By observing only a verse here and there, it is possible to emphasize the personal dimension of the "love" between David and Jonathan. The inclusion of the wider context of 1 and 2 Samuel, however, draws attention to what may be called the political overtones of the word. The word may be used in a political sense, as seen by the reference to 1 Kings 5:1—"Now Hiram King of Tyre sent his servants to Solomon, when he heard that they had anointed him king in place of his father; for Hiram always loved David." David and Hiram were involved in diplomatic and commercial arrangements for a number of years. The word "love" here describes the political amity between the states.

Thompson has suggested that another context where the political meaning of the word is found are the David-Jonathan narratives in 1 Samuel.[75] The word describes the various covenants and friendships which David made en route to the throne. Saul "loved" David greatly, made him his armor bearer and even gave him his armor (1 Sam 16:21; 17:38, 39). Here the narrator is preparing his readers for the later political use of the term.

Jonathan did a similar thing after the battle with Goliath (1 Sam 18:4). The passing of arms and armor from the lesser to the greater seems to have had political implications in the ancient Near East. Jonathan seems well aware that David will inevitably become king (1 Sam 20:13-16), and makes David swear by his "love" for him (1 Sam 20:17). Saul was also aware of the popularity of David with the people and himself declared, "What more can he have but the kingdom?" (1 Sam 18:8). It must have been clear to Saul and Jonathan that "all Israel and Judah loved David; for he went out and came in before them" (1 Sam 18:16). Thompson remarks, "In this con-

---

separably devoted to Benjamin as Jonathan was vitally devoted to David in affection and loyalty.
73 J. Bergman, A. O. Haldar, G. Wallis, *"ahabh"* in *TDOT* 1 (1974): 104.
74 Ibid., p. 107.
75 J. A. Thompson, "The Significance of the Verb Love in the David-Jonathan Narratives in 1 Samuel," *VT* 24 (1974): 334-35.

text, the verb love expresses more than natural affection. It denotes rather the kind of attachment people had to a king who could fight their battles for them."[76]

A similar connotation may be seen in the message Saul sends to David, "'Behold, the king has delight in you, and all his servants love you'" (1 Sam 18:22). David is offered Saul's daughter in marriage but refuses on the grounds that he is poor and cannot afford the bride price. Saul asks for one hundred foreskins of the Philistines as the bride price and David brings two hundred. Saul realizes "that the Lord was with David, and that all Israel loved him" (1 Sam 18:28).

In this context it is not out of place to suggest that the word love has political rather than sexual overtones.[77] The transferring of clothes from Jonathan to David has royal overtones suggesting a legal symbolism relegating the privilege of succession willingly to David.[78] In this setting Jonathan moves beyond personal feelings of a friendly disposition and makes a solemn "covenant" concluded under the eyes of Yahweh in a fixed cultic form.[79]

We also see in this passage that covenant, league, agreement—*(berith)* is not necessarily a marriage covenant but simply a pact or agreement between the two men, each protecting the life of the other. Jonathan protected David from his father whereas David protected Jonathan, or rather his descendants, as he had promised. Due to the changing political fortunes of both men, the solemn vow was a necessary assurance for both of them.[80]

Finally, the claim that David and Jonathan had sexual intercourse *(gadal)* appears to be more an assertion than an interpretation. First Samuel 20:41b reads, "and they kissed one another, and wept with one another, until David recovered himself." The expression "recovered himself" is a translation of the hiphil perfect of *gadal*. It is an obscure expression at best as evidenced by the various translations of it—recovered, exceeded, etc. The lexicons do not give a sexual meaning for this verb. Holladay gives the translation, "take courage."[81] Gesenius, followed by Brown, Driver and Briggs sees an ellipsis with an implied infinitive and translates, "they both wept—until David wept most violently"

---

76 Ibid., p. 337.
77 P. K. McCarter Jr., *1 Samuel: A New Translation With Introduction, Notes and Commentary*, AB 8 (Garden City, NY: Doubleday & Co., 1980), p. 305.
78 Ibid.
79 H. W. Hertzberg, *I and II Samuel: A Commentary* (Philadelphia: Westminster Press, 1964), pp. 154-55.
80 Josephus, *Ant.* VI. 229-31, interprets the entire episode in a clearly political light.
81 W. L. Holladay, *A Concise Hebrew and Aramaic Lexicon of the Old Testament* (Leiden: E. J. Brill Pubs., 1971), p. 56.

(Brown, Driver, and Briggs, "wept greatly").[82] The Septuagint translates into Greek with a similar idea using the word *sunteleia*[83] which Delling interprets in this context as "satiety."[84] Based on this interpretation the text means that David wept violently or until he could weep no more. There is neither philological nor contextual warrant for the translation of *gadal* as "sexual intercourse."

The larger context supports a sociopolitical interpretation of the particular verses involved, rather than personal or sexual. Upon examination we conclude that the homosexual interpretation of David and Jonathan's relationship is read into the text rather than out of it. There simply is no warrant for the assumption that David and Jonathan had a homosexual love affair. Consequently, neither is there evidence inferring that, since this alleged homosexual affair stands uncondemned in the Bible, all loving homosexual relationships can be justified on the basis of Scripture.

Noah and Ham

> Genesis 9:20-24. Noah was the first tiller of the soil. He planted a vineyard; and he drank of the wine, and became drunk, and lay uncovered in his tent. And Ham, the father of Canaan, saw the nakedness of his father, and told his two brothers outside. Then Shem and Japheth took a garment, laid it upon their shoulders, and walked backward and covered the nakedness of their father; their faces were turned away, and they did not see their father's nakedness. When Noah awoke from his wine and knew what his youngest son had done to him, he said, . . .

Bruns interprets this event in the light of the Contendings of Horus and Seth.[85] Parts of that story already have been narrated. The essence of the Seth-Horus story, as Bruns interprets it, is that while Horus sleeps, Seth commits an act of sodomy upon him. Subsequently in the council of the gods, he claims superiority over Horus due to his "doughty deeds of war" against Horus. According to Bruns,

> It would seem that the original story of Noah and Ham followed the same lines. By committing sodomy upon his father—who

---

82 W. Gesenius, *Hebrew and Chaldee Lexicon to the Old Testament Scriptures,* tr. S. P. Tregelles (Grand Rapids: Wm. B. Eerdman Publishing Co., 1964), p. 159; and F. Brown, S. R. Driver, C. A. Briggs, ed., *A Hebrew and English Lexicon of the Old Testament* (Oxford: Clarendon Press, 1976), p. 152.
83 A. Rahlfs, ed., *Septuaginta I* (Stuttgart: Württembergische Bibelanstalt, 1962), p. 544.
84 G. Delling, *"sunteleia," TDNT* 8 (1977): 65.
85 J. Edgar Bruns, "Old Testament History and the Development of Sexual Ethic," *The New Morality: Continuity and Discontinuity,* ed. W. Dunphy (New York: Herder, 1967), p. 75.

was the ancestor of all men after the flood—Ham (Egypt) could also claim the right to dominate all mankind. Both Ham and Seth take advantage of the unconscious condition of their victims.[86]

He thinks the biblical editor's revision of the story omits explicit mention of a sexual act and makes Canaan rather than Ham the recipient of Noah's curse. This was done because the Canaanites were the most immediate threat to Israel's political and religious survival. Ham, however, was retained as the sexual aggressor because the editor realized that the Canaanites never had been a real threat to Israel.[87]

Although, as Bruns concedes, there is no explicit mention of a sexual act here, is such an act implicit in the narrative, as some seem to think? The story relates how Noah became intoxicated and lay "uncovered" *(galah)* in his tent. Here the verb is in the hithpael imperfect form; that is, Noah exposed himself. Although the verb *galah* can be a euphemism for sexual intercourse (cf. Lev 18:7), it must be in the Hebrew piel construction to have this meaning. Even in the piel to "uncover the nakedness" of someone, is not necessarily to have intercourse with them. This was especially true where the other person was also male. In this case the Levitical code is careful to explain what is meant, meaning to "uncover the nakedness" of a male was to have intercourse with his spouse. For example we read:

> Leviticus 18:7. You shall not uncover the nakedness of your father, which is the nakedness of your mother; she is your mother, you shall not uncover her nakedness.
>
> Leviticus 18:14. You shall not uncover the nakedness of your father's brother, that is, you shall not approach his wife; she is your aunt.
>
> The law in Leviticus 18:7 is rephrased in Deuteronomy 27:20. Cursed be he who lies with is father's wife, because he has uncovered her who is his father's.[88]

Here the verbs "lies with" and "uncovered" both are euphemisms for sexual intercourse. The verb "uncovered" is not used in the Old Testament to describe sexual intercourse with males; for this the terms "lie with" and "know" are employed.

These observations raise the possibility that Ham had intercourse with

---

86 Ibid.
87 Ibid., p. 76.
88 Cf. Lev 20:11, 20. The most frequent object of *galah* in the piel is *'erwah* ("shame," "nakedness"). It can mean to commit fornication, to flaunt nakedness, to rape. See H. J. Zobel, *galah*, in *TDOT* 2 (1974): 479.

his mother, which in the technical language of Leviticus would be termed "uncovering the nakedness" of his father. The text says, however, that Ham "saw the nakedness" of his father, an expression used only once in the Old Testament for sexual intercourse in Leviticus 20:17, that being with one's sister.

Some have suggested that Ham's sin was the invasion of the privacy of his father while he was having intercourse, that is, he watched them during the act. If so, there is no suggestion of that in this particular word. The clear meaning of *galah* here is that Noah exposed himself in his tent. Even here, some read "her tent," assuming that Noah was about to or more likely had just completed intercourse with his wife and fallen asleep. In antiquity it was possible for wealthy wives to own their personal tent. However, the reading "her tent" rather then "his tent" requires a change in the vowel pointing of the Masoretic text.

The story continues by relating that "Ham the father of Canaan, saw the nakedness of his father, and told his two brothers outside." To see the nakedness of another was a great humiliation to the one seen.[89] The nakedness *('erwah)* of Noah was seen by Ham. Wood comments:

> Uncovering the nakedness usually meant displaying the genitals and was almost akin to sexual intercourse, and therefore where a parent or relative was concerned, to incest. Ham, it will be remembered, was cursed for seeing the genitals of his father when the latter was drunk.[90]

In Leviticus 20:17, the expression "to see the nakedness of" appears to be synonymous with the phrase "to uncover the nakedness of," in which case it means sexual intercourse.

---

[89] It was customary for ancient conquerors to humiliate their captives by marching them naked into exile. See Isaiah 20:4; 47:2-3; Jeremiah 13:22, 26; Ezekiel 23:29. Numerous views of what Ham actually did have been proposed by the rabbis and others. The Midrash and Talmud agree that Ham castrated Noah. Others think that Ham believed that by looking he acquired Noah's potency or that Ham caught Noah in the act of intercourse and watched till he fell asleep. For these and other discussions of the event see, H. H. Cohen, *The Drunkenness of Noah* (Tuscaloosa, AL: Univ. of Alabama Press, 1974), pp. 13-21. Others suggest that Ham's sin was incest, that is, while Noah was asleep Ham slept with his mother. See F. W. Basset, "Noah's Nakedness and the Curse of Canaan: A case of Incest?" *VT* 21 (1971): 232, 237. As a result of this incestuous relationship Canaan was born, hence the curse on Canaan rather than Ham. Problems with this interpretation are spelled out by V. P. Hamilton, *Handbook on the Pentateuch* (Grand Rapids: Baker Book House, 1982), pp. 77-79.

[90] L. R. Wood, "Sex Life in Ancient Civilizations," in *The Encyclopedia of Sexual Behavior* 1, ed. A. Ellis and A. Abarbanel (New York: Hawthorn Books, 1961), p. 127. Speiser suggests that the term relates to exposure and does not necessarily imply sexual offenses. E. A. Speiser, *Genesis: Introduction, Translation and Notes* (Garden City, NY: Doubleday and Co., 1964), p. 61.Pentateuch (Grand Rapids: Baker Book House, 1982), pp. 77-79.

If a man takes his sister, a daughter of his father or a daughter of his mother, and sees her nakedness, and she sees his nakedness, it is a shameful thing, and they shall be cut off in the sight of the children of their people; he has uncovered his sister's nakedness, he shall bear his iniquity.[91]

Ryle suggests a want of delicacy and uncalled-for levity on the part of Ham who had no regard for his father's honor.[92] He emphasizes the carefulness and modesty of the two brothers as contrasted with immodesty of the younger son and adds, "Possibly the narrator suppressed something even more repulsive than mere looking (cf. vs. 24: 'What his youngest son had done to him')."[93]

If the expression, "saw the nakedness of his father" is used in Genesis 9:22 as a euphemism for sexual intercourse, it would be the only such instance in Scripture where this term is used for male-with-male intercourse. However, it cannot be absolutely ruled out as a possibility on that account alone. Consequently, this text could be interpreted to mean that Ham made a homosexual assault on his father. On the other hand Ham may have seen his father lying uncovered in the tent and instead of discreetly covering up his exposed body, took his garment so that he was left naked. The text may suggest this by saying, "Shem and Japheth took a garment, laid it upon both their shoulders, and walked backward." Here the passage refers to something specific, in this case the garment that Ham took from his father as evidence that he had seen the nakedness of his father with all that it implied.

Whatever Ham did to his father, whether he only saw him and made light of the matter or whether he physically assaulted him, it is difficult to see how this text could be seen as condoning homosexual acts in any way. The withering curse of Noah against Canaan scarcely commends the act. That the curse is directed against Canaan, a descendant of Ham (Gen 10:6) suggests that Noah saw this act as marring the inheritance of Ham. This flagrantly unfilial act "is the obverse of the fifth commandment, which makes the national destiny pivot on the same point."[94]

Although there may be a hint of homosexual conduct in the Ham-Noah account the entire episode is denounced and the perpetrator severely

---

[91] G. von Rad, *Genesis: A Commentary,* tr., J. H. Marks, (Philadelphia: Westminster Press, 1961), p. 133.
[92] H. E. Ryle, *The Book of Genesis: With Introduction and Notes* (Cambridge, MA: Cambridge University Press, 1921), p. 127.
[93] Ibid.
[94] D. Kidner, *Genesis: An Introduction and Commentary* (Downers Grove, IL: Inter-Varsity Press, 1973), p. 103.

cursed as one who has dishonored a parent. Contrary to condoning homosexual acts this suggests instead a strong condemnation of them, especially here where a father/son relation is also involved.

Ruth and Naomi

> Ruth 1:16-18. But Ruth said, "Entreat me not to leave you or to return from following you; for where you go I will go, and where you lodge I will lodge; your people shall be my people, and your God my God; where you die I will die, and there will I be buried. May the Lord do so to me and more also if even death parts me from you." And when Naomi saw that she was determined to go with her, she said no more.

Johnson, referring to this passage, comments: "The most beautiful love song ever written was composed by one woman to another and is still sung at weddings (Ruth 1:16)."[95] Foster refers to the account as a great short story, a masterpiece of narrative act. Concerning the details of the story she says, "the author, however, was . . . seemingly blind to their full significance, of an attachment which, however innocent, is nevertheless still basically variant."[96] The story, she believes, must be read against the background of a primitive tribal custom. Ruth was willing to abandon not only her native soil, her own family and burial with her ancestors, but even her god.

Alongside these considerations, the emotional force of the story is clarified by three other factors. First of all Ruth had been married about ten years at the time of her widowhood and must have been in her midtwenties. Consequently, her clinging to Naomi

> cannot be counted as clinging of a bereaved adolescent to the bridegroom's mother. Furthermore, it was Naomi who schemed to get Ruth married to Boaz at which time the women said to Naomi, ". . . he shall be unto thee a restorer of life and a nourisher of your old age; for thy daughter-in-law who loves you, who is more to you than seven sons, has borne him" (Ruth 4:14, 15).

Finally, Orpah, who remained in Moab, apparently had every prospect of finding a second husband there. Foster summarizes the narrative as follows:

---

95 P. R. Johnson, T. F. Eaves Sr., p. 107.
96 J. Foster, *Sex Variant Women in Literature* (Baltimore: Diana Press, 1975), p. 22.

Viewed without prejudice, this is a masterly portrait of a somewhat passive young woman, twice playing the heterosexual role with success, but dominated by another love at least as compelling as that for the men she successively married.[97]

Homer finds it impossible to demonstrate a relationship of physical love between them, but "all the right words are there" he says. "Certainly no other sexual relationship was possible for either of them at the time these words were expressed."[98]

The difficulty with this interpretation is that any similar close relationship would allow some speculation about a homosexual bond. Close friendships, however, need not be necessarily homosexual. Furthermore, the difficulty is compounded by Foster's suggestion that the author was seemingly blind to the full significance of the events related.[99]

Indeed, not only did the Bible writer miss this deviant significance, but almost everyone else since has missed it also. The homosexual interpretation appears to be a speculation read into the text rather than an interpretation arising from or suggested by the text and context of the book itself. This is even more apparent when the passage is placed in context and the purpose of the author taken into consideration.

In part, the aim of the author was to portray the idyllic scene of a God-fearing pastoral community. The main characters stand out against this background. Further points the author was trying to make were, (1) the fact that a Moabite woman could be a pattern of the highest virtues and faithful to the laws and customs of her adopted country; (2) that marriage within kin was a commendable piety; (3) that Ruth became the grandmother of the great King David himself.[100] It seems that the last thing the author would wish to do here is to introduce a foreign person whose character could be questioned in any way in the light of Jewish morality.

The theological context of the narrative portrays the activity of God not by intervention, "but by a lightly exercised providential control."[101] There is also an emphasis on *chesed* living. *Chesed* living meant a life lived in the light of God's covenant loyalty and loving kindness. It includes adherence to covenant loyalty and covenant morality by the individual. This lifestyle of caring responsibility appears not as a forgone conclusion among God's

---

97 Ibid.
98 Homer, *Jonathan Loved David*, p. 20.
99 V. L. Bullough, *Sexual Variance in Society and History* (New York: John Wiley & Sons, 1976), p. 86. See his comments on Foster's interpretation.
100 G. A. Cooke, *The Book of Ruth* (Cambridge, MA: Cambridge University Press, 1918), p. xii.
101 E. F. Campbell, Jr., *Ruth: A New Translation With Introduction Notes and Commentary* (Garden City, NY: Doubleday & Co., 1975), p. 29.

people but something to be strived after. "Living out a righteous and responsible lifestyle is a matter of determination to do so."[102]

The story of Ruth is the quiet commendation of a lifestyle that can be blessed by God. It is especially effective because it is not preached but lived out by the characters in the story.

Campbell argues that the narrative portrays covenant life as applied to a particular social situation in a way that custom is adapted and given new applications to meet arising needs. However, "All of the decisions to be made and acts to be taken are governed by the overarching commitments of honoring God by caring for neighbors."[103]

The immediate context of our passage becomes clearer when seen against the purpose and context of the book. Naomi has lost her status as a wife and mother of sons. In itself this was a serious, devastating turn of events for an older woman in the ancient Near East. She was forced to return to her home bereft of almost everything, reduced to the position of a beggar. Ruth's presence with her meant that at least the two destitute women could look after each other.

In the narrative Naomi well understands the difficulties Ruth will face in a strange land and discourages her from following. This leads into the famous passage quoted above. It is unfortunate, however, that the context frequently is ignored.[104] Although the passage is a perfect expression of human devotion, it also exemplifies *chesed* and covenant loyalty. Ruth determines to go, that is, to leave her nation and country. She determines to stay in her newly adopted country. The change is permanent. She will become totally identified with a new people and a new God. It is notable that Ruth does not say *'Elohim* ("God"), as a foreigner might, but Yahweh. Thus the author "emphasizes that the foreigner is a follower of the true God."[105]

Proselytism and conversion are not obvious in the narrative, although Ruth's pledge to become one people with Naomi and to accept one God cannot be ignored.[106] Human devotion and religious fervor combine in the moving statement made by Ruth. No injustice is done to Scripture by the conclusion that Ruth's statement, seen against the background of the book as a whole and in its immediate context, does not require a homosexual interpretation. Indeed we found sincere human devotion informed by covenant loyalty and religious fervor, the idea of *chesed* in practice.

---

102 Ibid., p. 30.
103 Ibid., p. 31.
104 W. J. Fuerst, *The Books of Ruth, Esther, Ecclesiastes, The Song of Songs, Lamentations* (Cambridge, MA: Cambridge University Press, 1975), p. 14.
105 L. P. Smith, J. T. Cleland, "The Book of Ruth," *IB* 2 (1953): 837.
106 Except in the Targum, which reads like a catechism on verses 16 and 17.

As we have seen, if the Old Testament Scriptures are to be treated as an accurate historical record of God's dealings with His people in the past, and if they are considered to be a reliable guide in morals and ethics, then homosexual acts stand condemned in them both directly and by implication. The primary Old Testament texts, those that describe or imply homosexual acts, never condone those acts but condemn them as an infringement of covenant morality.

Nevertheless the Old Testament does not present homosexual acts as the sole mark of decadence and iniquity that merits the direct punishment of God. Sodom witnessed many grievous sins besides the attempted homosexual acts in Genesis 19. Homosexual acts in antiquity frequently were connected with exploitation, violence, or idolatry, but such circumstances only compounded the problem.

Secondary Old Testament texts are those where homosexual acts are possible but not probable. As we interpret them their nature neither condemns nor condones homosexuality, since the presumed acts for the most part are read into the texts. The sole text in this category where a homosexual act may have occurred contains a terrible curse against the perpetrator of the act.

By ignoring the larger context and historical background of some of these passages, some cite isolated texts which can be interpreted to condone loving homosexual relationships. Similarly, others isolate a few texts out of context in an effort to show that God destroyed nations because of homosexual acts. In the Old Testament, although God does not countenance homosexual acts, neither does he make them the only reason for pouring out His judgments on humanity.

Chapter 4
New Testament Historical Background— The Classical Setting

Homosexuality in Classical Greece

We are not certain when homosexual practices first appeared in Greek history. Some authors trace homosexuality back to the Mycenaean civilization (fl. 1400 B.C.). This thesis stems from an interpretation of various passages in Homer (ca. 850 B.C.) as clearly homosexual, although homosexuality as such is not mentioned in Homer.[1] Others find the Dorian invasion (ca. 1100 B.C.) as the decisive event that introduced homosexuality into Greek civilization.[2]

The Spartan lifestyle and the social pattern of the descendants of the Dorian invaders came to manifest itself in the exclusive and dominant male warrior class. Whatever its origin in Greece, there is no reason to doubt Dover's suggestion that it was widespread by the sixth century B.C.[3]

Lesbianism in Greece

Perhaps the best known name in Greek antiquity to be connected with homosexual activity is that of Sappho from the island of Lesbos. Sappho was a poetess from Mitylene. After a childhood exile in Sicily, she returned to Mitylene where, some scholars believe, she functioned in some manner in a school for girls which honored Aphrodite and the Muses. She was married and had a child named Cleis. In a powerful and direct manner she

---

1 D. M. Robinson, E. J. Fluck, *A Study of the Greek Love-Names, Including a Discussion of Paederasty and a Prosographia,* The Johns Hopkins University Studies in Archeology, No. 23 (Baltimore: Johns Hopkins Univ. Press, 1937), pp. 18-19; also J. A. Symonds, *Male Love: A Problem in Greek Ethics and Other Writings* (New York: Pagan Press, 1983), pp. 1-2.
2 R. Flaceliere, *Love in Ancient Greece,* tr. J. Cleugh (New York: Crown Pubs, 1962), p. 64. Crete was frequently considered as the place of origin since the legend of Zeus and Ganymede was centered there. Plato, *Laws,* 1:636. For the connection between Crete and the Dorians see C. O. Muller, *The History and Antiquities of the Doric Race,* tr. H. F. Tufnell, G. C. Lewis, J. Murray (Oxford, 1839), 1:37-38.
3 K. J. Dover, *Greek Homosexuality* (Cambridge, MA: Harvard University Press, 1978), p. 1.

writes candid accounts of her feelings for the girls in her circle of companions and their feelings for each other.

She was a woman ahead of her time. She wrote contemptuously to an uneducated woman in a day when most were uneducated (frag. 55). She wrote a poem with great feeling and intimacy to an unnamed girl, a poem some think was inspired as Sappho witnessed the girl's wedding and saw her standing by the bridegroom (frag. 31). The possibility is strengthened by the fact that Sappho wrote a number of poems to her girls in celebration of their weddings.

Sappho writes in the vernacular dialect of Lesbos: her language is bold and straightforward but never coarse or erotic. Over the years Sappho and her "school" have become a symbol and name for homosexual activity among women—"Lesbianism," being taken from the name of the island Lesbos. Thus "Lesbian," in modern parlance and popular literature, almost invariably is not the name given to an inhabitant of Lesbos but the name given to a homosexual woman.

Scholarly opinion, however, is neither certain nor unanimous about the matter. Some writers hold that Sappho's relationship with the girls of her group was similar to that of Socrates and his companions.[4] In this case the word *hetaera* should be translated as "companion" rather than "harlot" or "prostitute." Homosexuality here, it seems, was of the refined "spiritual" nature found in Plato, which later became sullied by Sappho's detractors.

Other writers see a gradual development of a certain degree of obloquy in connection with her name beginning about three centuries after her death.[5] This gathered force until the genius of Sappho was subverted, her name coming to connote decadence and depravity.

For at least two hundred years after her death she was praised as the queen of beautiful song. The first burst of calumny against her came from the Athenian comic dramatists, which in turn stigmatized her in the minds of later Latin poets. The rapturous lines in Sappho's poems are explained by one writer as innocent "crushes" existing in that young ladies' seminary as they do in many girls' schools today.[6] Sappho's love of beauty of person in man or woman was purely aesthetic. She loved her disciples as Socrates did his; fondling the curly locks of Phaedo as he leaned against his knee. Robinson maintains that the moral purity of Sappho shines in its own light.

---

4 B. Saklatvala, *Sappho of Lesbos: Her Works Restored* (London: C. Skilton Ltd., 1968), pp. 11-13, 15.
5 E. M. Cox, *The Poems of Sappho: With Historical and Critical Notes, Translations, and a Bibliography* (London: Williams and Norgate, 1924), p. 19.
6 M. M. Miller and D. M. Robinson, *The Songs of Sappho: Including the Recent Egyptian Discoveries* (Lexington, KY: Maxwelton Co., 1925), pp. 78-79.

A woman of bad character and certainly a woman of such a variety of bad character as scandal has attributed to Sappho might express herself passionately and might run on indefinitely with erotic imagery. But Sappho is never erotic. There is no language found in her song which a pure woman might not use.[7]

According to Robinson the Renaissance revival of Sappho was unfavorable to her, as was her popularity among the Romans. The fifteenth century witnessed discovery of what was dubbed "Ovid's perverse epistle" which from that time forward biased all Sapphic literature.[8]

The great German classical scholar, Ulrich von Wilamowitz-Moellendorf, likewise argued that "love of maidens" does not necessarily translate into "Lesbianism" in the modern sense of the word.[9] Page,[10] on the other hand, finds precious little evidence for the interpretation of von Wilamowitz-Moellendorf. The latter theorized that Sappho was the leader of a formal cult-association *(thiasos)* and that her companions were pupils. To them she gave lessons on moral, social, and literary topics. She was, therefore, a highly respected member of society, a lady of official capacity and unblemished character.

But Page rightly argues that the evidence for a cult association is nonexistent. He, like von Wilamowitz-Moellendorf, rejects "the gossip of comedians, rakes, pedants and bigots" who smear the name of Sappho; yet he recognizes at the same time that the problem of the nature of Sappho's relation with her girl-companions cannot be ignored. So little is known, and that little is, as he describes it, "confused with mythology and turbid with the scandal of comic poets."[11]

The fact remains, however, that any evidence for Sappho's amorous converse with men is scant. Although many of her poems discovered later reveal a different mood and do not display the high flame of passion of the earlier works, the earlier works cannot be ignored.

Of the longer pieces, number 31 is the only one that seems to come from

---

7 D. M. Robinson, *Sappho and Her Influence* (New York: Cooper Square Pubs., 1963), pp. 43-44.
8 Ibid., pp. 136-37.
9 U. von Wilamowitz-Moellendorf, *Sappho und Simonides Untersuchungen Über Griechische Lyriker* (Berlin: Weidmann, 1966), pp. 17-78, esp. pp. 72-73. See also *Lexikon der Klassischen Alterthumskunde*, ed. O. Seyffert (Leipzig: Verlag des Bibliographischen Instituts, 1882), p. 557, where Sappho is characterized as a pure and strict woman, unwarrantably scandalized by later generations. Agreeing with Moellendorf is C. M. Bowra, *Greek Lyric Poetry from Alcaeus to Simonides* (Oxford: Clarendon Press, 1961), p. 188.
10 D. Page, *Sappho and Alcaeus: An Introduction to the study of Ancient Lesbian Poetry* (Oxford: Clarendon Press, 1983), p. 32, nn. 2, 110, 111. A more balanced picture of Sappho's character is also found in W. Mure, *A Critical History of the Language and Literature of Ancient Greece* (London: Longman, Brow, Green and Longman's, 1954), 3:272ff.
11 Ibid., p. 142.

the heart without reserve and speaks of an overwhelming passion for a girl-companion. But as Page notes, "It is a lover's passion, not sisterly affection or maternal benevolence which Sappho describes in 31, the overwhelming emotion of intensest love."[12] For Page this statement does not necessarily imply that Sappho and her companions were involved in homosexual practices, although for him poem 31 clearly suggests she had homosexual inclinations.

> Such was the nature of Sappho, not to be altered. To the further question—so often propounded, so seldom considered without prejudice whether evidence for practice as well as inclination is to be found in the fragments of Sappho's poetry, a negative answer must be returned. It is at least probable that Lesbos in her lifetime was notorious for the perverse practices of it's women: but in all that remains of Sappho's poetry there is not a word which connects itself or her companions with them, and at most a half word which reveals her awareness of their existence. The question then is not one which can be discussed at all on the basis of reliable evidence. I therefore take my leave of it.[13]

The newer Egyptian discoveries fail to dampen speculation on this matter. The biographer in P. Oxyrynchus states that Sappho was "accused by some of being disorderly and a lover of women."[14] Page comments, "I find it remarkable that this biographer should say 'she is accused by some,' if the fact were manifestly proved in her works, which were abundantly preserved into the biographer's era."[15] On the other hand, Page suggests in another footnote that although there is no reliable evidence in the fragments of Sappho for any impropriety in the conduct of herself or her companions, new evidence suggests that the story might be different if the bulk of the Alexandrian collection of Sappho's poems had survived intact. At least there would be much more to say on the topic.[16] As it is, the claim of the practice or non-practice of homosexual relations by Sappho is clearly in the realm of speculation. Whatever the intimacies of her private life, it is clear that in Lesbos in her own day her repute was unblemished.[17]

Although today's Lesbianism is connected with Sappho and her school

---

12 Ibid., p. 143.
13 Ibid., pp. 144-45.
14 XV, 1800, fr 1, cd. 1.16 f.
15 Ibid., p. 142, n. 3.
16 Ibid., p. 144, n. 1.
17 J. B. Bury, "Greek Literature From the Eighth Century to the Persian War," *The Cambridge Ancient History* 4, ed. J. B. Bury, et al. (Cambridge, MA: Cambridge University Press, 1939): 498.

and she is offered as an example of homosexual practice in ancient Greece, evidence is almost nonexistent. Earlier scholars of modern times defended Sappho's morality. They suggest that the Greek comic poets read into her writings the upper-class morality and practices of their own society and time. The only evidence subject to interpretation as same-sex desire are a half dozen or so lines in poem 31 of the older writings. The tendency among scholars is to interpret these lines as love of women, but in the sense of the so-called elevated pederasty of the Academy. Here, ethical restraint and consideration of the welfare of the object of desire played a part in the relationship.

Page, the most recent scholar to assess Sappho's writings, suggests that poem 31 shows an inclination on the part of Sappho to "love of women," but declines to comment on her practice of Lesbianism due to lack of evidence.

The Development of Pederasty in Classical Greece

The most common form of homosexuality among Greek males was pederasty. This term refers to a plan of education for boys in which they were placed by their fathers under the care of another man to be trained. As a feature of the system the boy, called the *eromenos,* could be expected at times to provide his mentor, the *erastes,* with homosexual favors.

The Greeks themselves were divided in their understanding of the origin of pederasty among them. Herodotus, a widely travelled Greek historian and lecturer born about 484 B.C., assumed that the Persians had learned it from the Greeks, whereas Plutarch of Chaeronea, a philosopher and bibliographer writing in the Hellenistic period (ca. A.D. 120), traces the practice to Persia.[18] It is possible these two authors are referring to two quite different things under the same name.

In Athens pederasty already was deeply imbedded in the social structure by Solon's time (fl. 600 B.C.). Generally it was felt to be an honorable institution. The regulations of the legislation produced by Solon show that by that time boy-love was something customary for an Athenian.[19] Solon, an Athenian statesman and poet, was himself of noble descent. But in his reform of the Athenian constitution he substituted wealth for birth as the principal criterion for political privilege. By this means he was able to mute the discontent of the unprivileged classes which had risen to a dangerous level because of their exploitation by the nobility.

The more one learns of classical Greek pederasty, however, the clearer

---

18 Herodotus, I, 135. Plutarch, *On the Malice of Herodotus,* 13.
19 Robinson and Fluck, p. 24.

it becomes that early Greek homosexuality was considered a strictly controlled convention rather than a "natural" and uncontrollable condition. Legal regulations stipulated that slaves could not traffic with freeborn, nor could a young man sell himself for money. This was no great barrier to the practice of homosexuality since it was generally accepted that anything mutually agreeable was excusable. Also, as time passed, this law fell into a dormant state.

Foreigners and slaves were not affected by this law, but no freeborn Athenian or Athenian citizen was to sell himself. Those who made a living from homosexual prostitution would be predominantly non-Athenians since foreigners were considered to be of less worth than citizens.

The adult Greek male who indulged in a homosexual relationship was expected to have that relationship with a young boy up to the age of puberty. The boy was not expected to enjoy the erotic aspect of the relationship, but merely endure it for the sake of, and out of respect for, the *erastes*. If the boy sought bodily pleasure from the experience, he incurred disapproval as a *pornos* ("prostitute") or as perverted.[20]

What the *erastes* hoped to engender in the boy was not love primarily in a physical sense *(eros)* but a kind of love inspired by admiration and gratitude toward the *erastes (philia)*. Such gratitude coupled with compassion would induce the *eromenos* to grant "favors" and perform the "services" which the *erastes* desired. In public the behavior of the two was expected to be decorous and circumspect. Consequently, except for the *eromenos* and *erastes* any homosexual activity between them remained to others a matter of conjecture.[21] Ideally such a relationship was conducted in a most responsible manner and discussed only with reticence and decorum if at all.

The gymnasium, a center for the training of youth in academic, physical, and military discipline became famous (or infamous, depending on the point of view) for pederasty. Here young men came to exercise in the nude and older men came to look at them and sometimes to seduce them.[22] But society frowned upon this ogling and peeping at boys merely with a view to seducing them. The true *erastes* had the boy's physical and mental welfare in mind as well as the emotional and erotic aspects of the relationship.

Once the young lad had come of age, he was not to submit himself homosexually to any man as a passive partner. If a young Greek citizen did so, he made himself liable to charges of *porneia* or *kinaidia*.

---

20 Ibid., p. 52.
21 Ibid., pp. 53-54.
22 This situation as well as homosexuality in general is frequently the subject of ribald comedy in Aristophanes; see, *Peace,* p. 762; and *Birds,* pp. 139-42.

Charges of Homosexuality As Political Handicap

Laws against selling oneself for homosexual acts could be revived if necessary to embarrass a political enemy. Precisely such an occurrence appears in the controversy between Aischines and Timarchos (fl. 350 B.C.). These two men were orators (lawyers) and statesmen in Athens. Timarchos was a political ally of the great orator Demosthenes in his persistent opposition to the attempts of Philip of Macedon to control Greece. Hence Demosthenes and Timarchos were the political enemies of Aischines, who sought to reconcile Athens to the Macedonian proposals.

It was Timarchos who began prosecution of Aischines for his part in the peace negotiations. Aischines replied by charging Timarchos with a breech of law that forbade those guilty of notorious conduct from addressing the assembly where Demosthenes and Aischines were members. These disagreements between Demosthenes and Aischines led to sixteen years of enmity between two men.

Aischines sought to advance his case against Timarchos by citing law against Timarchos, who, he claimed, had sold himself as *hetaira-kenai* or *pornos* ("prostitute") for the sake of homosexual intercourse.[23]

Perhaps encouraged by his earlier success against Timarchos, Aischines tried to prevent Demosthenes from receiving a crown from the city by leveling similar charges against him.

The story is this: Demosthenes is about to be honored for his services to the city by being awarded a crown in the theatre during the festival known as Dionysia. Aischines charges Demosthenes with *kinaidia*, that is, homosexual submission.[24] In the clash he attempts to show that Demosthenes is unworthy of the crown. Demosthenes replies in a speech, *de Corona* ("Concerning the Crown") with all the power and devastating effect which his great rhetorical gifts could command, and he then wins the case.

The extraordinary effort by Demosthenes indicates the seriousness of the charge in the minds of Athenians. The idea that the younger partner would seek to initiate a homosexual act for his own sake was not a possibility allowed by any Greek enthusiast or apologist for homosexual *eros*.

---

23 Dover, pp. 20-21; also H. Licht, *Sexual Life in Ancient Greece* (New York: Barnes & Noble Books, 1952), p. 438. Boys could be bought with or without girls in Athenian brothels.

24 Dover, p. 75. Generally relationships were between young men and teenagers 12-18 years. Reciprocal desire between partners of the same age group was almost unknown in Greek homosexuality. The relationship was essentially that of the ruler and the ruled. See L. P. Wilkinson, *Classical Attitudes to Modern Issues* (London: Kimber, 1979), pp. 116-17, 121.

Plato and Pederasty

Plato (429-347 B.C.), a disciple and student of the great Socrates, gives the rules for the relationship.

> When *erastes* and *eromenos* meet, each observing a rule, the *erastes* (sc. the rule) that it would be right for him to subordinate himself in any way to an *eromenos* who has granted him favors, and the *eromenos* (sc. the rule) that it would be right for him to perform any service for one who improves him in mind and character (lit., "who makes him *sophos* and *agathos*") ... then ... in these circumstances alone, and in no others, it is creditable for an *eromenos* to grant favors to an *erastes*.[25]

Consequently, according to Plato, "It is creditable to grant any favor in any circumstances for the sake of becoming a better person (lit. 'for the sake of goodness')."[26]

It is clear that in Athens at the time of Aischines, whoever had sold his body while a boy or prostituted it, either unwillingly by force or wantonly, lost his citizenship rights; he could not be one of the nine archons, neither could he be a priest. He could not be a herald, an ambassador, an orator, nor could he wear a crown.[27]

The Greeks were not entirely consistent in their attitude to pederasty. A law of Solon forbade adult men entrance to the *palaistra*, an arena for exercise connected with the gymnasium. But before the end of the fifth century this law had fallen out of use or was no longer enforced. Plato could speak approvingly of pederasty in the *Symposium*[28] yet suggest in the *Republic* that there should be laws against it. Indeed, in *Republic* III, 403, he suggests that there should be "a law to the effect that a friend should use no other familiarity to his love than a father would use to his son." This ambiguity may stem from the difference between a rigidly controlled and sublimated boy-love emphasizing physical and intellectual development and, in contrast, what was considered a degenerate sort of relation formed simply for erotic satisfaction.

Karlen sees the chief justification of pederasty as being of the higher sort, as Cretan and Dorian homosexuality. Here the relationship between

---

25 Plato, *Symposium*, 184 (I have followed Dover's translation).
26 Plato, *Symposium*, 185 (Dover's tr.).
27 Robinson and Fluck, p. 42.
28 In *Symposium* 181, Plato, perhaps with tongue in cheek, had stated that there should be a law against pederasty because of the waste of zeal and effort on an object so uncertain as youth. He attributes the uncertainty to the impossibility of predicting whether a youth would end in vice or virtue of mind and body. Even in his praise of pederasty the erotic element is not paramount in Plato's thinking.

a man and a boy was supposed to be pedagogic, the interest being to produce brave men and good citizens. He concludes,

> Now, if the relationship continued, it was the man's job to mold the boy into a good citizen and brave warrior. Here as in Sparta, says Plutarch, it was considered shameful for a wellborn boy of twelve or thirteen not to have a lover. The phrase "wellborn," like the assumption of having city and country homes and time for a long honeymoon, indicates an upper class phenomenon.[29]

Karlen's negative judgment results partly from his conviction that intellectual Athenian homosexuals attempted to justify homosexuality by rewriting myth and history to produce homosexual gods and heroes in abundance. He finds the culmination of this tendency in Plato's *Symposium* where the author attributes everything virtuous and desirable to homosexuality.

Although there may be some truth in Karlen's thesis, he overstates the case. There can be no doubt that intelligent Greeks attempted to sublimate and elevate the conventional *eromenos-erastes* relationship to a high ethical plane which few men reached in actual practice.[30] In the story of Socrates and his young student, Alcibiades, we have the student attempting repeatedly to seduce the teacher but without success. Clearly, the nature of the *eromenos-erastes* relationship and the amount of erotic invested in it would depend heavily on the nature and character of the individuals involved.

Some argue that the love of men for boys was never quite sanctioned by society, consequently both laws and parents united in their efforts to check and control it.[31] From this perspective the very institution of the *paedagogos* (a guardian or custodian who protected the boy) is proof enough of the attitude of parents toward *paederastia*.

Bryant also takes a different view of the *Symposium* of Plato. True, Plato's work is a beautiful defense of love between men, but Plato distin-

---

29 A. Karlen, *Sexuality and Homosexuality: A New View* (New York: W. W. Norton & Co., 1971), p. 26. Müller defends the Dorian military custom described by Karlen as a manly, martial influence on the education of Spartan youth. The older man enjoyed watching the youthful beauty and vigor of his charge. It is doubtful, he thinks, that this custom was "identical with the vice to which in its name and outward form it is so closely allied." For the whole discussion see Müller, 2:306-313.
30 Ferguson points out that the true meaning of "Platonic Love" "is not the absence of physical attachment but its sublimation. The stories about Socrates are pointless unless he has strong physical urges over which he had still stronger control." (J. Ferguson, *Moral Values in the Ancient World* [New York: Arno Press, 1979], p. 89.)
31 A. A. Bryant, "Boyhood in Athens," *Harvard Studies in Classical Philology* 18 (1907): 101-2.

guishes two orders of love. First, the love manifested in the senses and second, the love of the soul. He places *paederastia* in the latter. Here the ideal as the perfect philosopher friend, "We cannot deny that, as he refines it, the relation approaches that perfect friendship which has been the dream of so many philosophers."[32] According to Plato about all the care and attention some boys' education received was derived from the interest of their erastes in getting the best for them.[33] Many a lad grew to manhood watched over and guided by maturer wisdom and looked upon with admiration and respect by his *erastes*. This at least was the ideal, though not all relationships kept to this high a plane. As Bryant concludes, not all reached the high ideal, but not all abused the convention either.

> Even the temperate and high-minded Socrates requires all his iron will at times to banish unholy desires, as he confesses himself, with humility. To too many *erastae* the paramount interest was the body and not the soul of the boys for whose favor they sued. For such a relation even Plato has nothing to say, though he admits its prevalence, at least outside of Athens. It is easy, of course, to overdraw the part which abuse of the relation played in the community life; just as it is idle to deny that its influence was on the whole bad. And yet those who threw away all restraint must have been in the minority.[34]

Again, it probably is true that "the Greeks never 'canonized' the physical act of sodomy. They always kept up the fiction of 'educational' paederasty."[35] But to be fair to the sons of Hellas, however, we need to add that homosexual practice was largely the result of an approving social convention and the weakness of human nature on the part of most Greeks rather than a deliberate plan or personal decision.[36] It is possible to see many of the Greeks as being, from Paul's point of view, ignorantly well-intentioned. Their times of ignorance God winked at. Devereux adds the insight that "pre-Platonic homosexuality, while behaviorally real, was psychologically spurious."[37] What he is saying is that the Greeks were not "perverts" (a

---

32 Ibid., p. 105.
33 Plato, *Alcibiades* I, 103, 135; *Symposium*, 213, 215-16.
34 Bryant, pp. 106-7.
35 Karlen, p. 33.
36 J. J. Chapman, *Lucian, Plato and Greek Morals* (Boston: Houghton Mifflin Co., 1931), p. 132. Chapman sees the degeneration in question as not necessarily personal, but racial, a thing indigenous and ingrown.
37 G. Devereux, "Greek Pseudo-Homosexuality and the Greek Miracle," *Symbolae Osloensis* 42 (1967): 69. The expression "PseudoHomosexuality" in Devereux should not be confused with the modern use of the term which refers to a psychological condition. See L. Overssey, "Pseudohomosexuality and Homosexuality in Men: Psychodynamics as a Guide to Treatment," *Sexual*

word which actually appears to mean in his article what we have described as "invert"). He explains,

> A contemporary adolescent, courted by adult men, taught to glory in such attentions, and subjected to homosexual practices would, in most cases, become a genuine and permanent pervert [i.e., invert?]; in the rest of the cases he would become a neurotic. The Greek adolescent, however, ended up as a non-neurotic, completely (or predominantly) heterosexual adult.[38]

Devereux concludes that the Greeks saw the *eromenos* experience as a stage in the child's development toward masculinity and, although it may not have been the best way, it was encouraged by inadequate fathering. The Greeks, consequently, were not inverts in the sense we have described, involved in homosexuality from deep personal need or even underlying perverted fantasies. Neither was there an anti-hedonistic aggressivity involved.

For Devereux the average Greek was not an invert.[39] Rather in the typical youth culture in classical Greece, homosexuality was but one way to prolong youth and keep in touch with the privileged, admired, and irresponsible world of adolescence. This produced a strange convention where another man brought up and educated one's sons. We read:

> The Greek father usually failed to counsel his son; instead, he counseled another man's son, in whom he was erotically interested. As for the boy, who needed an effective father to model himself upon, he had to rely on his erastes, who also served as a father surrogate.[40]

In Sparta the *erastes* was responsible even for the misconduct of the *eromenos;* the father having no responsibility. The expectation for the Greek youth after the *eromenos* stage, however, was that he would marry and rear a family.[41] Although he might have an *eromenos* himself, he would by no means subject himself passively to another man without receiving

---

Inversion, the Multiple Roots of Homosexuality, ed. J. Marmor (New York: Basic Books, 1965), pp. 211-33.
38 Ibid., p. 70.
39 Ibid., pp. 71-73.
40 Ibid., p. 78; cf. Plato, *Laches,* 179-180.
41 W. Churchill, *Homosexual Behavior Among Males: A Cross-Cultural and Cross-Species Investigation* (Englewood Cliffs, NJ: Prentice Hall, 1971), pp. 140-41. Malloy also notes, "Greek men considered exclusive homosexuals as odd and degraded. Most of those who engaged in pederasty were married and fulfilled the prevailing expectations of family life." E. A. Malloy, *Homosexuals and the Christian Way of Life* (Lanham, MD: University Press of America, 1981), p. 32.

scorn. Whatever the origin of this convention in which a stranger raised and educated the sons in another's family, receiving as his fee certain sexual favors from the youth and association with him, certain classes of Greeks countenanced the practice for some time.

However, the presence of a privileged and powerful oligarchy in Greece unwittingly fostered a double standard in pederasty; one for the nobles and citizens where youths were protected by ethical, social and political considerations; another for unfranchised Greeks and foreigners where lust was the only limit. In time the latter tended to overshadow the former.

As we have seen, Greek society appears to have had an ambivalent attitude to pederasty. Citizens were protected from homosexual exploitation. Any man who had submitted himself to another merely for gain was scorned and his reputation sullied. Any youth tutored by an older man was expected to allow him sexual favors, but the boy was not to indulge in it for enjoyment or gain, but out of respect for the older man. In intellectual circles there was a tendency to elevate and ethicize the relationship so that it became a "Platonic" friendship. This was not always successful. Even Plato recognized that outside the Academy the practice of boy-love degenerated to licentiousness.

Plato's Defense of Pederasty
Versus Sensualism and Licentiousness

Whatever high spiritual ideals may have been attached originally to the practice of pederasty, its tacit licensing of erotic expression as a reward for services offered damaged the social fabric. No matter how charming, innocent and quietly intimate it may have been at first, it did not take long for less sensitive souls to legitimate their lustful and sometimes violent activities as pederasty. Those who did not believe, like Plato, that the unseen Soul and Ideas were the only reality quickly gravitated to an intense and exclusive preoccupation with outward physical beauty. This development of pederasty in two directions is summarized nicely by Robinson and Fluck:

> To sum up, then, the path of development which pederasty had taken, I quote John Addington Symonds: "We find two separate forms of masculine passion clearly marked in early Hellas—a noble and a base, a spiritual and a sensual." As Maximum Tyrius says: "The one is Greek, the other barbarous; the one is virile, the other effeminate." The mixed form *(poikilos)* on which the Greeks prided themselves and on which Plato was decisive, was a passionate and enthusiastic attachment between

man and youth, recognized by society and protected by opinion. Though it was not free from sensuality, it did not degenerate into mere licentiousness.[42]

This dual tradition of boy-love coupled with the Greek appreciation of attractive physical form was easily misunderstood and perverted by those who followed the practice. Even in the Academy the overemphasis on outward form and beauty meant that the gangling Athenian youth with acne had less chance of receiving a good education than his comely counterpart, at least with an *erastes*.

Plato attempted to uphold an idealistic pederasty governed by ethical self-control. Socrates' advice to Hippothales is reported in Plato's *Lysis* 222. Plato recognizes that there are many more nonlovers than lovers.[43] It is not only the lover who can be a firm friend. Indeed, true love does not seek the effeminate and submissive youth. Plato even describes the *erastes* ("older male") as a wolf who forces his attention upon the younger man, not with real kindness but because he has an appetite and wants to feed on the youth.[44]

How then can Plato defend this relationship at all? He defends it philosophically (theologically) on the basis of divine madness *(manike)*, the immortality and transmigration of the soul, recollection, and idealism.[45]

Plato's dualism always leaves an element of doubt or ambiguity about bodily pleasure. At times he seems to spiritualize the entire relationship while on other occasions it becomes physical.[46] In the *Symposium*, Plato considers pederasty the greatest of blessings: "For I know not any greater blessing to a young man who is beginning life than a virtuous lover, or to the lover than a beloved youth."[47]

Plato then makes clear the far-reaching ethical and social ramifications of this ideal relationship:

> And I say that a lover who is detected in doing any dishonorable act or submitting through cowardice when any dishonor is done to him by another, will be more pained at being detected by his beloved than at being seen by his father or by his

---

42 Robinson and Fluck, p. 42.
43 Plato, *Phaedrus,* 231-32.
44 Ibid., 240-41.
45 Ibid., 244-256.
46 Ibid., 255-56.
47 Plato, *Symposium,* 178. Quotations from the *Symposium* are from Jowett's translation. B. Jowett, *The Dialogues of Plato: Translated Into English With Analyses and Introduction* (London: Oxford University Press, 1924).

> companions, or by anyone else. The beloved, too, when he is found in any disgraceful situation has the same feeling about his lover. And if there were only some way of contriving that a state or an army should be made up of lovers and their loves, they would be the very best governors of their own city, abstaining from all dishonor, and emulating one another in honor; and when fighting at each other's side, although a mere handful, they would overcome the world. For what lover would not choose rather to be seen by all mankind than by his beloved, either when abandoning his post or throwing away his arms? He would be ready to die a thousand deaths rather than endure this. Or who would desert his beloved or fail him in the hour of danger? The veriest coward would become an inspired hero, equal to the bravest at such a time; love would inspire him. That courage which, as Homer says, the god breathes in the souls of some heroes, love of his own nature infuses into the hero.[48]

At this point Plato begins to enumerate Homeric heroes who were inspired with this love, a process that Karlen calls a rewriting of history to glorify homosexuality.

Plato distinguishes between the heavenly Aphrodite and the common or earthly Aphrodite. The love of youths comes from the heavenly Aphrodite. Aphrodite, the goddess of love, inspired love in human beings. Normally it was male for female and vice-versa.

Plato, however, in his typical dualistic pattern divides Aphrodite into a heavenly Aphrodite and an earthly Aphrodite. For Plato only the heavenly ideas were reality. Matter was transient, deceptive, evil. He subsumes heterosexual relations under the earthly Aphrodite.

> But the offspring of the heavenly Aphrodite is derived from a mother in whose birth the female has no part, she is from the male only; this is the love which is of youths, and the goddess being older, there is nothing of wantonness in her. Those who are inspired by this love turn to the male, and delight in him who is the more valiant and intelligent nature; anyone may recognize the pure enthusiasts in the very character of their attachments. For they love not boys, but intelligent beings whose reason is beginning to be developed, much about the time at which their beards begin to grow. And in choosing young men to be their companions, they mean to be faithful to them, and pass their

---

48 Ibid., 178-79.

whole life in company with them, not to take them in their inexperience, and deceive them, and play the fool with them, or run away from one to another of them.[49]

In contrast, followers of the earthly Aphrodite, whether in love of women or youths, are the foolish and ignoble who do good and evil indiscriminately. Plato's statement, already quoted, suggests that boy-love should be outlawed since it is uncertain how their souls will turn out and much noble enthusiasm may be wasted on them. The statement itself testifies to a male dominant culture and in general displays almost a misogynist attitude.

Plato was well aware that pederasty was practiced by two very different groups of people for whom he tries to present a rationale. He recognizes that not all parents approve of the relationship and place their children under a tutor's care. Plato insists, however, that such practices are honorable if followed honorably. "Evil is the vulgar lover who loves the body rather than the soul, inasmuch as he is not even stable, because he loves a thing which is in itself unstable."[50] For Plato the attachment must be voluntary and impart virtue.[51]

The Androgynous Myth

Plato's dualism and divine madness did not account for the attraction of men to youths, not even to Plato himself, so he goes into great detail on the androgynous man-woman myth to explain it.[52]

In this myth Plato explains that primal man was dual. He had four hands, four feet, two faces and two privy parts, that is, like two people back to back—the faces opposite directions. Some of these dual, primal creatures were male in both parts, others were female in both parts and yet others (a third sex) part male and part female. These primal creatures were so strong that they became insolent, attacking the gods. Because of their continued insolence, Zeus divided these dual four-legged creatures into two-legged creatures. A dual male became two males, a dual female two females and the male-female (androgynous) became a male and a female. On this basis he accounts for the differing sexual desires apparent in society, for each creature searches out its own or opposite kind, according to its original orientation. When dual parts encounter each other they fall in love. By the creation of this myth Plato attempts to explain the the attrac-

---

49 Ibid., 181.
50 Ibid., 183.
51 Ibid., 184.
52 *Symposium*, 189-192.

tion some men and women have for persons of the same sex.[53]

However, dualism has the last word. Those pregnant in the body only betake themselves to women and beget children, whereas pregnant souls wander about seeking beauty in souls. Those having an affinity of soul have a closer union and friendship than those who beget mortal children. Hence beauty of soul is more important than beauty of form. Taken at face value there is a defensible element here; but for Plato the immortal, invisible soul (Idea) is the only reality.

In the *Republic* Plato would have no more familiarity between *erastes* and *eromenos* than between father and son, and in the *Laws* he recommends the death penalty for violence done to a free woman or a youth.[54]

Plato himself was aware that the controlled aesthetic pederasty he advocated was not followed by the majority. Therefore he goes to great lengths to show that this type of love and this alone is the one which is philosophically (theologically) defensible. For Plato this kind of pederasty is "natural" since he defends it with a myth of origins and from a philosophical-theological perspective.

Aristotle, a student of Plato, also recognized that pederasty may be practiced for various reasons—either from custom, habit, or nature.[55]

Homosexuality in Greek Drama

A brief word is appropriate about the use of Attic Comedy as historical evidence in a serious and accurate account of homosexuality. The idea that drama always represents reality is a misleading notion. Poets in ancient Greece pictured the gods as enjoying sodomy, masturbation and fellatio.

A first glance at Old Attic Comedy might lead one to believe that the Greeks lived in "a rosy haze of uninhibited sexuality."[56] There is reason to believe that the Greeks themselves, at least Athenian audiences, did not suppose that the figures in tragedy represented normal human beings in normal family circumstances. On the other hand comedy generally dealt with normal people in comic situations.[57] Ehrenburg demonstrates that

---

53 Ibid., 189-192. Plato tries to clinch his argument with the example of Socrates and Alcibiades, 217-19.
54 Plato, *Republic*, III 403; *Laws*, IX 874. Symonds suggests that in the *Phaedrus*, the *Symposium*, the *Charmides*, the *Lysis*, and the *Republic*, Plato gave liberal scope to his own sympathy for pederasty: "As a young man, Plato felt sympathy for love as long as it was paederastic." As an old man, Plato denounced carnal pleasure of all kinds, as reflected in the *Laws*. Symonds believes this is moral growth on Plato's part rather than a disapprobation of the pederastic passion. (Symonds, p. 52.) Of course, it could have been both.
55 Aristotle, *Nichomachean Ethics*, VII 5.
56 K. J. Dover, *Greek Popular Morality in the Time of Plato and Aristotle* (Oxford: Basil Blackwell, 1974), p. 205.
57 W. K. Lacey, *The Family in Classical Greece* (Ithaca, NY: Cornell Univ. Press, 1968), p. 10.

Old Attic Comedy is truthful about all real facts, especially those relating to the general conditions of life.[58] He takes the comedies to be a good source of reality; reality in essence here meaning the everyday life occurrences which are not displaced in comedy (as in tragedy), by myth.[59]

Men of all classes are attacked and ridiculed in Old Attic Comedy. Comedy pictures the reality of everyday life as background, for the average spectator of comedy must have familiar ground to stand on if the dramatist is to make his point.[60] David shows that political satire, likewise, was not simply the dramatist's personal response to a political treatise or philosophical arguments. Authors dealt with subjects familiar to the populace and popular subjects of discussion.[61]

Sexual matters were unduly prominent in comedy and the outstanding quality that characterized noblemen was the practice of pederasty.

> It was one of the most favored (and most exaggerated) themes of comedy. . . . There were, of course, very different types of paederasty, from fashionable liaisons down to venal love; but from comedy one gets the impression that the differences had almost disappeared. The comic writers again and again sneer at the members of the aristocratic circle as paederasts.[62]

Though this bias of comedy concerning aristocracy and pederasty should not be construed as a moral judgment per se, it is hard to escape the idea that even here the attitude of comedy echoes a feeling held by many. In comedy a slave is never the object of homosexual love. All those ridiculed for practicing it come from the upper classes. Both pederasty and misogyny are attacked in comedy; treated as upper-class practices which went hand in hand but did not represent urban and rural middle-class views.[63]

In poor and middle-class families there was much more opportunity for boys and girls to get acquainted with each other and carry on love affairs. The upper classes, on the other hand, made it extremely difficult for a young man to establish contact with the daughter of another citizen. Even if he managed to do so, he might place himself in considerable danger.[64]

---

58 V. Ehrenburg, *The People of Aristophanes: A Sociology of Old Attic Comedy* (Oxford: Basil Blackwell, 1943), p. 6.
59 Ibid., p. 7.
60 Ibid., pp. 19, 26-27. On this point see also, L. Pearson, *Popular Ethics in Ancient Greece* (Stanford, CA: Stanford Univ. Press, 1962), p. 2.
61 E. David, *Aristophanes and Athenian Society of the Early Fourth Century B.C. Memnosyne bibliotheca classica batava supplementum octogesimum primum* (Leiden: E. J. Brill, 1984), pp. 21, 27.
62 Ehrenburg, p. 77.
63 Ibid., pp. 133, 143. There is no mention of Spartan homosexuality involving all of society.
64 Dover, pp. 209, 211.

Furthermore, pederasty was expensive, which also tended to limit its practice to the upper classes and wealthy. At least in comedy, it was the practice of aristocrats and those who cared to imitate them. Consequently, it was held suspect by the common people and at times became a means of arousing prejudice in legal cases, as we have seen.

In comedy, then, we find a tendency to exaggerate sexual (particularly homosexual) matters. In addition it gives evidence for a degree of class bias, including, to a certain extent, bias against homosexuality itself. This needs to be kept in mind as we approach the texts.

Aeschylus, the prolific Greek playwright of about 500 B.C., in *Seven Against Thebes,* speaks of "man, woman—or some despicable thing halfway twixt them both,"[65] a reference to the effeminate male. Aristophanes, the great poet of Old Attic Comedy (b. ca. 457 B.C.), speaks derisively of the effeminate, "O thou young shaver of the hot-souled rump, with such a beard, thou monkey, dost thou come tricked out amongst us in a eunuch's disguise?" Here of course, is a reference to the youth who remains passive after puberty and shaves his buttocks to retain the appearance of prepubertal youth. Another reference in the same work describes such a character as,

> the little fop we all despise, The young Cratinus neatly shorn with single razor wanton-wise, That Artemon-engineer of ill, Whose father sprang from an old he-goat, And father and son, as ye all may note, Are rank with its fragrance still.[66]

In *The Knights* Aristophanes pronounces what may have been only too true of homosexual relations outside the Academy, that is, purely erotic and indiscriminate, "You yourself, Excuse me sir, are like boys with lovers. The honest gentleman you won't accept, yet give yourself to lantern-selling chaps, to sinew-stitchers, cobblers, aye and tanners."[67] He also speaks of boy-love as associated with "vile degrading crimes."[68] He portrays the obviously low-class sausage-seller in *The Knights* as having "sold sausages ... and myself."[69]

Toward the end of *The Knights* is a play on words and possibly a jibe at what we have described as situational homosexuality, "First, when the sailors from my ships of war come home, I'll pay them all arrears in full." To which the sausage-seller answers, "For that, full many a well-worn rump

---

65 Aeschylus, *Seven Against Thebes,* 193-94; he also implies the death penalty for the activity.
66 Aristophanes, *The Acharnians,* 123-25; 153-59.
67 Aristophanes, *The Knights,* 696-99.
68 Ibid., 883-86.
69 Ibid., 1250-52.

will bless you."[70] Of course, this could mean that the sailor's posterior was tired from rowing, but the double-entendre is clear.

Aristophanes contains references to the beardless boys in the agora whom he identifies with the striplings in the perfume mart,[71] and in *The Clouds* he bemoans the loss of the good old days of the manly aesthetic pederasty of the gymnasium, which has degenerated into effete customs and practices.[72] The former seems to have been held in a certain amount of respect by some Greeks, whereas the latter was generally despised. Of these two classes it was unfortunately also the latter, featuring effeminacy and prostitution, that was predominantly received by the Hellenistic world as the legacy of classical Greece.

Briefly, pederasty developed along two lines. First, a more refined version practiced among intellectuals in which affection for boys led older men to care for and train them. Sometimes this involved a sensual element but it was supposed to be a controlled and elevated relationship that took the boys' interests into consideration. Some ancient critics claimed that this was not always the case, which probably is correct.

The second direction in which pederasty went was toward sensualism, licentiousness, exploitation, and prostitution. Since all men had sexual drives but not all had the education, philosophy and bent of those who attended the academies, such an outcome was inevitable.

Aside from the androgynous myth, Plato's defense of "ethical" pederasty is based on an anthropology that is fundamentally a metaphysical dualism. This entire philosophical premise now is widely recognized as alien to the biblical understanding of the nature of man. For the Christian, therefore, the practice of pederasty as explained by Plato is founded on an erroneous concept of the nature of man and on that premise alone it is unacceptable. Plato does not present an accurate picture of the nature of homosexuality or an accurate statement of its origins because his immortal soul doctrine does not give an accurate picture of the nature of man.

Although they exaggerate and are biased, the dramatists provide some

---

70 Ibid., 1364-68.
71 Ibid., 1373-76.
72 Aristophanes, *The Clouds*, 965-1018. Much of the coarseness in the Greek dramatists is euphemized by many modern translators, or in some instances omitted. Often it depends on a play on words or the use of the feminine form of a man's name or the feminine article used with a man's name as well as terms which may be translated obscurely or literally in a more coarse manner to get across their meaning. In Aristophanes' *The Clouds*, 1085-1104, Wrong compels Right to admit that *europroktoi* are in the majority in Athens. Europroktos actually means "wide-arsed," a reference to someone who habitually offers himself for homosexual intercourse. Some translators simply render the expression "probed adulterers," whereas Aristophanes speaks of them as "wide-arsed adulterers," i.e., homosexual adulterers. Dover gives a more literal translation of the comic dramatists which brings out the meaning. See Dover, pp. 135ff.

clues to social life in Athens with respect to homosexuality. We cannot conclude that homosexuality existed only among the noble and intellectual classes, but it was common enough among them that jibes were well understood. Any indiscretion in this direction also was eagerly picked up and used as a political tool against them by their peers. At any rate the dramatists show us that pederasty was not limited to the refined type described, defined, and defended by Plato.

Chapter 5
New Testament Historical Background— The Hellenistic World

Pederasty and Prostitution in Later Greek Practice

No major change in attitude or activity concerning homosexuality stands between the earlier Greek and Hellenistic periods. Pausanius, a character in Plato's dialogue, *Symposium* 182, observes that in Greece as well as abroad there were cities that frowned on homosexuality and others whose laws favored it. This was increasingly true following the fourth century B.C. when Alexander carried Greek influence to many new regions, beginning what is called the Hellenistic era.

Cities with large Jewish populations frequently were anti-homosexual. Although during the Hellenistic era even Jewish mores eroded considerably in some areas, there is no evidence of general Jewish acceptance of this practice.

The manly ideal of pederasty continued in the gymnasia of the Hellenistic world with their all-male emphasis, military training, sports and nudity for exercises. In some of the countries and cities where gymnasia were established, however, there already existed a tradition of effeminate homosexuality.

Furthermore, the status of women in many countries occupied by the Greeks was higher than that of Greek women. Consequently, the invading Greeks and their descendants who remained on foreign soil were required to deal with women whose status was equal or almost equal to their own.[1]

The effeminate actor-dancer also was well-known outside of Greece.[2] In short, both the high status of women and practice of effeminate homosexuality outside Greece were serious factors to contend with when

---

1 R. E. White, "Women in Ptolemaic Egypt," *JHS* 18 (1898): 238-66, C. C. Edgar, "A Women's Club in Alexandria," *JEA* 4 (1917): 253-54.
2 C. C. Edgar, "Records of a Village Club," *Publicazioni di Aegyptus-Serie Scientifica* 3, Raccolta di Scritti in onore di Giacomo Lumbroso 1844-1925 (Milan, 1925): 369-76.

Greeks ventured abroad. The result was development of both the female and effeminate erotic elements in the Hellenistic life. As Licht observes,

> the more the foreign element penetrates the Greek spirit the more pederasty retires into the background; the female element begins to occupy more space when, especially in the large cities, the intercourse of young men with hetaerae increased.[3]

As a result the meaning of homosexuality in the Hellenistic world broadened to include everything from the sublimated educational process between *erastes* and *eromenos* to extremes of rape and prostitution of adult effeminates. The manly and academic ideal still was held in theory, but probably was practiced in the breech rather than as the rule. In Hellenistic times a debate developed that compared the virtues and vices of pederasty vis-a-vis sexual relations with women. Scroggs has described the homosexual scene in the Hellenistic era as composed of sublimated pederasty, slave prostitution and the effeminate callboy. All of this met stern opposition from Judaism, particularly Diaspora Judaism.[4]

Sublimated pederasty in the Hellenistic milieu was similar to the Greek phenomenon. Hellenistic epigrams in *The Greek Anthology* show that the same concerns, emotions, and social conventions continued into later times.

Perhaps one new twist is that of a *hetaira* dressing up as a boy to attract the young *ephebes* in the gymnasium.[5] In a unique way it demonstrates that in that bastion of Greek culture, the gymnasium, pederasty was in vogue. Here also we find the typical Greek defense of homosexual love,[6] as well as a poem to a boy whose charms are beginning to fade.[7] Callimachus produces a series of epigrams on *eromenoi*[8] and Rhianus on the diverse charms of different boys.[9] Even the large number of anonymous epigrams dwell on homosexuality and the relation between *erastes* and *eromenos*.[10] In them we find scarcely anything but the transference of the Greek pederastic tradition to foreign soil.

Slave prostitution was practiced in Greece, and it acquired an effemi-

---

3   H. Licht, *Sexual Life in Ancient Greece* (New York: Barnes and Noble, 1952), p. 438. Hetairae are "high-class" prostitutes or mistresses.
4   R. Scroggs, *The New Testament and Homosexuality: Contextual Background for Contemporary Debate* (Philadelphia: Fortress Press, 1983), pp. 29-98.
5   Asclepiades, XX. The epigrams are found in A.S.F. Gow and D. L. Page, *The Greek Anthology, Hellenistic Epigrams,* 2 vols. (Cambridge, MA: Cambridge University Press, 1965).
6   Asclepiades, XXXVII.
7   Asclepiades, XLVI.
8   Callimachus, V-XI.
9   Rhianus, III.
10 Anonymous, VIII-XXIII.

nate nature in the expanded Greek empire. Young slave boys often were castrated before or after puberty in order to prolong their youthful appearance and subsequently their usefulness for homosexual activities. This clearly was not a part of the old Greek ideal although increasingly it became characteristic of the Hellenistic age.[11] These pathics or effeminates were sometimes used commercially in brothels or as household servants for wealthy men to whom they provided sexual favors.[12]

The servants of wealthy men frequently acted as procurers of beautiful boys and girls for the sexual indulgence of their masters. The beauty of Aristobulus, the young son of Herod the Great, was reported to Mark Antony by his servant who hoped to procure the lad and his sister for the sexual satisfaction of his master. The Jewish historian, Josephus, writing about A.D. 93, reports that Herod,

> decided that it would not be safe for him to send Aristobulus, who was the most handsome—being just sixteen—of a distinguished family, to Anthony, who was more powerful than any Roman of his time, and was ready to use him for erotic purposes and was able to indulge in undisguised pleasure because of his power.[13]

Unbridled lust may not have been more prevalent in Hellenistic times than in the early Greek experience; but it was written about more, and in extremely frank, vulgar, and sometimes obscene language. The treatment of sex and homosexuality in Roman authors such as Lucilius, Horace, Persius, Petronius, Juvenal, Catallus, and Ovid leaves little to the imagination. Seemingly unobtainable objects of lust could be obtained by stealth and trickery by means of a procurer or procuress for the right sum of money. Sometimes it was done with the connivance and cooperation of personnel in a temple under the guise of religious ritual.[14] Although worship in many pagan temples was not necessarily a sex act, it was customary to use temples in search of love-adventures with men or women.[15]

Roman homosexuality usually was connected with the baths. In addition, actors and mimes were expected to have a homosexual disposition.

---

11 Th. Hopfner, *Das Sexualleben der Griechen und Römer von den Anfängen bis ins 6. Jahrhundert nach Christus* (New York: AMS Press, 1975), pp. 418-20 (reprint of Prague 1938 edition).
12 Petronius, *Satyricon*, II, 79f.; Lucian, *Timon*, 22; Seneca, *Epistle*, XLVII 7; Suetonius, *Nero*, XXVIII.
13 Josephus, *Ant.* XV. 26-30.
14 Josephus, *Ant.* XVIII. 65-80.
15 O. Kiefer, *Sexual Life in Ancient Rome* (London: G. Routledge and Sons, 1934), p. 129. Juvenal mentions hetero- and homosexual love affairs taking place in temples, Juvenal, *Satires*, 6, 489; 9, 22-24.

A prolific literature grew up describing various sexual experiences, saturated with salacious puns. The result is an extensive Roman sexual vocabulary.[16] However, although adultery and homosexuality are mentioned in the literature without censure, Veyne observes that "the interested parties would be discreet enough to admit nothing, and pretend to know nothing."[17]

Satire and literary invective frequently employed sexual imagery and obscenity became an art form, asserting the claims of nature against convention. In such works men and women were reduced not merely to sex objects but to sex organs.[18]

In Roman literature sexual and homosexual activity appears at times as sheer voluptuousness, degenerating on occasion to sadomasochism. It involved the exploitation of slaves and other defenseless persons. Emperors such as Nero and Caligula led the way. Nero castrated a youth named Sporus and married him, declaring the boy to be his "empress." Churchill contrasts this effeminacy with the Greek masculine ideal:

> While the Greeks were charmed by the masculinity of their favorites and looked upon their passion as an opportunity to better the condition of the beloved, it was necessary for Nero to remove the clearest evidence of masculinity in Sporus, to feminize him and to degrade rather than elevate him. Such cruel and eccentric acts were not at all uncommon among the Romans, but had virtually no precedent in the history of the Greeks.[19]

Karlen suggests that this came about by the Roman mind's equating eunuchism and homosexuality with Eastern religious cults, particularly that of Cybele and her eunuch priests, the Galli.[20] In his *Metamorphoses* Apuleius describes the eunuch-priests of Cybele as passive homosexuals with insatiable appetites for sexual gratification, who rape a dinner guest. This is significant in itself, for Roman invective assumed that there was only one main kind of male homosexual, that is, pathic (those who were anally penetrated). These are frequently identified as *effeminatus*.

---

16 J. N. Adams, *The Latin Sexual Vocabulary* (Baltimore: Johns Hopkins Univ. Press, 1982). Jews were sometimes the object of satire. They were considered sexually well-endowed and lustful by the Romans. (See p. 13.)
17 P. Veyne, "Homosexuality in Ancient Rome," *Western Sexuality Practice and Precept in Past and Present Times,* ed. P. Aries and A. Bejin, tr. A. Forster (Oxford: Basil Blackwell, 1985), p. 32.
18 L. C. Curran, "Nature, Convention and Obscenity in Horace's Satires," *Arion* 9 (1970): 221, 235.
19 W. Churchill, *Homosexual Behavior Among Males: A Cross-Cultural and Cross-Species Investigation* (Englewood Cliffs, NJ: Prentice Hall, 1971), p. 143.
20 A. Karlen, *Sexuality and Homosexuality: A New View* (New York: W. W. Norton and Co., 1971), p. 61.

If the Romans wished to hint at underlying sexual profligacy or perversion, they had a full vocabulary at their command to do so. Besides speaking of a man as *pathicus* or *effeminatus,* he might be called *mollis* ("soft"), or any of a dozen or more adjectives connoting weakness or delicacy.[21]

One of the most common accusations in graffiti, political slanging matches, political lampoons, and courtroom attacks is "pathic." Usually it designated three kinds of behavior: (1) having been the boy of some older man previously; (2) as an adult, continuing to enjoy being penetrated anally by other men; and (3) enjoying fellatio. In Rome as in Greece, a man seeking to discredit another could do so by claiming that he had been or still was sexually passive. Sexual intercourse with young slave boys was regarded not only socially acceptable but normal, whereas sexual intercourse with free-born boys was shameful and illegal, no doubt out of consideration for the boy's pride and future reputation. The aggressive position carried no stigma; what bothered the Romans most in male homosexual behavior was assumption of the female role. It was disgraceful for a Roman citizen to act as the passive instrument for another's pleasure.

Artemidorus (second century A.D.) traveled widely in the ancient Near East in a study of dreams. Eventually he wrote a treatise on the interpretation of dreams. This man, a good representative of the majority opinion, described intercourse with wife, mistress, male or female slave as normal behavior. But he stopped short of accepting the passive role, "to let oneself be buggered by one's own slave is not right. It is an assault on one's person and leads to one being despised by one's slave."[22]

It was the sodomite *(cinaedus)* held up to ridicule in Petronius, a Roman novelist of the first century A.D.[23] Often these were pathics who danced and cut lewd capers at banquets. Often they were free-born youths or men who sold their services to individuals for sexual gratification.

Cicero informs us that Mark Anthony of Anthony and Cleopatra fame, played this role as a youth.[24] He asserts that Anthony played the passive role and was basically the harlot "mistress" of another man to whom he functioned as a wife.

---

21 A. Richlin, *The Garden of Priapus: Sexuality and Aggression in Roman Humor* (New Haven, CT: Yale University Press, 1983), pp. ix, 92.
22 Ibid., pp. 220-21, 225. Roman satirists were not inventing the content of their poems as a literary exercise. Each poet reflects his own times, although he may search for striking ways to say things that had been going on for some time. See E. S. Ramage, D. L. Sigsbee, S. C. Fredericks, *Roman Satirists and Their Satire: The Fine Art of Criticism in Ancient Rome* (Park Ridge, NJ: Noyes Press, 1974), pp. 4-5. Artemidorus, *Oneirocritica,* pp. 88-89.
23 Petronius, *Satyricon,* II, 21; or passive boys, II, 81.
24 Cicero, *Philippics* II, 44-45.

Such practices often could be quite remunerative. If youths remained indefinitely in such a role, they emphasized their effeminate position by imitating the toilette of women. They mimicked feminine hair styles, make up, depilation of masculine body hair and sometimes feminine attire.[25]

Scroggs notes that among several words used to refer to such persons was *malakos,* a Greek word meaning "soft" (1 Cor 6:9-10), that Paul uses to refer to this specific category of person.[26] He continues by surveying the Hellenistic arguments for and against pederasty.[27] The debate in Hellenistic times survives today in two authors—Plutarch of Chaeronea (ca. A.D. 50-120), and Lucian of Samosata, from the late second century A.D.

Arguments for pederasty included the Platonic ideal of a non-sexual relationship, illustrated in ancient times by the relationship between Socrates and Alcibiades, and a second view that allowed sexual gratification in the pursuit of wisdom. Pederasty, it was thought, contributed in some way to the growing wisdom of the youth involved in it. Thus Protogenes in Plutarch's *Erotikos* speaks of the love of women as an effeminate and bastard love, but true love brings young and talented souls to virtue, that is, boy-love.[28] Pederasty clearly is touted as more masculine than heterosexuality and more worthy, since men are more worthy than women. Protogenes appears not merely as a pederast but as a misogynist.

Daphnaeus advances arguments against pederasty. He argues for what to us seems obvious, that intercourse between men and women is natural and conducive to friendship,[29] that the love of men and the love of women is of the same sort. If anything, male effeminacy is an affront to Aphrodite. Daphnaeus rejects Plato's heavenly Aphrodite versus earthly Aphrodite dichotomy. So did Philo of Alexandria, who thought of the idea as humorous.[30] Boy-love can be thought of as the late born son of an old man who tries to disinherit true love. He comes slinking into the gymnasium to corrupt the boys there.

Plutarch exposes academic pederasty as a sham:

> It plays the highbrow and publicly proclaims that it is a philosopher and disciplined on the outside—because of the law. But when the night comes and all is quiet, "Sweet is the harvest when the guard's away."[31]

---

25 Philo, *Laws,* III, 37-42; Clement of Alexandria *Paedagogus,* III, 3.
26 Scroggs, p. 42.
27 Ibid., pp. 44-65.
28 Plutarch, *Erotikos,* 750c.-751a.
29 Ibid., 751c.
30 Ibid., 751d.; cf. Philo, *The Contemplative Life,* 59-62.
31 Ibid., 751; 752a.

Protogenes counters these arguments by arguing that the young man must be ruled by someone during his youth, who better than his *erastes?* Were not the heroes of old susceptible to this kind of love and does not the true lover use the beautiful body simply as an instrument to memory?[32] Of course these are Platonic arguments posited to counter the picture of pederasty as a lascivious assault.

> That is why we class those who enjoy the passive part as belonging to the lowest depth of vice and allow them not the least degree of confidence or respect or friendship.[33]

The arguments alternate between the two antagonists, but Plutarch ends the debate with an endorsement of heterosexuality,

> There are very few examples of a durable relationship among boy lovers, but countless numbers of successful unions with women may be enumerated, distinguished from beginning to end by every sort of fidelity and zealous loyalty.[34]

Lucian, a later writer, favors pederasty. Lucian admits that some men give the appearance of devotion to physical training in the wrestling schools while their real interest is boy-love.[35] He grants that Aphrodite made men for women and vice versa. He despises eunuchism for homosexuality and espouses the ideal concept of pederasty.[36] His misogynist leanings surface in the following statement: "And how much better that a woman should invade the provinces of male wantonness than that the nobility of the male sex should become effeminate and play the part of a woman."[37]

Lucian concedes that marriage is necessary for the perpetuity of the race. That is why boy-love did not appear in earlier times. But with leisure came the pursuit of wisdom and knowledge and men have found boy-love to be the stablest of loves.[38] Lucian considers idealistic pederasty to be bred into people from childhood and enacted by divine laws.[39] This is of interest since most Hellenistic writers considered it contrary to nature. Lucian's view of pederasty is summed in one of his concluding statements.

---

32 Ibid., 758b; 761d; 766a.
33 Ibid., 768e.
34 Ibid., 770c.
35 Lucian, *Erotes,* 9.
36 Ibid., 19-20.
37 Ibid., 28.
38 Ibid., 33-36.
39 Ibid., 48.

Marriage is a boon and blessing to men when it meets with good fortune, while the love of boys, that pays court to the hallowed dues of friendship, I consider to be the privilege only of philosophy. Therefore, all men should marry, but let only the wise be permitted to love boys, for perfect virtue grows least of all among women. And you must not be angry Charicles, if Corinth yields to Athens.[40]

Of course, Corinth was notorious for its female prostitutes whereas Athens was the center of academic pederasty.

In brief, the basic arguments against pederasty were that law and public opinion opposed it, that philosophy was a sham cover-up for erotic escapades, that it encouraged boys to become effeminate, that the relationships were brief, that it fostered jealousy in the youth and that it was contrary to nature.

Throughout the Hellenistic period the ideal of sublimated pederasty continued, especially in the gymnasia, the centers of Greek culture and influence. Outside these areas homosexuality combined with eunuchism and effeminacy frequently degenerated into unbridled lust with elements of sadomasochism. Homosexuals prostituted themselves publicly and privately. The activity became so widespread that even the most eminent men in society prostituted themselves and sought to use others. Eventually pagan authors debated the wisdom of the entire practice of pederasty. Some defended it while admitting abuses, others found no value in it at all.

The Reaction of Hellenistic Judaism

1. Palestine. Palestinian Judaism consistently rejected homosexuality. From legal injunctions of the Torah to the Targums, translations of the Torah, we meet general opposition. The Neofiti text and Targum Jonathan, for example, interpret Genesis 19 as homosexual rape and Deuteronomy 23:18 as prohibiting male homosexual prostitution outside any cultic setting.[41]

In Rabbinic literature, the Mishnah summarizes and explains Pentateuchal law. In this document homosexuality is one of the crimes punishable by death.[42] To the rabbis homosexuality was a Gentile sin and Jews were not under suspicion of it, although certain precautions were made to avoid temptation or the appearance of evil. Only one clear mention of

---

40 Ibid., 51.
41 Scroggs, pp. 75-77. As Scroggs notes there is no definitive answer yet which tradition the Neofiti text represents. See S. Lund, and J. A. Foster, *Variant Versions of Targumic Traditions Within Codex Neofiti* 1 (Missoula, MT: Scholars Press, 1977): 1-13.
42 Mishnah, *Sanhedrin* 7, 4.

Jewish homosexuality occurs in the rabbinic literature.[43] Palestinian literature discusses homosexuality in terms of homosexual acts, not other facets such as intention or motive.

2. The Diaspora. The best known document from Judaism outside Palestine during the Hellenistic period is the Septuagint, the Greek translation of the Old Testament, from the period 300-100 B.C. Scroggs believes that the language of the Septuagint in Leviticus influenced Paul's terminology. It reads, "With a male *(arsen)* you shall not lie the intercourse *(koite:* lit. 'bed') of a woman" (Lev 18:22). Also, "And whoever lies with a male *(arsen)* the intercourse *(koite)* of a woman, both have done an abomination; they shall be put to death, they are guilty" (Lev 20:13). Scroggs believes this juxtaposition of the two words, *arsen* and *koite,* reached a semitechnical status among the rabbis in the expression *mishkav zakur* ("lying with a male") and *arsenokoites* (1 Cor 6:9), an almost exact Greek parallel to the Hebrew.[44] Deuteronomy 23:17-18 is translated in the Septuagint in such a way to oppose male homosexuality more clearly than the Masoretic text does.

Philo, a Jewish writer and philosopher of Alexandria (fl. A.D. 40), rejects homosexuality. He especially abhors the effeminate male.[45] Philo accuses both active and passive partners of acting against nature, pursuing unnatural pleasure. For Philo the greatest sin is the channeling of semen away from the natural, divinely intended purpose of procreation. Such a man is an enemy of nature.[46] Philo applies Deuteronomy 23:1 to the effeminate castrated male, attacking this form of homosexuality at every opportunity.[47] He also attacks the ancient Sodomites and accuses them of homosexual practices.[48]

Josephus, another Jewish Hellenistic author originally from Palestine but later a pensioner in Rome (fl. A.D. 70), cites the pride, arrogance, and wealth of Sodom as the reason for God's destruction of the city. He turns the account of the two angels into one of intended pederastic rape, speaking of the angels as two "young" men.[49]

Apocryphal and pseudepigraphal literature is mixed in its interpretation of homosexual episodes in the Old Testament. The book of *Jubilees,* assumed to be written by a Pharisee between 135 and 105 B.C., mentions the destruction of Sodom but attributes it to general wickedness, fornica-

---

43 *Sanhedrin* 623c, 4.
44 Scroggs, p. 86.
45 Philo, *Special Laws,* III, 37.
46 Ibid., 36.
47 Philo, *Special Laws,* I, 325.
48 Philo, *On Abraham,* 133-41; *Questions on Genesis,* IV, 37.
49 Josephus, *Ant.* I. 194-204.

tion, and uncleanness.[50] The Letter of Aristeas, which purports to give a firsthand account of the translation of the Septuagint about 270 B.C., depicts homosexuality as a Gentile vice from which the Jews have been kept by their adherence to the law of Moses.[51] The Testaments of the Twelve Patriarchs, another Pharisaic work dated 109-106 B.C., mentions Sodom in a context of idolatry but also in a context of creation.

> The Gentiles went astray, and forsook the Lord, and changed their order, and obeyed stocks and stones, spirits of deceit. But ye shall not be so, my children, recognizing in the firmament, in the earth, and in the sea, and in all created things, the Lord who made all things, that ye become not as Sodom, which changed the order of nature.[52]

The last statement here is likely a reference to the homosexual episode of Genesis 19. The Sibylline Oracles, a collection of prophecies begun by Jews and later added to by Christian writers, speak of an empire that follows the Greeks (Rome), characterized as allowing "male to draw near to male and they shall set their children in ill-famed houses."[53] In another passage the Oracle prophesies that a holy race of men will appear who are not given to idolatry,

> nor do they hold unholy intercourse with boys as do the Phoenicians, Egyptians, and Latins and spacious Hellas and many nations of other men, Persians and Galatians and all Asia, transgressing the holy law of the immortal God which he ordained.[54]

To the Oracle the transgression of God's law by idolatry and pederasty precipitates woes and calamities. Men should shun "adultery and confused intercourse with males," for this brings the wrath of God.[55]

Rome in particular is condemned. "Adulteries are with thee and unlawful intercourse with boys, effeminate and unjust, thou wicked city, most ill-starred of all."[56] Rome is castigated repeatedly for abuse of boys, harlotry, irregular unions within the degrees of consanguinity, fellatio and bestiality.[57] Sometimes these evils are connected with idolatry, sometimes

---

50 *Jubilees,* 16, 5. Edition cited or consulted in this section, R. H. Charles, *The Apocrypha and Pseudepigrapha of the Old Testament,* 2 vols. (Oxford: Clarendon Press, 1976).
51 *Letter of Aristeas,* 152.
52 *Testament of Naphtali,* 3:1-5.
53 *Sibylline Oracles,* III, 185.
54 Ibid., 584-606; 596-600 cited.
55 Ibid., 762-766.
56 *Sibylline Oracles,* V, 166-67.
57 Ibid., 386-393, 428-430.

not. The Oracle describes Rome as full of the basest evils of which idolatry and various sexual crimes seem to be the worst.

The apocryphal book of Wisdom, produced in Egypt about 116-50 B.C. by a conservative Jewish author, makes idolatry the beginning and cause of every evil, including what the RSV translates as "sex perversion."[58] This is a translation of the obscure expression *geneseos enallage,* which translates literally as "changing of order" or "changing of kind." It is similar to the expression "changed the order of nature" in the Testament of Naphtali,[59] and it is difficult to see what else it could refer to except the change of sex roles in homosexuality.

In brief, the judgment against homosexual acts in Judaism is so universal and deeply rooted that arguments against it seem to have been considered superfluous. Judaism excluded homosexuality by definition; therefore, it was non-Jewish authors who brought detailed arguments against it in the Hellenistic period.

---

58 *Wisdom,* pp. 14, 26.
59 The verbal form of *enallage* is used in T. Naphtali, 3, 4.

Chapter 6
The New Testament and Homosexuality

The Social Background of Early Christianity: Form and Context of Anti-homosexual References

Outside Palestine Christianity took root first in provincial towns and cities of the Roman Empire. For the most part the apostle Paul walked Roman roads and sailed Roman trade routes. The aim of Roman policy was to unify and acculturate the provinces to Roman ideas. In pursuit of these goals Rome worked in alliance with Greek civilization, especially in the heavily-populated Eastern provinces. As Ramsey observes, "The Greek influence was, on the whole, European and Western in character; and opposed to the oriental stagnation which resisted Roman educative efforts."[1]

Christianity was doubtless envisaged by many in the East as a force in social life arrayed on the side of imperial policy. The new religion worked against ignorance, stagnation, social anarchy, and enslavement of the people to priests. At the same time it stood for universal citizenship, universal equality of rights, universal religion, and a universal church. Almost all of these concepts already were developing slowly in one way or another within the empire.[2]

Paul took advantage of elements in Greek education. The best in Greek ethics, learning, and forms of polished courteous address he did not disdain. In his speeches at Lystra and Athens there was nothing overtly Jewish or Christian. Paul could speak as a Jew and a Christian; also he could express the truths of Scripture in the language and ideas of educated Romans.

The first churches were in cities and towns, and the first Christians urban dwellers. Cities were small by modern standards, however population density in many cities rivaled that of modern city slums.[3] Under such

---

1 W. M. Ramsey, *St. Paul the Traveller and Roman Citizen* (Grand Rapids: Baker Book House, 1979), p. 131.
2 Ibid., p. 138.
3 W. A. Meeks, *The First Urban Christians, the Social World of the Apostle Paul* (New Haven, CT: Yale University Press, 1983), p. 28. If we were to find out how early Christians actually lived we should probably find a diversity of lifestyles co-existing, see L. E. Keck, "On the Ethos of Early

circumstances privacy was rare; no social group could remain anonymous.

So it is not surprising that Christians in the larger cities were extremely sensitive to public opinion. Their safety as Christian groups depended to a certain degree on their religious activities' largely escaping public attention. Abnormal behavior in the community of believers would encourage circulation of rumors to the discredit of the entire community. As Judge indicates, "The basic problem for Christians was thus not their relations with the government, but with the communities within which they lived."[4] Early Christian writers responded more to social criticism than questions about the legality of the Christian's status or actions in relation to the state.

It is a mistaken judgment to consider the triumph of Christianity as tantamount to the triumph of the lower classes, or "proletariat," as some Marxist exegetes prefer to say, over the upper classes.[5] Early Christian churches represented a cross section of society. If anything, the small intense clusters of Christian communities were largely middle class in origin.[6] "The triumph of Christianity in a hierarchically organized society necessarily took place from the top down."[7]

Christians and Social Structure

The form which early Christian communities assumed was present already in the environment. The early church did not build structures especially for its own religious activities. The meeting places of a great number of Paul's converts in the diaspora were private houses. Several times Paul mentions Christian assemblies in connection with a specific household. The conversion of a person with "all his/her household" is mentioned several times in Acts also.

In New Testament times the term "household" meant more than in modern Western societies. It included not just immediate relatives but

---

Christians," *JAAR* 42 (1974): 442. There must have been wide divergences at first between lived morality and preached morality in early Christian circles, eg. Corinth. However the private morality of the Christian circle, informed by preached morality, exerted its influence on the community and eventually on society. On "private morality," see W. Den Boer, *Private Morality in Greece and Rome: Some Historical Aspects* (Leiden: E. J. Brill, 1979), pp. 2, 3.

4 E. A. Judge, *The Social Pattern of the Christian Groups in the First Century* (London: Tyndale Press, 1960) pp. 71, 73.
5 K. Kautsky, *The Foundation of Christianity,* tr. H. F. Mins (New York: S. A. Russell, 1953).
6 R. M. Grant, *Early Christianity and Society* (San Francisco: Harper & Row Pubs., 1977), p. 11; see also, E. A. Judge, "St. Paul and Classical Society," *Jahrbuch für Antike und Christentum* 15 (1972), 30-31; also, A. Robertson, *The Origins of Christianity,* rev. ed. (New York: International Pubs Co., 1962), p. 132; and G. Theissen, *The Social Setting of Pauline Christianity: Essays on Corinth,* ed. and tr. J. H. Schutz (Philadelphia: Fortress Press, 1982), pp. 69-110. Other references in R. Scroggs, "The Sociological Interpretation of the New Testament: The Present State of Research," *NTS* 26 (1980): 169-170.
7 Ibid.

slaves, freedmen, hired hands, even partners in crafts or trades, and could be extended to include virtually anyone who depended on the group for livelihood and sustenance.[8] The household was a basic political unit whose loyalties could rival those toward the Roman republic. The head of the household had a certain amount of legal responsibility for his/her charges. But as Malherbe points out, the solidarity of such groups, "was based more on economic, and especially psychological, social and religious factors."[9] New Christian groups were thus superimposed upon an already existing network of relationships.

The household, probably 30-50 persons at the most, afforded privacy, intimacy, and stability of place for early Christian communities. However, when several households existed in one community, a potential for factions existed. Households were hierarchical. The head of the household, who was legally responsible, no doubt also exercised certain political and moral influence over the group. Paul seems to take this for granted in his epistle to Philemon. Household factions also may be the source of the trouble in 1 Corinthians 1-4. It was not unusual for households to be the center of a cult or society under the patronage of the head of the household. Under these circumstances the solidarity of Christian groups as a whole is indeed remarkable and points to other inner cohesive factors at work beyond the exclusivity of the household.

Social intercourse with those outside the Christian group was not discouraged, but a clear line of demarcation was drawn between the ethical-moral behavior expected of those outside and that expected of those inside the group (1 Cor 5:9-13). Paul also discouraged any activity that might involve participation in another cult (1 Cor 8 and 10).

It is clear from the advice given in 1 Corinthians 5 and 6 that Paul considered the Christian community a pure and holy place over against the impure and profane world outside. Christians were to avoid the abhorrent sexual practices and other vices practiced in the pagan world.

The *Haustafeln* ("house rules") in Ephesians 4:17 and onward state (in the positive) what is expected of Christian communities (cf. Col 3:12ff.). These regulations were essential to the solidarity and cohesiveness of Christianity as a whole (1 Cor 1:2). They also highlight Paul's conviction that the purity of the community "is contaminated only from within, not by contact with outsiders, even though the latter are considered typically immoral."[10] Nevertheless, the *Haustafeln* were composed with an eye toward how outsiders perceived the community (Col 4:5).

---

8   Meeks, 75-76.
9   A. J. Malherbe, *Social Aspects of Early Christianity* (Philadelphia: Fortress Press, 1983), p. 69.
10 Meeks, p. 105.

New Testament Vice Lists: Christian and Non-Christian

Regulations for Christian ethical behavior also are stated negatively in the New Testament. This was achieved by listing vices that Christians were exhorted to avoid.[11] It is possible that such lists were used in catechetical instruction beginning at a very early period.[12] These lists existed in the popular moral teaching of the period, and parallels among Stoics are unmistakable.

The cataloging of virtues and vices in such lists is familiar enough in classical, Hellenistic, and early Christian literature.[13] Of course this is not to say that Paul took his ideas directly from the teachings of the great classical schools of philosophy studied by the privileged elite with the requisite time and inclination. A careful analysis shows that Paul has much in common with philosophical thought in general but not with any regular system of thought.[14] Judge proposes another approach to illuminate how the niche Paul filled related to popular ethics. This is not a system of ethics as such, he says, "but the way in which a loose body of general principles for life develops among thoughtful people in a community."[15] This "body of general principles" is not directly subject to the discipline of the schools, although it may draw from them and feed into their systems.

Christians also found precedent for ethical lists in the Hellenistic Jewish literature. They are abundant in Philo, and an excellent example of a vice list is found in Wisdom 14:25-26: "Blood and murder, theft and fraud, corruption, faithlessness, tumult, perjury, troubling of good, unthankfulness for benefits, defilement of souls, confusion of sex, disorder in marriage, adultery and wantonness." Easton observes that in accord with Jewish custom actions rather than thoughts are enumerated here.[16] In contrast, a Stoic list would center on sins of disposition.

Likewise, Wisdom's characteristically Jewish emphasis on idolatry as the

---

11 New Testament vice lists include: Matt 15:19; Mark 7:21-22; Rom 1:18-32; 13:13; 1 Cor 5:10-11; 6:9-10; 2 Cor 12:20; Gal 5:19, 21; Eph 4:31; 5:3, 7; Col 3:5, 9; 1 Tim 1:9-10; 6:4-5; 2 Tim 3:2, 5; Titus 3:3; 1 Pet 2:1; 4:3-4; Jude 8:16; Rev 9:20-21; 21:8; 22:15.

12 C. H. Dodd, "The Ethics of the New Testament," *Moral Principles of Action—Man's Ethical Imperative*, ed. R. N. Anshen (New York: Harper Bros., 1952), pp. 544-45.

13 E. N. O'Neal, "De Cupiditate Divitiarium" *(Moralia 523c- 528b)*, *Plutarch's Ethical Writings and Early Christian Literature*, ed. H. D. Betz., *Studia ad Corpus Hellenisticum Novi Testamenti* 4, eds. H. D. Betz, G. Delling, and W. C. Van Unnik (Leiden: E. J. Brill, 1978): 309.

14 Judge, "St. Paul and Classical Society," p. 32. The extent to which the philosophical vice lists had penetrated the popular consciousness may be seen in Deissmann. Roman game pieces contain all of Paul's vice list in 1 Corinthians 6:9-10 except for two words. The comic dramatist Plautus contains a considerable number of the vices listed in 1 Timothy 1:9-10. A. Deissmann, *Light From The Ancient East, The New Testament Illustrated by Recently Discovered Texts of The Graeco-Roman World*, tr. L.R.M. Strachan (New York: G. H. Doran Co., 1927), pp. 314-17.

15 Ibid., p. 33.

16 B. S. Easton, "New Testament Ethical Lists," *JBL* 51 (1932): 2.

cardinal defect differs from Greek and Roman moralists who would choose ignorance.[17]

Paul's line of thought in Romans 1:26-31 parallels much of Wisdom's thesis and language. Yet this longest of the New Testament catalogs of vices does not simply repeat the list in Wisdom. Of the 15 terms in Wisdom and the 21 in Romans only two—murder and deceit—are common to both lists.[18] Indeed most of the lists are conventional and the particular sins listed have little to do with the immediate context.

Non-Jewish precedent, particularly Stoic, as well as Jewish precedent inform most lists. Easton postulates non-Jewish precedent for Romans 1:29-31 and somewhat less so for 2 Timothy 3:2-4.[19] Other lists probably have Jewish-Greek influence in the immediate background. McEleney[20] finds no pattern of terms followed in the vice lists of the pastoral epistles. He concludes,

> Thus the vice lists of the Pastorals have been influenced by more or less of these elements: (1) reference to the Decalogue or other commands of the Law; (2) polemic against immoral pagan idolaters; (3) Hellenistic conceptions of virtue and vice as qualifications of a man; (4) moral dualism due to various inclinations of spirits in a man causing him to walk in one of two ways; (5) the theme of eschatological punishment.

Here again the Stoic and Jewish background stand out. The similarities with Stoicism, however, should not be overemphasized. The pagan concept of *philanthropia* ("love for mankind"), while present in Wisdom is notably absent in the New Testament. The Christian concept of patience *(makrothymia)*, on the other hand, is absent in Stoicism, and qualities such as mercy *(eleos)* and humility *(tapeinotes)* are Christian virtues but Stoic vices.

The differences are determined by different views of man, his nature, and purpose in life. The Christian concept of human relationship with God is determinative in Christian lists. Therefore it is vital to understand the conceptual framework in which the terms are used in the New Testament—also to recognize that these terms are not used in that framework outside of it. As Easton has noted, "avoidance of the sins cataloged in these lists is never identified with Christian morality. Life as a Christian hardly begins

---

[17] Marcus Aurelius, *Meditations* II, 1. "Say to thyself at daybreak: I shall come across the busy-body, the thankless, the overbearing, the treacherous, the envious, the unneighborly, all this has befallen them because they know not good from evil."
[18] Easton, p. 3.
[19] Ibid., p. 8.
[20] N. J. McEleney, "The Vice Lists of the Pastoral Epistles," *CBQ* 36 (1974): 218.

until such temptations have been put to death."[21] It is most significant, therefore, that all major references to homosexuality in the New Testament occur in vice lists.

In creating vice lists the Stoics tried to demonstrate that one is not controlled by the logos—the universal world soul—and which are therefore improper or unethical for the man of reason or philosophy. Avoiding them produces an ethical man of logos.

For Christians, however, mere avoidance of vice is not the essence of an ethical or moral person. Morality and ethics cannot begin until these acts are removed from the lifestyle. Christian ethics and morality involve the doing of positive things, not merely removal of negatives.

Homosexual activity never appears in any positive list in the New Testament, although numerous other activities are listed. When homosexuality is mentioned it is always included in the negative vice lists. This fact cannot be ignored by those who claim that loving homosexual relations are condoned in Scripture. Nowhere does Paul issue instructions for the homosexual couple or tell how they are to be integrated into the church. He does this for slaves, for families where only one spouse is a believer, for those coming from pagan cults and worldly associations, for those who are virgins and those who are not, and for Jews and/or Pharisees with all their religious and cultural baggage. But homosexual acts are listed as one of the lifestyles left behind, discontinued upon acceptance of Christ.

Primary New Testament Texts Cited
With Reference to Homosexuality

> Romans 1:26-28. For this reason God gave them up to dishonorable passions. Their women exchanged natural relations for unnatural, and the men likewise gave up natural relations with women and were consumed with passion for one another, men committing shameless acts with men and receiving in their own persons the due penalty for their error. And since they did not see fit to acknowledge God, God gave them up to a base mind and improper conduct.

These verses are followed immediately by the longest vice list in the New Testament (Rom 1:29-32). It includes no sexual sins. Apparently Paul was satisfied with his treatment of them in verses 24-28, the whole of which (vss. 24-32) may be seen as an extended vice list.

Numerous interpreters of these verses see homosexual acts totally

---

21 Easton, p. 8.

condemned in them, others find only a certain kind of exploitive homosexual practice condemned here. Among the latter by far the most prevalent view is that which sees Paul opposed to homosexual lust but not homosexual acts per se. The text, they claim, could not have been written against the "natural" or permanent homosexual because Paul was ignorant of the distinction between the primary or constitutional homosexual and other perverted forms of homosexual activity.[22] Accordingly, Paul is concerned with exploitation, prostitution, and unbridled homosexual lust.

In fact he must refer to those who are not permanent homosexuals, because the text states that those involved do so against their nature. It would not violate the nature of a constitutional homosexual to indulge in homosexual activity, but it would be against the nature of a heterosexual to do so. Therefore, Bailey interprets this text to speak about perverted heterosexuals who indulge in homosexual acts for kicks out of lust. Consequently, it cannot refer to the loving homosexual relationship of the constitutional homosexual where affection and responsibility are the marked criteria and not unbridled lust.[23]

Another common interpretation, sometimes held in conjunction with Bailey's view, is that Paul here is condemning those who were idolaters, not homosexual activity as such. Paul is speaking out against those who were idolaters-and-homosexuals, not against those who were homosexuals but not idolaters.[24] Various assumptions are involved here. Among them, that homosexuality was practiced in conjunction with idolatry in Paul's day and was, therefore, a conscious voluntary choice, or that homosexuality is in some way the result of idolatry or that it is God's punishment for idolatry.[25]

Other interpreters zero in on the word "nature." They reject the idea that Paul's use of the word is tied in some way to Greek philosophical usage.[26] Others read it to mean simply "convention," the generally

---

[22] D. S. Bailey, *Homosexuality and the Western Christian Tradition* (Hamden, CT: Shoe String Press, 1975), pp. 38, 157.

[23] H. K. Jones, *Toward a Christian Understanding of the Homosexual* (New York: Association Press, 1966), p. 70; also, R. Woods, *Another Kind of Love: Homosexuality and Spirituality* (Chicago: Thomas More Press, 1977), pp. 104-6; and R. L. Treese, "Homosexuality: A Contemporary View of the Biblical Perspective," *Loving Women/Loving Men: Gay Liberation and the Church,* ed. S. Gearheart, W. R. Johnson (San Francisco: Glide Publications, 1974), p. 38.

[24] R. W. Wood, "Homosexual Behavior in the Bible," *Homophile Studies: One Institute Quarterly* (Winter 1962), p. 16; N. Pittenger, *Time for Consent: A Christian's Approach to Homosexuality* (London: SCM Press Ltd., 1976), p. 82.

[25] Jones, D. L. Bartlett, "A Biblical Perspective on Homosexuality," *Homosexuality and the Christian Faith: A Symposium* (Valley Forge, PA: Judson Press, 1978), pp. 30-31.

[26] Particularly Plato's view that homosexuality was "unnatural" because animals did not do it. Scanzioni and Mollenkott take pains to point out that sea gulls and other creatures display lesbian and homosexual behavior. See L. Scanzioni and V. R. Mollenkott, *Is the Homosexual My Neigh-*

accepted practice in a particular time and place. These frequently quote 1 Corinthians 11:14 where Paul says, "Does not nature itself teach you that for a man to wear long hair is degrading to him?" Here Paul uses the word "nature" in what is considered a conventional sense.

In the Graeco-Roman culture, it was generally accepted practice for men to have short hair and be close shaven. However, among the Jews the practice was quite different. Longer hair and beards, cropped or uncropped, were not considered degrading. "Nature" here seems to mean the nature of the situation in a particular time and place. Neither long hair nor short hair was wrong per se; its appropriateness depended on a particular time and place. The implication is, of course, that the homosexual acts that Paul says are "against nature" are practices simply not accepted in some societies but accepted in others, and this is what he means here.[27] He is not saying that God condemns homosexual acts but simply that homosexuality is behavior contrary to Jewish culture and practice.

Finally, some adduce an argument more theological than historical, lexical, or philological. For them some forms of homosexual behavior are legitimate. Romans 1 is seen as incidental to the book and even incidental to Paul's attack on false righteousness in Romans 2, especially among Jews who believed they kept the law.

According to this interpretation Paul adopts a Jewish list of vices from apocryphal literature, but he does not seriously endorse all of it. He can point out the same sins among contemporary Jews. Homosexuals are not the only ones under criticism since Paul speaks of covetousness, malice, envy, deceit, gossip, and so forth. All men are sinners, and Paul is not isolating one group for special condemnation. All sinners can be saved by Christ, and there is no biblical basis for singling out homosexuals more than gossips and fornicators. Since fornicators, adulterers, and thieves are accepted into church fellowship, why not homosexuals? One cannot always be

---

bor: *Another Christian View* (San Francisco: Harper & Row Pubs., 1980), p. 65; also Plato, *Laws* VIII, 836-840.

27 J. Boswell, *Christianity, Social Tolerance and Homosexuality: Gay People in Western Europe from the Beginning of the Christian Era to the Fourth Century* (Chicago: University of Chicago Press, 1981), pp. 110-11. Also T. D. Perry, *The Lord is My Shepherd and He Knows I'm Gay* (Los Angeles: Nash Publishing Co., 1972), p. 152. According to Scroggs, all that can be gathered from this text is that Paul opposes homosexuality. Paul gives no reason. His Greek sources who opposed it likewise gave no reason. Paul's judgment here ultimately is dependent on Greek sources, not Jewish. It is not based on the doctrine of creation or philosophical principles, but on what appears to be common sense observation. See R. Scroggs, *The New Testament and Homosexuality Contextual Background for Contemporary Debate* (Philadelphia: Fortress Press, 1983), pp. 116-17. Wright points out that no fewer than twenty-two recent critical commentaries fail to make the distinctions on which Boswell bases his interpretation here, most of them generally reinforcing the opposite point of view. See, J. R. Wright (Review Article) "Boswell on Homosexuality: A Case Undemonstrated," *ATR* 66 (1984): 86-87.

certain whether Paul addresses the condition or the acts. Some would include both, others would not. This interpretation is summed up in Bartlett's paraphrase of Galatians 5:6: "In Christ Jesus, neither heterosexuality, nor homosexuality—in themselves—are of any avail, but faith working through love."[28]

If the above interpretations are accepted those who believe Paul is condemning all forms of homosexual activity will find their position difficult to defend. Perhaps it is wise to look at the entire context in which Paul is speaking, better to determine just what he is or is not saying.

Those with even a scanty knowledge of Romans know that here Paul deals in considerable detail with the doctrine of justification by faith. The theme of the book, as announced in Romans 1:16-17, is that the righteousness of God is revealed in the gospel about His Son Jesus Christ. Then Paul illustrates the need for this righteousness by showing that sin carries a retribution in life and eventually culminates in death. The arena where sin operates is universal. Those who drank the dregs of pagan vice and crime as well as those pagan moralists who considered themselves superior to the outcasts of society needed righteousness. Even the Jews, the chosen people of God who considered themselves supremely enlightened in contrast to the rest of mankind, fell under the stern judgment of God. In short, all mankind stands wanting and guilty before God. None has reason for complacency and congratulatory self-righteousness.

> Paul's aim is to show that the whole of humanity is morally bankrupt,... He begins with an area of human life whose moral bankruptcy was a matter of general agreement among moralists of the day—the great mass of contemporary paganism.[29]

But in placing both pagan moralists and Jews in the same category with the pagan masses Paul is not claiming that moralists and Jews practiced the same forms of immorality. What he is saying is that even the most degraded pagan can know enough from Creation itself to avoid confusing the Creator with the creatures (including man as a creature).

If, however, they deliberately confused the two, inevitably they fell into errors of thought and action. Paul is not suggesting that the pagan masses or any other group were not intelligent enough to understand, but that by resolute moral obduracy they failed to do that which they knew to be right.

As a group the Jews demonstrated that the essential problem was not

---

28 Bartlett, p. 39; also, Scanzioni and Mollenkott, pp. 70-71.
29 F. F. Bruce, *The Epistle of Paul to the Romans: An Introduction and Commentary* (London: Tyndale Press, 1969), pp. 81-82. Suetonius, *The Twelve Caesars*, reports homosexual activity on the part of all the emperors he writes about except one—Claudius.

ignorance but something quite different. The Jews are under the judgment of God because, exactly as they boasted, they are supremely enlightened. Consequently, they should have done that much better than those not so advantaged. But they failed to do so. Privilege brings responsibility and they failed in the latter when God provided the former.

Righteousness, or a right relationship and standing before the Holy God, was not to be found in the actions of the pagan masses, among the moralists, or even among the Jews; for all showed the same fundamental failure, a stubborn disobedience to what they already knew to be right.

It is here that Paul introduces the new principle of the gospel (Rom 3:21—5:21). God does not expect man to become righteous before He declares him such. Such a requirement would pose a hopeless situation. Rather God gives right status, or declares a person righteous, initiates a right relationship, then helps him grow up to its full potential. For Paul freedom from a system of law or religious activity to set oneself right with God and freedom from death (Rom 7:1—8:39) come before freedom from sin (Rom 6:1-23). He vigorously opposes the idea that the outpouring of God's grace means a life continued in sin. In baptism we die to sin, and changing the analogy to the slave market he sees the Christian as a redeemed slave working for a new master—God, not the old master Sin.

Paul's remarks encompass all humanity. It is not against merely a Jewish or Greek background that he writes, but against a cosmic background. He deals with the broad canvas of Creation, sin, Fall, and redemption. For Paul, Adam was a historical person involved in the process (Rom 5). Since all have sinned and come short of God's original glorious intention for man, God offers to all the opportunity to come into right relationship with Him through Jesus. The relationship is to be maintained thereafter to the best of one's ability in cooperation with God, in good faith. The ultimate aim is that man will be restored to God's image as He intended in Creation.

In the section under consideration (1 Rom 1:24-32) Paul is showing how far mankind has fallen from this ideal or original state. In verse 24 he first uses the words, "God gave them up." We doubt that these words, repeated in verses 26 and 28, imply that the abandonment of the heathen to the dominion of sin represents a punitive act inflicted by God.[30] If God withdraws the restraints of His providence and grace from the wicked He may be described in biblical terminology as giving them over to sin. But "the permission to sin is not necessarily a judicial or punitive act."[31] The

---

30 C. Hodge, *Commentary on the Epistle to the Romans* (Grand Rapids: Wm. B. Eerdmans Publishing Co., 1977), p. 40.
31 W.G.T. Shedd, *Commentary on Romans* (Grand Rapids: Baker Book House, 1980), p. 25.

sin of Adam was permitted, but scarcely as a judgment or penalty for sin. The issue here is one of free relationship between God and humans. God allows the wicked to "enjoy forever the horrible freedom they have demanded, and [they] are, therefore, self-enslaved."[32]

To some extent sin is exposed and punished by its own results, but this is because God has so constituted natural process that wrong inevitably gravitates to wretchedness. God leaves men where they place themselves—in the fatal region of self-will and self-indulgence.[33] "There is a moral law in life that men are left to the consequences of their own freely chosen course of action; and unless this tendency is reversed by divine grace, their situation will go from bad to worse."[34]

It is not helpful then to consider homosexuality a punishment for sin. Such an opinion may lead to judgmental questions as asked by the disciples, "Rabbi, who sinned, this man or his parents that he was born blind?" (John 9:2). As with blindness, so with the homosexual condition the answer may be "neither, but that the glory of God might be revealed in him."

There is no doubt that in verse 25 Paul sees the vices of paganism as the product of idolatry. This was commonplace in Jewish apologetic of the time (see Wisdom of Solomon 12-14; The Epistle of Aristeas). For him the vices of paganism with their inevitable results are in themselves retribution for the fundamental error of taking up an irreligious attitude to life—that is, of placing the reason and will of the creature at the forefront in spite of the knowledge of God native to the human mind. Idolatry cannot be reduced in this context simply to pagan practices and cultic life. In essence it is an attitude toward God that places human will above His will, human authority above His sovereignty (Rom 1:28, 32).

To say that homosexuality is a result of idolatry is to say, therefore, in the wider sense of the word that it is the result of the sinful human condition in which we all live, to which any specific individual may or may not contribute by his/her actions.

In verse 26 Paul specifies some of the things that result from and contribute to the fallen existence common to man. God gives man up to the dishonorable passions that spring from his attitude toward God. Specifically, Paul mentions homosexuality as a dishonorable passion. It needs not be the only one. The fact that men may believe they serve God by indulging in these passions is part of the ultimate irony in idolatry—the ultimate foolishness of those who claim to be wise (vs. 19).

Paul begins with women, or "females" *(thelus)* as he designates them,

---

32 C. S. Lewis, *The Problem of Pain* (New York: Macmillan Publishing Co., 1961), pp. 115ff.
33 H.C.G. Moule, *The Epistle to Romans* (London: Pickering and Inglis, 1925), p. 49.
34 Bruce, p. 81.

who exchange natural relations for unnatural. The meaning of this brief verse is clarified by the next (vs. 27). Men likewise gave up natural relations with women and were consumed with passion for one another: men (actually "males," *arsen*) committing shameless acts with men.

Natural Versus Unnatural

The two key terms in these verses are the expressions "natural" and "unnatural," and much depends upon what Paul meant here. The crux of the issue turns on why Paul concludes that homosexuality is unnatural. Paul uses the terms *para phusin* ("against," "beside," or "contrary to") nature and *kata phusin* ("according to") nature. (Cf. expressions in Rom 11:24.) There is no doubt that these terms are common Greek usage and that they are used at times to express an ethical judgment on homosexuality. This is true in Plato (*Laws* I, 636; VIII, 836-841), who repeatedly uses the term "natural" to describe heterosexual intercourse, and "unnatural," for homosexual intercourse.

Plato attempts a reason why it is unnatural, that is, because men cannot fall below the level of the animal world where homosexuality does not take place (Laws VIII, 841). These expressions are common in the Hellenistic period, as we see in Diodorus Siculus (ca. 49 B.C.). In his *History* 32, 10, 8-11, he uses the term *kata phusin* of natural intercourse with a woman. However, in a case where the woman was in reality a man, he speaks of the intercourse as having taken place "as with a man" and the marriage as "against nature" *(para phusin gamou)*. In any event the woman (in reality a man) had to submit to "unnatural embraces" *(para phusin homilian)*.

Musonius Rufus, a Roman Stoic philosopher sometimes referred to as the Roman Socrates, was Paul's contemporary (ca. A.D. 30-102). His works show "the typical characteristics of the popularized philosophical treatise."[35] He is one of the few real supporters in antiquity of equal standing for women.

For Musonius, life in accordance with nature is life in accordance with virtue. Musonius identifies *kata phusin zen* ("to live according to nature") with *en arete zen* ("to live according to virtue"). Because men and women may have equal virtue they should have equal training.

It is not surprising then that Musonius sees marriage as the most venerable relationship. One of Musonius' arguments is that marriage is *kata phusin*. "In the later Stoics marriage is always said to be *kata phusin*."[36] He allows for sexual intercourse only within marriage and then

---

35 A. C. Geytenbeck, *Musonius Rufus and Greek Diatribe*, tr. B. L. Hijmans Jr. (Assen: Van Gorcum and Co., 1963), p. 13.
36 Ibid., p. 68.

only for procreation. All other instances are "indecent relationships," adultery because it is unlawful, and other unmarried relations as being unlawful and dissolute. Also when he speaks on sexual relationships, he refers to pederasty as *para phusin tolmema* ("an outrage against nature").[37]

Another contemporary of Paul, the Jewish historian Josephus (ca. A.D. 37-97), speaks of sodomy as "unnatural vice" *(para phusin)* and "unnatural pleasure" *(para phusin)*.[38] Examples of such vices spoken of as *para phusin* occur also in Plutarch and other Hellenistic writers but none of them attempts to define what they mean by these expressions. After reading them all, we still do not really understand what they meant. Under these circumstances, it might be easier to determine what Paul did *not* mean by these expressions and to clarify the ideas that separate him from the late Stoics who also used the same terms.

Paul's God was transcendent, wholly above and beyond the world, as was Aristotle's. Like Plato's God, however, Paul's also was the creator of nature, nevertheless separate from the natural world. On the other hand the Stoics believed that God was immanent in ways that Paul could not at all agree with. For them, not only was the world controlled by God, but in the last resort, it *was* God. For the Stoics, existence goes on forever in endlessly recurring cycles following a fixed "law" or "formula" *(logos)*. This law is Fate or Providence ordained by God.

The Stoics thought that the *logos* is God or the mind of God, the universal world soul. The Stoic system, therefore, was basically determinist. Cicero, the Roman orator, statesman, and Stoic philosopher (106-43 B.C.), claimed that according to Zeno "the law of nature is divine," that Cleanthes held that "the world itself is god," and that Chrysippus said that "the divine power resides in reason and in the soul and mind of the universe."[39] There is little doubt that the late Stoics deified "Nature."[40] Marcus Aurelius spoke of Nature as "the eldest of deities."[41]

It is clear that Paul uses Stoic philosophical terms in Romans 1 and 2. But it is equally clear that Paul does not simply repeat the terms and concepts of the Stoa with the same meanings they had in Stoicism or even in Hellenism.[42] It is probable that for Paul the word "nature" meant the

---

37 Fr. XII, 8-10. The Greek text with translation and introduction is found in C. E. Lutz, *Musonius Rufus "The Roman Socrates"* (New Haven, CT: Yale Univ. Press, 1947).
38 Josephus, *Against Apion,* II 273, 275; further references may be found in H. Köster, *"Phusis, Phusikos, Phusikos,"* in *TDNT* 9 (1977): 251-77.
39 Cicero, *Of the Nature of the Gods* I, 14, 15. On Stoic determinism see, E. Bevan, *Stoics and Skeptics* (New York: Arno Press, 1979), p. 53.
40 C. S. Lewis, *Studies in Words* (Cambridge, MA: Cambridge University Press, 1975), p. 41. See the whole chapter on *Phusis.*
41 Marcus Aurelius, *Meditations IX,* 1.
42 A. J. Malherbe, "The Apologetic Theology of the Preaching of Peter," *Restoration Quarterly* 13

providential ordering of the natural world, as with the Stoics.[43]

Apart from this agreement, however, the term has a completely different function for Paul. The meaning of the term in Romans comes from a Stoic-Jewish storehouse. The direct influence of non-Jewish Hellenistic thought upon Paul has been exaggerated. His main background is Jewish, or better, that of Hellenistic Judaism. Paul, writing as a moralist and having occasion to deal with vices, ordinarily follows the classification used by popular moralists of the time. Customarily they were classified as sensual and antisocial. Many of the vice lists in Paul's epistles demonstrate that he was familiar with this mode of classification.[44]

Paul's God, however, was not nature, but the supremely transcendent one, the Creator who formed the earth and made man in perfection, whose work was blighted subsequently by the entrance of sin. Consequently, for Paul nature at present does not represent humanity's true nature. In a fallen world an appeal to nature to determine what humans should do or be is at best relative and at worst useless. In the context of fallen nature only relative distinctions can be made between the natural and the unnatural. For the Christian contemporary natural life is prelude to life with Christ, and it is validated as natural only because Christ Himself entered into the fallen natural life through the incarnation.

> Through the fall the "creature" becomes "nature." The direct dependence of the creature on God is replaced by the relative freedom of natural life. Within this freedom there are differences between the true and the mistaken use of freedom, and there is therefore the difference between the natural and the unnatural. In other words there is relative openness and relative closedness for Christ.[45]

The natural, from this point of view, is recognized as the form of life preserved by God in the fallen world. It is that life directed toward jus-

---

(1970): 211. Paul does not share the ideal underlying the Stoic terms, "because for him there is no nature either detached from God or identifiable with God." Also, E. Käsemann, *Commentary on Romans,* tr. and ed. G. W. Bromiley (Grand Rapids: Wm. B. Eerdmans Publishing Co., 1980), p. 48.

43 A. J. Herschbell, *De Virtute Morale (Moralia 523c-528b), Plutarch's Ethical Writings and Early Christian Literature,* ed. H. D. Betz., *Studia ad Corpus Hellenisticum Novi Testamenti* 4, ed. H. D. Betz, G. Delling, and W. C. Van Unnik (Leiden: E. J. Brill, 198), p. 167. Also Köster, p. 273. For the Stoics, to be in agreement with nature was to be in harmony with God. For Paul this would not necessarily be so, for nature too was fallen. Even for the Stoics what was natural for animals was not necessarily natural for man. See Bevan, pp. 55, 60-61.

44 C. H. Dodd, *The Epistle of Paul to the Romans* (London: Harper & Row Pubs, 1932), pp. xxxii, 26-27.

45 D. Bonhoeffer, *Ethics,* ed. E. Bethge (New York: Macmillan Publishing Co., 1968), p. 145.

tification, redemption, and renewal through Christ. Reason itself is embedded in the natural; reason then is nothing more than the conscious perception of the content of the natural in this world. Thus reason, after the Fall, has not ceased to be reason, but is now fallen.[46]

> From this there follows a conclusion that is of crucial importance, namely, that the natural can never be something that is determined by any single part of any single authority within the fallen world. And indeed whatever is set up in this arbitrary manner by an individual, a society or an institution will necessarily collapse and destroy itself in the encounter with the natural which is already established. Whoever does injury to the natural will suffer for it.[47]

Here we see that the natural, even in the form preserved by God after the Fall, is a given. In the fallen world nature reflects the splendor of the glory of God's creation and points forward to the restitution of all things.

But Paul's perspective in the passage under consideration is not limited to the relative distinctions between natural and unnatural in the fallen world. Only God's original intention for humans can be considered determinative for human essence, and this is revealed as His will in Scripture.

It is difficult to see what else Paul could mean by "Nature" in our text if not the world and man as intended and as created by God. The "unnatural" comes as a consequence of the Fall and, therefore, not God's original intention and will for man.

The cosmic context of Romans 1:18-32 is generally recognized. Scroggs even suggests that in these verses the universal Fall is under discussion, which includes Jews as well as Gentiles.[48] For these reasons homosexuality is not treated here merely as an expression of cultic idolatry, rather both practices are traced to the bad exchange that man made in departing from the Creator's original design.[49]

As Field observes,

> In writing about "natural relations," Paul is not referring to individual men and women as they are. His canvas is much broader. He is taking the argument back, far more radically, to man and woman as God created them. By "unnatural" he means "unnatural to mankind in God's creation pattern." And that pat-

---

46 Ibid., p. 146.
47 Ibid., p. 147.
48 Scroggs, p. 110.
49 D. H. Field, "Homosexuality," *The Illustrated Bible Dictionary* 2, ed. J. D. Douglas (Wheaton, IL: Tyndale House Pubs., 1980): 657. See Köster, p. 266.

tern he clearly understands to be heterosexual. So the distinction between pervert and invert (which Paul could have hardly made anyway) is undercut.[50]

Paul has in mind not only the casual and capricious sex swapping of the pervert, driven by lust and desire for flesh stimulation, but the basic divergence from God's original creation scheme which all homosexual behavior represents. The invert or constitutional homosexual may be seen as an aberration of God's original creation. He may be considered depraved (as all are to some extent) in the theological sense but not in a moral sense.[51]

The constitutional homosexual who has physical and emotional attraction to other males may be less culpable morally than the lustful heterosexual who constantly fantasizes adulterous relationships. Neither may act out their inner drives. The excessive sexual drive of the heterosexual may be due to some physical predisposition, but it is a perversion of God's intention and design. Both are culpable if the drives are acted out. The nymphomaniac whose impulses cannot be sexually satisfied by one man falls into the same category.

Paul uses the homosexual practices of his day to illustrate the depravity that follows departure from God's will. If homosexual acts could gain divine approval in any sense, surely Paul would have indicated how and drawn the distinction.[52]

Paul must have known the distinctions between the homosexual relationships in Plato, Sparta, prostitution, pederasty, and so forth, as well as adult relationships of a more permanent kind. For example the Roman emperor Galba (A.D. 68-69), considered a conservative and supported by many of the Stoic leaders, is described by the Roman historian, Suetonius:

---

50 D. Field, *The Homosexual Way—A Christian Option?* (Grove Books; Bromcote Notts., new ed. 1980), p. 16. On this point see also, D. Atkinson, *Homosexuals in the Christian Fellowship* (Grand Rapids: Wm. B. Eerdmans Publishing Co., 1979), pp. 87-88; P. Coleman, *Christian Attitudes to Homosexuality* (London: SPCK, 1980), p. 90; Coleman sees a strong relationship to the Noachian Law, p. 93; R. F. Lovelace, *Homosexuality and the Church* (Old Tappan, NJ, Fleming H. Revell Co., 1978), p. 92; R. Moss, *Christians and Homosexuality* (Exeter, CA: Paternoster Press, 1977), p. 27; E. A. Malloy, *Homosexuality and the Christian Way of Life* (Lanham, MD: University Press of America, 1981), p. 194; J. Murray, *The Epistle to the Romans, the English Text with Introduction, Exposition and Notes* (Grand Rapids: Wm. B. Eerdmans Publishing Co., 1971), pp. 47-48; E. Brunner, *The Divine Imperative*, tr. O. Wyon (Philadelphia: Westminster Press, 1947), p. 126.

51 H. Thielicke, *The Ethics of Sex*, tr. J. W. Doberstein (Greenwood, SC: Attic Press, 1978), p. 282.

52 G. L. Bahnsen, *Homosexuality: A Biblical View* (Grand Rapids: Baker Book House, 1979), p. 50. Paul is able to draw fine distinctions at other places in his epistles. We cannot entirely agree with Furnish when he says, "To Paul it represented a rebellion against the Creator and his creation, a surrender to one's lusts, the debasement of one's own true identity and the exploitation of another's. It is no longer possible to share Paul's belief that homosexual conduct always and necessarily involves all these things" (V. P. Furnish, *The Moral Teaching of Paul* [Nashville: Abingdon Press, 1979], p. 81.)

A homosexual invert, he showed a preference for mature and sturdy men. It is said that when Icelus, one of his old-time bedfellows, brought the news of Nero's death, Galba openly showered him with kisses and begged him to get ready and have intercourse with him without delay.[53]

In a day when homosexual acts were commonly practiced and widely known, Paul could hardly have been ignorant of the variety of relationships existing in the first century Hellenistic world. An interpretation of his words that allows homosexual activity would have to allow also any sin in the list of vices which follows.

We need to emphasize, however, that Paul is speaking of homosexual acts, not temptations to homosexuality or disposition to homosexuality of whatever intensity. Paul concludes verse 27 by observing that those who practice such acts, "receive in their own persons the due penalty for their error." The apostle may refer to spiritual moral erosion in the life or the physical deterioration that results from a dissolute life or both. At the end of the vice list (verse 32) he notes finally that "they not only do them but approve those who practice them." We must keep in mind that in Paul's day male-with-male sexual relationships not only went largely uncondemned but were sometimes glorified as a stage of love higher than that between man and woman.[54]

Paul came from a Semitic culture that held marriage and family in high esteem for centuries and homosexual acts were condemned. For him and many early Jewish Christians, homosexual acts produced revulsion. It is understandable to find him reacting as he does. Lovelace observes, "Paul's target in Romans 1:26 and 27 is, therefore, not a few dissolute heterosexual experimenters, but the Gentile culture whose male aristocrats could use women as chattel and child rearers but reserve their most refined erotic passion for other males."[55]

One might argue that as a conservative Jew Paul was merely reacting to the Gentile culture around him in typical Jewish fashion. But Paul was the most liberated of the apostles. He was most open and accepting of the Gentiles and willing to reject Jewish tradition where he saw it in conflict with the will of God. Other reasons have to be found for Paul's rejection of homosexuality. He was no conservative reactionary. Based on evidence, there is no "Pauline privilege" for homosexual activity in Romans 1:26-28.

---

53 Suetonius, *Galba*, 21., tr. Robert Graves. *The Twelve Caesars*, rev. with an introduction by M. Grant (Penguin Books, Harmondsworth, 1979), p. 258.
54 E. Best, *The Letter of Paul to the Romans* (Cambridge, MA: Cambridge University Press, 1967), p. 23.
55 Lovelace, p.92.

1 Corinthians 6:9, 10. Do you not know that the unrighteous will not inherit the kingdom of God? Do not be deceived; neither the immoral, nor idolaters, nor adulterers, nor [homosexuals], nor thieves, nor the greedy, nor drunkards, nor revilers, nor robbers will inherit the Kingdom of God.

The old city of Corinth was destroyed in 146 B.C. by the Roman consul L. Mummius. A hundred years later Julius Caesar rebuilt it and established a Roman colony there. Both old and new cities had one thing in common, they were notorious for their depravity and immorality.[56]

From this city Paul wrote his vivid description of the moral corruption of the pagan world (Rom 1:18-23). Nearly every religious cult and rite of the Mediterranean region was practiced and excavations have uncovered the sacred objects of Greeks, Romans, Orientals, Anatolians, and Egyptians.[57] Corinthian depravity was paralleled, if not surpassed by the social polarization in the city. The most abject poverty stood adjacent to immense wealth and extravagant luxury (1 Cor 11:17-34).

In his first epistle to the Corinthians, written from Ephesus about A.D. 57, Paul attempts to correct a number of abuses in the church. He must deal with factions in the church (1 Cor 1:10—4:21), with moral abuses (5:1—6:20), and in the last part of the epistle, with various questions and problems raised by the members there. Our passage falls within the section 6:1-11 where Paul is remonstrating with the Corinthians for their litigation before pagan law courts.

Both the Greeks and the Romans prided themselves in litigation. Many reputations were made at court and fortunes won or lost at the bar. Paul censures the church members for entering this arena. Matters between the brethren should be settled amicably within the confines of the church. In addition, the attitude manifest in litigation for trivial causes did not exhibit the mind of Christ in the believers. Christ would rather allow Himself to be deprived or wronged.

The Corinthian believers, on the other hand, still were manifesting the character of their previous way of life in this matter. Rather than patiently enduring a wrong as Christ would, they were doing wrong. The apostle censures them sternly because they know better than this: "Do you not know" (vs. 2) and "Do you not know" (vs. 3) and again "Do you not know?" (vs. 9). This expression is used often by Paul when he wants to bring to mind some important truth his readers knew but disregarded.[58]

---

56 Strabo, VIII, 6, 20; Horace, *Epistles,* I, 17, 36.
57 For the last mentioned, see D. E. Smith, "The Egyptian Cults at Corinth," *HTR* 70 (1977): 201-231.
58 C. Hodge, *Commentary on the First Epistle to the Corinthians* (Grand Rapids: Wm. B. Eerdmans

Looking at the passage in greater detail, we see that Paul picks up the word "unrighteous" *(adikoi,* vs. 9), from the previous verse, "But you yourselves wrong *(adikeo)* and defraud." The Corinthians treated standing up for one's rights, even in trivial matters, as an assertion of Christian freedom. It was likely the wealthy who went to court with high confidence of winning. They could afford the costs. The poor would have neither the bribes, lawyer's fees, nor court fees necessary for a successful suit in those days. What Paul labors to point out here is that unrighteousness in all its forms is a survival from the wretched past all Corinthians ought to have left behind them. So he says plainly, Evil-doers such as you were cannot enter the kingdom of heaven.

Pagan religions tended to divorce religion from morality. One could be a devotee of many gods and goddesses and scrupulously perform many religious rites without changing lifestyle. Some converts may have been prone to look upon Christianity as just another religion. The closest to what we call religious conversion among ancient pagans was joining a philosophical sect where ethical and moral demands were made on the person.[59]

Using the vice list format, Paul begins to enumerate the evils that should belong to the past of any Christian. It is possible that some in the Corinthian church were advocating the idea that the deeds of the body were irrelevant to salvation. Paul warns them, "Do not be deceived" *(planao).* There was danger that some were being deceived or led astray by a form of gnostic teaching that considered the body intrinsically evil and not subject, therefore, to redemption. Again, this view may have appealed to the few aristocratic families in Corinth since it allowed them to justify their customary lifestyle, one they enjoyed and could well afford. Such people would have taught that faith in the heavenly Christ and knowledge of the true nature of the things were sufficient for salvation.

Paul enumerates ten kinds of offenders. They represent sins no doubt prevalent at Corinth, but the list is largely conventional. Of the first five, three (or four) are sins against purity. Fornicators or immoral persons, adulterers, and homosexuals are the first three in some versions. Idolaters usually are mentioned separately and second in the list.

"Homosexuals" is in some ways a misleading translation. As the RSV footnote points out, the word is a translation of two Greek words *malakoi* and *arsenokoitai.* The translation and meaning of these two words is vigorously debated. The primary meaning of *malakos* is "soft."[60] The word

---

Publishing Co., 1976), p. 94.
59 A. D. Nock, *Conversion, the Old and New in Religion from Alexander the Great to Augustine of Hippo* (London: Oxford University Press, 1969).
60 H. G. Liddell and R. Scott, *A Greek Lexicon* (London: Oxford University Press, 1973), pp. 1076-77; W. F. Arndt and F. W. Gingrich, *A Greek-English Lexicon of the New Testament and other*

is used to describe fabrics (Matt 11:8; Luke 7:25), skin, and many other items. It can be used of persons in the sense of "soft of nature," "delicate," or "tender." In a more derogatory sense the word means "effeminate" or "voluptuous." Moffatt translates the terms separately as catamite and sodomite:[61] catamite is usually defined as a boy used for pederasty.

Other translators see no connection at all with homosexual acts and suggest that the word means loose, morally weak, or lacking in self-control.[62] These non-homosexual translations are usually picked up by the prohomophile literature. The idea at work here is that if the word *malakos* is not a reference to homosexual activity, then such acts are not a form of iniquity that prevents entrance to the kingdom of God.

The vast majority of commentators and lexicographers of the New Testament, however, see this as a reference to passive homosexuals, that is, to those who yield themselves to be used for homosexual purposes.[63] Some quote papyrus Hibeh 54, "And send us also Zenobius the effeminate with tabret, and cymbals, and rattles." "Effeminate" here equates to *malakos*. On this papyrus Deissmann comments, "The word is no doubt used in its secondary (obscene) sense as by St. Paul in 1 Cor. VI, 9. It is an allusion to the foul practices by which the musician eked out his earnings."[64] The fact that *malakoi* are mentioned between two other sexual sins in our text lends weight to the argument that "softness" here is not merely self-indulgence in general but, as the lexicographers, Arndt and Gingrich suggest, males who allowed themselves to be used homosexually.[65]

The other word translated "sodomites" by the Jerusalem Bible and Moffat is *arsenokoitai*. Outside of our reference it is used only in 1 Timothy 1:10. Some argue that the word refers only to homosexual prostitutes.[66] Boswell, a Yale scholar, argues in a lengthy appendix that the compound word *arsenokoitai* means males involved in sexual activity, that is, it simply

---

Early Christian Literature (Chicago: Chicago University Press, 1957), p. 489.
61 J. Moffatt, *A New Translation of the Bible* (New York: Harper and Brothers Publishers, 1935).
62 J. J. McNeill, *The Church and the Homosexual* (Kansas City, MO: Sheed, Andrews and McMeel, 1976), p. 52; and G. G. Findlay, "St Paul's First Epistle to the Corinthians," *The Expositors Greek Testament* 2, ed. W. R. Nicoll (Grand Rapids: Wm. B. Eerdmans Publishing Co., 1967), p. 817; also, Boswell, pp. 106-7.
63 Among them, F. F. Bruce, *1 and 2 Corinthians* (London: Oliphants, 1971), p. 61; C. K. Barrett, *A Commentary on the First Epistle to the Corinthians* (New York: Harper & Row Pubs., 1968), p. 141; F. W. Grosheide, *Commentary on the First Epistle to the Corinthians* (Grand Rapids: Wm. B. Eerdmans Publishing Co., 1953), p. 140; W. F. Orr and J. A. Walker, *1 Corinthians a New Translation Introduction With a Study of the Life of Paul, Notes, and Commentary* (Garden City, NY: Doubleday & Co., 1976), pp. 198-99; H. Conzelmann, *A Commentary on the First Epistle to the Corinthians,* tr. J. W. Leitch (Philadelphia: Fortress Press, 1975), p. 106.
64 Deissmann, p. 164, n. 4.
65 Atkinson, p. 91. Also P. M. Ukleja, "Homosexuality in the New Testament," *BSac* 140 (1983): 350-51.
66 Boswell, p. 107; McNeill, p. 53.

means male sexual agents, not those who have sex with males. Boswell stresses the coarseness and active licentiousness of the word, connoting thrusting activeness, denoting a male performing the sexual act. Hence, he concludes that it is not necessarily a reference to homosexuals at all.[67]

The word is first found in the Palatine Anthology (IX, 686), and the verb form is in the Sibylline Oracles II, 73.[68] Boswell contends that the word is rare in Greek literature and, therefore, it is difficult to compare references as to its usage. Consequently, there are no guidelines in Greek literature which might help to determine whether the first element of the word "male" is the subject or the object of the last element suggesting "marriage bed" or "sexual relations."

He also makes a distinction between the *arreno* and *arseno* compound words. *Arreno* compounds, he believes, are employed objectively. *Arreno* ("male") being the object of *koitai* ("bed" or "sex"), that is, one who has sex with males, males being the object of sex. This compound is a reference to homosexual relations. But the compound found in the Scriptures, *arseno-koitai*, is different, he thinks, that is, a male (subject) who has sex—the object not specified here. He concludes that it cannot be demonstrated that any of these New Testament uses of the word is objective, or therefore, implies homosexuality.

Wright, however, in a lengthy article on *arsenokoitai*, shows that Boswell's presentation contains numerous flaws.[69] First, he does not give sufficient attention to *arsen* and *koite* in the Septuagint of Leviticus 18:22; 20:13. Second, he does not take account of the fact that the *arreno* and *arseno* compounds are word variations in Greek dialects, and there is no evidence of any semantic difference between them. Third, there is no lexical evidence for the active, male thrusting connotation that is attached to the compound *arsenokoitai*. Fourth, there are many more occurrences of the word in Hellenistic literature than Boswell allows which do reveal the meaning it bore for the writers in question. Wright discusses these references in detail and concludes that in 1 Corinthians and 1 Timothy, male prostitution (with females) is out of the question as the word's meaning,

---

67 Ibid., pp. 338-53.
68 J. H. Moulton and G. Milligan, *The Vocabulary of the Greek New Testament Illustrated From the Papyri and Other Non-Literary Sources* (Grand Rapids: Wm. B. Eerdmans Publishing Co., 1963), p. 79.
69 D. F. Wright, "Homosexuals or Prostitutes? The Meaning of *ARSENOKOITAI* (1 Cor 6:9, 1 Tim 1:10)," *Vigiliae Christiannae* 38 (1984), pp. 126, 129, 130, 134, 136, 144, 145, 146. Also P. Zaas, "1 Cor. 6:9ff.; Was Homosexuality Condoned in the Corinthian Church?" *Society of Biblical Literature 1979 Seminar Papers* 2, ed. P. J. Achtemeier, SBL Seminar Papers Series 14 (Missoula, MT: Scholars Press, 1979): 208-9. Zaas rightly sees that the etymology of the word is "one who lies with a male," but he goes on to claim, mistakenly, that the majority of occurrences are in Hellenistic moral and astrological literature and he connects the activity with idolatry.

but what is intended is male homosexual activity with youths or adults.

In the Septuagint, *koite,* the last part of the word *arsenokoite,* frequently refers to sexual relations or the marriage bed. It is used four times in the New Testament, three times referring to sexual intercourse (Rom 9:10; 13:13; Heb 13:14).

Scroggs suggests that *arsenokoites* may come from the rabbinic technical term *mishkav zakur* ("lying with a male"). *Arsenokoites* could be seen then as the literal translation of the Hebrew phrase. As we have seen, parts of the Greek compound appear in the Septuagint.

> This provides the Greek linguistic link between the rabbinic phrase and the term in the vice catalog in 1 Corinthians. Thus the word *arsenokoites* originated in Hellenistic Jewish circles as an attempt to translate the rabbinic quasi-legal term into understandable Greek, perhaps with the deliberate intention of avoiding contact with the usual Greek terminology.[70]

On this basis Scroggs concludes, correctly in our opinion, that the first element of the word "male" is indeed the object of the action implied in the last part of the word "sexual relation." The *arsenokoites,* then, is the active partner in the homosexual relation while the word *malakos* points to the effeminate call-boy who acts as mistress. Scroggs, however, applies this only to dissolute homosexual practices of the kind indulged in by Timarchus, who was hired or kept by a number of adults with the usual jealousies and quarrels, a model not aspired to by the gay community today.[71]

Although many commentators agree with Scroggs' exegesis, not all agree with his interpretation. If Paul was condemning only a crude form of homosexual activity here, by implication allowing other types, he surely would have been more explicit. Coming from a Jewish background and tradition, Paul knew that his readers would understand him against that background. If, as proposed, Paul was flying in the face of Jewish teaching, he could have and would have made himself much clearer. Conzelmann rightly observes that "The Jewish verdict on the latter [homosexuality] is unequivocal."[72] Is Paul here making a clear, single-handed departure from the traditional Jewish interpretation of Scripture by removing the taint of immorality from *mishkav zachur?* From the evidence provided, this must be seriously doubted.

Some scholars agree that Paul is speaking here of both passive and active

---

70 Scroggs, p. 108.
71 Ibid., p. 109.
72 Conzelmann, p. 106.

homosexual acts, but they claim he is not referring to the invert, the constitutional homosexual involved in a loving relationship.[73] Instead he is condemning dissolute homosexuals. By loading the terms *malakos* and *arsenokoites* with the connotations of exploitation and dissoluteness, a favorable comparison then can be drawn between them and the invert in a loving relationship. This is a distinction Paul would not have drawn, not because of his ignorance of inversion but because of his conviction that all such acts were immoral.

Finally, the point is sometimes argued that if we were to take this catalog of vices seriously, none of us would enter the kingdom because we are all, for example, covetous.[74] This conclusion completely overlooks the biblical distinction between repentant believers prone to sin but striving against the inner and outer expression of it (see 1 John 1:6-10) and unrepentant sinners, on the other hand, who follow a steady and largely unresisted program of deliberate disobedience (see 1 John 2:4; 3:6-9.[75]

The constitutional homosexual is not barred from the kingdom of God any more than the inveterate adulterer or the kleptomaniac. All, however, must resist the temptation to act out their impulses. As Paul says, "And such were some of you. But you were washed, you were sanctified, you were justified in the name of the Lord Jesus Christ and in the Spirit of our God" (1 Cor 6:11). Such reasoning would undermine any attempt at repentance or reformation in the church by arguing that "we are all sinners."

Meeting the Gnostic Approach

> 1 Timothy 1:8-10. Now we know that the law is good, if any one uses it lawfully, understanding this, that the law is not laid down for the just but for the lawless and disobedient, for the ungodly and sinners, for the unholy and profane, for murderers of fathers and murderers of mothers, for manslayers, immoral persons, sodomites, kidnapers, liars, perjurers, and whatever else is contrary to sound doctrine.

Readers who accept the authenticity of the first epistle to Timothy usually date it about A.D. 63-65. They believe that Paul dispatched it while staying in Macedonia shortly after a visit to Ephesus—in other words that Paul wrote the epistle between his first and second Roman imprisonments. A quick reading of the epistle shows that it is primarily concerned with the

---

73 Bailey, pp. 38-39.
74 Mollenkott and Scanzoni, p. 70.
75 Lovelace, p. 96.

issues of heresy and church order. The heresy seems to have been a form of Judaizing Gnosticism based on metaphysical dualism. Matter was held to be essentially evil, and God is the supreme good. Therefore God could have no direct contact with matter. A series of emanations was posited between man and God.

The danger of Gnosticism was not simply theological: it also had serious moral and ethical consequences. If matter is essentially flawed and evil and the spirit/soul is good, then physical bodies are essentially evil. In ethical belief and conduct, this produced two results. First, if the body is evil it must be subjugated, thwarted, held down. This type of Gnosticism ended in rigid asceticism.

But the same basic assumption, the evil nature of the body, could result in exactly the opposite ethical belief. If the body is evil, then it does not really matter what one does with it. The body is unimportant; all that really matters is spirit. Therefore, a person may indulge his body in the most gluttonous, licentious, and uninhibited manner possible, and it makes no difference to salvation. If the body will not be resurrected (2 Tim 2:18), the deeds done in the body become irrelevant to the hereafter.

It is not hard to imagine the impact on the law of two such approaches. One group desired to be teachers of the law but understood neither what they were saying nor what they affirmed (1 Tim 1:7). Some of the false teachers evidently assumed that the law was designed for the righteous man and "urged their interpretations of it as necessary appendices to the Gospel."[76] These false teachers forbade marriage and ordered abstinence from certain foods (1 Tim 4:1, 5).

On the other hand, Paul finds it necessary to warn Timothy about those who are lovers of pleasure rather than lovers of God, that is, "those who make their way into households and capture weak women, burdened with sins and swayed by various impulses, who will listen to anybody and can never arrive at a knowledge of the truth" (2 Tim 3:4-7). These men also oppose the truth, they are "men of corrupt mind and counterfeit faith" (2 Tim 3:8).

Against such a background, Paul affirms that the primary purpose of the law is to condemn sin. The law is good (Rom 7:16) if it is used properly, and its purpose for Paul in this context is to reveal and restrain evil. In this sense the law is good *(kalos)*. In an ideal world there would be no need for law other than the love of God in the heart. But the present state of affairs calls for something quite different.

Paul then presents a catalog of sins which the law must identify and

---

[76] A. E. Humphreys, ed., *The Epistles to Timothy and Titus* (Cambridge, MA: Cambridge University Press, 1925), p. 85.

condemn.[77] In keeping with the context, the list of sins enumerated here follows the pattern of the Decalogue in that they move from general to specific. First he addresses the lawless and disobedient, or those who refuse to obey any law. Next are the ungodly and sinners or those who refuse to obey the law of God, followed by the unholy and profane who transgress specific requirements of the law.[78] These relate to the first four commandments of the Decalogue. Murderers of fathers and mothers correlate to the fifth commandment, representing an extreme violation of it.[79] Manslayers represent the sixth commandment whereas immoral persons and sodomites apparently are cited as extreme examples of the commandment not to commit adultery.80 So the list continues; men stealers (kidnappers, RSV), the grossest kind of theft representing the eighth precept, liars and perjurers the ninth, and so forth.

The key word in the passage is "sodomites" which is a translation of *arsenokoitai*. Most exegetes agree that this word refers to homosexual behavior. It is not a question of disposition or temptation.

We can make a number of significant observations about the vice list in 1 Timothy. First, the list deals with deeds: "only those sins have been enumerated of which the human law can take cognizance."[81] The tenth commandment warning against covetousness is covered by the final words in the list "and whatever else" and probably reflects Paul's disinterest at this point in sins of the mind and heart.

Pornos, translated "immoral persons," is a generic term in the New Testament for one acting against the virtue of chastity. Paul, however, specifies *arsenokoitai* ("sodomites") to be in the same category. Field remarks, "as an interpretation of the seventh commandment the parallel is striking. The implication is that homosexual conduct infringes the demands of the Decalogue as certainly as heterosexual adultery."[82] We also observe that Paul never connects homosexual acts with cultic or ceremonial law, or prohibitions against idolatry as such. In this context we see Paul attaching

---

77 *The Letters to Timothy, Titus and Philemon: With Introductions and Interpretations,* tr. W. Barclay, (Philadelphia: Westminster Press, 1960), p. 42; also, E. K. Simpson, The *Pastoral Epistles, The Greek Text With Introduction and Commentary* (Grand Rapids: Wm. B. Eerdmans Publishing Co., 1954), p. 31.

78 W. Lock, *A Critical and Exegetical Commentary on the Pastoral Epistles* (New York: Charles Scribner's Sons, 1924), p. 12. On the relation of the list to the Decalogue see also, McEleny, pp. 206-7.

79 D. Guthrie, *The Pastoral Epistles: An Introduction and Commentary* (Grand Rapids: Wm. B. Eerdmans Publishing Co., 1972), p. 61.

80 F. D. Gealy and M. P. Noyes, "1 Timothy," *IB* 11 (1955): 387.

81 J. H. Bernard, *The Pastoral Epistles* (Cambridge, MA: Cambridge University Press, 1906), p. 28; also F. Craddock, "How Does the New Testament Deal with the Issue of Homosexuality?" *Encounter* 40 (1979): 207.

82 Field, p. 17.

to this prohibition the kind of normative authority assigned to the Decalogue. If this is so, there can be no doubt that Paul regarded homosexual acts as sin and a perversion of the order of human existence as willed by God. "Even though within this catalog of vices it is not accented as being *especially* horrible, as many moral theologies would make it appear."[83]

By de-emphasizing the parallels to the Decalogue and the general context of combating "teachers of the law" some exegetes arrive at another interpretation. They see the words *pornos* ("male prostitute"), *arsenokoites*, which we know from the previous discussion, and *andrapodistes* ("kidnapper" or "slave dealer") as integrally related. The same relationship they believe to exist in 1 Corinthians between *malakos* and *arsenokoites* is proposed between *pornos* and *arsenokoites* in 1 Timothy. Just as *malakos* was the youth used and *arsenokoites* the one who used him, so here *pornos* could relate to *arsenokoites* in the same way. This view is strengthened, it is claimed, by the following word *andrapodistes*.

In the first century A.D. these three words could be related. A person kidnapped, particularly a handsome boy or beautiful girl, might be kidnapped to provide slaves for brothel houses. It is suggested that these three words fit together to mean "male prostitutes, males who lie [with them], and slave dealers [who procure them]."[84]

On these grounds Scroggs concludes that 1 Timothy is not a condemnation of homosexuality generally or even pederasty as such but of that specific form of pederasty that involved enslaving boys or youths for sexual purposes and the use of these boys by adult males. In this way this text is read to condemn only certain kinds of homosexual practices.

Although a scenario such as that described was common enough in Paul's day, it does not follow that Paul is discussing it here. The context of 1 Timothy 1:8-11 is the use and abuse of the law. The general consensus of opinion among commentators is that this list is modeled on the Decalogue. For Paul there was a time and a place for the preaching of the Law, and its precepts were to be set forth as "a means of awakening in human hearts the conscious need for salvation."[85]

The law is basically for criminals and rebellious offenders. Christians, however, who enjoy the liberty of love and grace in Christ Jesus must never forget that liberty is not license. Paul makes this point in his remarks at the end of verse 10, "and whatever else is against sound doctrine." These words come as a surprise after a list of criminal offenders against the law. "Sound doctrine" *(hugiainouse didaskalia),* are words found more frequently in

---

83 Thielicke, p. 278.
84 Scroggs, pp. 119-20.
85 C. R. Eerdman, *The Pastoral Epistles* (Philadelphia: Westminster Press, 1923), p. 24.

the Pastoral Epistles than anywhere else in the New Testament. This could be expected since the Pastorals are filled with instruction. In this context, however, they show that for Paul the law was not merely for criminals but contained teaching intended for the normal rule of life. Thus the description "sound doctrine" denotes "wholesomeness or healthiness of true Christian doctrine."[86]

The implication is that sound Christian teaching will not run contrary to the law of God. If it does, the law serves as a corrective showing that the moral nature is in violation of and in opposition to God's will. A person who thinks he is healthy may be shown by X-ray to be in mortal danger from disease. Likewise the law can point out sin and by so doing show man his need of righteousness, but law has no power to make him so. That is accomplished by the gospel. As Quinn notes,

> The upright believer is, on the other hand, not antinomian, anymore than he is a liar or a murderer (cf. 1 Timothy 1:9b). He does not reject all laws, divine and human. The point of the contrast here is that the law is "superfluous" for the believer who in virtue of the Spirit and faith in Christ (cf. Galatians 5:22-23) already does and more than does what the law can only command.[87]

The Law and the Gospel cannot be played off one against the other.

Furthermore, scholars have shown that the Decalogue has its theological and ethical foundation established firmly on the bedrock of the creation teaching of Genesis.[88] In other words, the appeal of the Decalogue is for men and women to live the lifestyle the Creator intended for his creation. And in that creation scheme, for Paul at least, homosexuality has no place.[89]

We see that the three major references to homosexuality in the New Testament clearly condemn homosexual acts. In Romans, 1 Corinthians, and 1 Timothy, male-with-male sexual acts are considered immoral. In Romans Paul illustrates the depravity of the pagan world by reference to such acts. At the same time the context in which it is discussed and the words used to describe this activity demonstrate that for Paul it was an

---

86 Guthrie, p. 62.
87 J. D. Quinn, "The Pastoral Epistles on Righteousness," in J. Reumann, *"Righteousness" in the New Testament* (Philadelphia: Fortress Press, 1982), p. 237.
88 C. F. Henry, *Christian Personal Ethics* (Grand Rapids: Wm. B. Eerdmans Publishing, Co., 1957), pp. 272ff.; F. D. Nichol, ed., *The SDA Bible Commentary* 1 (Washington, DC: Review & Herald Publishing Assn., 1953): 604-5; H. Thielicke, *Theological Ethics* 1, ed. W. H. Lazareth, tr. J. W. Doberstein (Philadelphia: Fortress Press, 1966), pp. 147ff.
89 Field, *The Homosexual Way,* p. 17.

aberration in human sexual conduct, the result of the entrance of sin. Homosexuality was not a part of God's plan for the sexes. To say that "natural" refers to what appears to be natural to fallen humanity today is to miss the cosmic perspective of creation against which Paul writes.

In 1 Corinthians Paul refers to activities, which although part of the individual's past, now are to be given up as the Christlike lifestyle takes command. Among them is the practice of homosexuality. Attempts to free the Greek words *malakos* and *arsenokoites* from homosexual connotations are not convincing. The evidence is too strong that homosexuality is indicated by these words. We can only conclude from this text that the homosexual lifestyle lies outside Christian sanctification..

This understanding is reinforced by the second mention of *arsenokoites* in 1 Timothy. Here the basic principles of the Decalogue are expanded and illustrated by listing various activities that the law forbids. The arrangement implies that the activities mentioned are forbidden, with the authority of the Decalogue standing behind the ban. This means that homosexual acts are forbidden by the same authority that prohibits adultery.

Once more, attempts to limit the word *arsenokoites* to certain limited kinds of exploitive prostitution by linking the words *pornos* and *andrapodistes* with *arsenokoites* are possible only if we dislodge the words from the context and consider them independently or in a compromising historical context.

Although there are only three major references in the New Testament relating to homosexuality, their meaning is clear. Homosexual acts are not a part of God's plan for the sexes. Neither are they a part of Christian sanctification which culminates with entrance into the Kingdom of God. They are forbidden by the same authority that prohibits murder and adultery.

Secondary New Testament Texts and Homosexuality

Of the many texts in the New Testament interpreted as pro- or anti-homosexual statements, on closer inspection, most are not really relevant at all. As examples we will examine two or three of these borderline references. Two texts in 2 Peter and Jude are virtually parallels, although one throws some light on the other.

> 2 Peter 2:6-10. If by turning the cities of Sodom and Gomorrah to ashes he condemned them to extinction and made them an example to those who were to be ungodly; and if he rescued righteous Lot, greatly distressed by the licentiousness of the wicked (for by what that righteous man saw and heard as he lived

among them, he was vexed in his righteous soul day after day with their lawless deeds), then the Lord knows how to rescue the godly from trial, and to keep the unrighteous under punishment until the day of judgment, and especially those who indulge in the lust of defiling passion and despise authority.

The second chapter of 2 Peter is essentially a warning against false teachers. Verses 1 to 3 describe these false teachers and their heresies. The succeeding verses through verse 10 assure readers that ultimate damnation and punishment of the false teachers is certain..

Three examples of previous punishment of the wicked and deliverance of the righteous are cited to confirm such assurance. First, the angels who sinned were consigned to pits of darkness to be kept until the judgment. Second, Noah was rescued from the Flood that destroyed the ungodly. Finally, according to our text, verses 6-10, Lot was rescued from Sodom and Gomorrah before the wicked cities were reduced to ashes.

Lot does not appear in the Old Testament as a particularly righteous man. However, based on Abraham's pleading in Genesis 18:23-33, we must conclude that Lot was one of the righteous whom God would not destroy with the wicked.

According to 2 Peter, Lot was wearied by the licentious behavior of the wicked, therefore he was rescued by God from Sodom. The expression "licentious behavior of the wicked" is a translation of three Greek words: *aselgeia* meaning "outrageous licentiousness" and "lasciviousness"; *anastrophe* which means "mode of life" or "conduct"; and *athesmos,* translated "wicked." *Athesmos* literally means "lawless" but differs from *anomos* which also means "lawless." *Thesmos* (here, from *athesmos*) implies a divine ordinance or a fundamental law.[90]

The point is that the wicked in their unbridled licence insolently disregard the most basic divine precepts. In verse 8 Peter repeats the theme that Lot suffered in Sodom and heightens it with stronger language. What Lot saw and heard as he lived among them on a day-to-day basis tortured *(basanizo)* his righteous soul. The lawless deeds *(anomoi)* here are the deeds elsewhere described in Scripture as deeds of persons not subject to law, that is, of Gentiles (Acts 2:23; 1 Cor 9:21) or of lawbreakers and malefactors (Luke 22:37).

Only verse 10 points up the same kind of licentiousness Jude emphasized in describing the sin of the "sons of God" and of Sodom as typical of the sin of the libertines. In verse 10 we read that God is able to keep the

---

90 J. B. Mayor, *The Epistle of St. Jude and the Second Epistle of St. Peter: Greek Text With Introduction, Notes and Comments* (Grand Rapids: Baker Book House, 1965), p. 125.

unrighteous under punishment until the day of judgment, especially those "who indulge in the lust of defiling passion." "Lust of defiling passion" is variously translated as "lust of defilement," "lust of pollution," or "polluting desire." All are translations of *epithumia miasmou*. Alford comments, "Here, all following after unlawful carnal lusts is meant, . . . hankering after unlawful and polluting use of the flesh."[91] It seems that those troubling those who worshipped God did so not only with false doctrines but also gross immorality.

The mention of Sodom and the strong language used in a number of these verses has led some commentators to think the apostle has in view here "the darker forms of impurity which were common throughout the Roman empire (Rom. 1:24-28),"[92] that is, homosexual lust. Peter's descriptions, however, are general and quite diffuse. It is possible that since he mentions Sodom and puts emphasis several times on sexual sins, he intends to include homosexual acts also, but we are not justified in singling out homosexual acts as alone intended by these verses. All sexual sins are included as well as the other lawless deeds of the people among whom Lot chose to live.

> Jude 7, 8. Just as Sodom and Gomorrah and the surrounding cities, which likewise acted immorally and indulged in unnatural lust, serve as an example by undergoing a punishment of eternal fire. Yet in like manner these men in their dreamings defile the flesh, reject authority, and revile the glorious ones.

It is generally accepted that the Jude who wrote this epistle is probably Jude the brother of Jesus, but it is not clear to whom the epistle is addressed. It is concerned with disruptive elements in the church, mostly a form of gnosticism, as in 2 Peter. Hints of Gnostic heresies appear in Colossians, the Pastoral Epistles, and Revelation. This kind of heresy was spreading through the churches of Asia Minor, and this epistle may have been sent to one or more of the churches there.

The writer begins what looks like a regular epistle intended to confirm the faith of the believers. Then he urges them to defend the faith against certain intruders and begins to expose the nature of these culprits by showing how they parallel earlier rebels against divine authority in Old Testament times. He assures the faithful that a similar fate awaits these contemporary rebels.

---

91 H. Alford, *The Greek Testament* 4, ed. and rev. by, E. F. Harrison (Chicago: Moody Press, 1968): 406.
92 E. H. Plumptre, *The General Epistles of St. Peter and St. Jude: With Notes and Introduction* (Cambridge University Press, 1926), p. 181.

Concerning the parallel passages in 2 Peter and Jude, it is not possible to determine whether 2 Peter used Jude or vice-versa. Our text is one of the parallel passages where Jude, like Peter, is explaining how sinners and rebels against God in antiquity were duly punished. The two lists are clearly related—both mention the fallen angels reserved unto judgment. Jude does not mention Noah and the antediluvian world but moves to Sodom and Gomorrah and the surrounding cities, five in all: Sodom, Gomorrah, Admah, Zeboim and finally Zoar, which was spared due to Lot's pleading (Deut 29:23; Gen 19:19-30). Lot himself is not mentioned in Jude.

These cities "acted immorally" *(ekporneusasai),* a term encompassing all kinds of immorality. The intensive use of the preposition *ek* suggests that immorality was practiced "to its fulfillment, thoroughly, without reserve."[93] Then, we are told, they "indulged in unnatural lust." This seems related to Paul's use of "unnatural," giving appearance of being a statement about homosexual acts. The original text, however, does not lend itself to this interpretation. It reads literally, "they went after other flesh," "other flesh" meaning flesh of a different kind *(heteros).*

Two interpretations of this phrase are possible, both appearing in different translations of Jude 7:

> Remember Sodom and Gomorrah and the neighboring towns; *like the angels,* they committed fornication and followed unnatural lusts [NEB].

> *In a similar way,* Sodom and Gomorrah and the surrounding towns gave themselves up to sexual immorality and perversion [NIV].

> *Just as* Sodom and Gomorrah and the surrounding cities, *which likewise* acted immorally and indulged in unnatural lust [RSV].

The NEB and RSV translations tell us that the citizens of Sodom and Gomorrah paralled the behavior of the angels mentioned in the previous verse. But that previous verse does not say specifically what the angels did; it says, "And the angels that did not keep their own position but left their proper dwelling have been kept by him . . . in the nether gloom until the judgment of the great day" (vs. 6).

Many commentators, however, relate verse 7 to Genesis 6:1-4 especially verse 4, which reads, "The Nephilim were on the earth in those days, and also afterward, *when the sons of God came in to the daughters of men,* and bore children to them. These were the mighty men that were of old, the

---

93 Alford, p. 532.

men of renown" (RSV). Here the "sons of God" who "came in to the daughters of men" are interpreted as angelic beings who have intercourse with human beings. This assumption is carried to Jude's statement as well.

Interpreters often assume that Jude is dependent on the non-canonical 1 Enoch for its ideas here. Clearly, Jude is familiar with pseudepigraphical works. He refers to the Jewish literary work, the Assumption of Moses in verse 9 and actually quotes 1 Enoch 1:9 in verse 14. First Enoch 6 is a tale of the fall of the angels based on Genesis 6:1-4. Passages in 1 Enoch read as follows:

> 1 Enoch 6:1, 2. In those days, when the children of man had multiplied it happened that there were born unto them handsome and beautiful daughters. And the angels, the children of heaven, saw them and desired them; and they said to one another, "Come let us choose wives for ourselves from among the daughters of man and beget us children."[94]
>
> 1 Enoch 7:1, 2. And they took wives unto themselves, and everyone (respectively) chose one woman for himself, and they began to go unto them. And they taught them magical medicine, incantations, the cutting of roots, and taught them (about) plants. And the women became pregnant and gave birth to great giants whose heights were three hundred cubits.[95]

If Jude simply follows these stories and claims that the Sodomites followed in the same manner as the angels, then, it is argued, he is not talking about homosexuality. Thus the "other flesh" the Sodomites went after was that of angels, just as the angels in 1 Enoch went after "other flesh," that is, women.[96] According to this account impurity as well as pride was involved in the fall of the angels, and Sodom represents an identical reverse repetition of their fall.

Another interpretation proposes that Jude refers to the apocalypse of Enoch without intending an exact comparison with it in every detail. Following this interpretation, the experience at Sodom was similar in certain ways to that in 1 Enoch. The angels went after that which was not divinely intended for them, and the men of Sodom did likewise. Unquestionably

---

94 E. Isaac, "1 (Ethiopic Apocalypse of) Enoch," *The Old Testament Pseudepigrapha* 1, ed. J. H. Charlesworth (Garden City, NY: Doubleday & Co., 1983): 15.
95 Ibid., p. 16.
96 J.N.D. Kelly, *A Commentary on the Epistles of Peter and Jude* (New York: Harper and Row Pubs., 1969), pp. 258-59. Kelly remarks that "it is probably legitimate to infer that he is snidely accusing the innovators of homosexual practices." See also, E. Schweizer, *"Sarx, sarkikos, sarkinos,"* *TDNT* 7 (1977): 143.

Jude uses the legend of fallen angels in 1 Enoch as some sort of analogy to Sodom and Gomorrah. His allusion to the story illustrates parenthetically the similarity between the judgment of the angels and that of Sodom.

This interpretation gains certain credence by the fact that there are basic differences in the two accounts. In Genesis 19 the men of Sodom apparently were unaware that Lot's visitors were angels and could not be accused of knowingly desiring celestial beings. But they did perceive of them as men and could be accused of desiring them as such. On the other hand, the angels in the 1 Enoch account of Genesis 6 knew that they were desiring and cohabiting with human beings. This aspect is neither accidental nor incidental in the 1 Enoch story.

The NIV translation, "in a similar way," points to the affinity between the events of Genesis 19 and the 1 Enoch story without requiring an exact correspondence.

> In the case of the angels the forbidden flesh (lit. "other than that appointed by God") refers to the intercourse with women; in the case of Sodom to the departure from the natural use (Romans 1:27).[97]

This interpretation of Jude assumes that he is using the 1 Enoch legend as an illustration or analogy to the Sodom experience. It need not be considered Jude's own interpretation of Genesis 6, in which it has at least two considerations in its favor.

First, it avoids interpreting Genesis 6:1-4 in a way that many readers of the Bible would find incomprehensible. The straightforward interpretation of Genesis suggests cohabitation between human beings.[98]

Second, it forestalls a flat contradiction between Genesis 6:4 and the words of Jesus in Matthew 22:30, "For in the resurrection they neither marry nor are given in marriage, but are like angels in heaven." So it is not necessary to translate "Sons of God" in Genesis 6:4 as angels, but simply as men. For Jude the 1 Enoch legend was an apt illustration of the Sodom event.

Finally, with another "likewise" or "in like manner" statement Jude addresses his own day and those troubling the church. Just as the men of Sodom could be compared with the angel legend in Enoch, so the heretics of Jude's day have parallels with the men of Sodom. These men are

---

[97] Mayor, p. 32; Alford refers to Leviticus 18:22-25 and suggests that the sin of Sodom went further then homosexuality. In this case "other flesh" becomes a tacit reference to bestiality. (Alford, p. 533.)

[98] See Nichol, p. 251, on the misunderstanding of the word *nephilim*, mistakenly translated "giants" in the Septuagint (LXX).

dreamers or visionaries *(enupniazomenoi)*. Not that they experience visions or dreams while asleep,[99] rather here is a metaphorical depiction of libertines as having a "nocturnal blindness" to the true faith.[100] Perhaps this is an allusion to the blind Sodomites groping for the door. They are children of the night, mere dreamers. These men live as if they were in a dream. The word "dream," therefore, is connected with all three words that follow and not simply with "defile the flesh." The Greek construction does not support the KJV reading, "filthy dreamers." These men live in an unreal world. The result is an impurity not unlike that of Sodom, in a rejection of authority and in the reviling (lit. "blaspheming") of glorious ones (cf. 2 Pet 2:10).

The expression "defile the flesh" is too general to allow application to homosexual acts alone. In the New Testament *miaino* usually designates moral defilement, also sexual immorality in general.[101] Once more it is clear that the writer is not singling out homosexual acts in these verses.

On the other hand, they cannot be entirely excluded. The reference to Sodom and to sexual irregularities calls to the minds of the readers the type of misbehavior for which this city had become proverbial. We must conclude, therefore, that in 2 Peter and Jude the full range of forbidden sexual relations is addressed and there is no scriptural basis for reading these texts as references to homosexual acts alone.[102]

> Revelation 22:14, 15. Blessed are those who wash their robes, that they may have the right to the tree of life and that they may enter the city by the gates. Outside are the dogs and sorcerers and fornicators and murderers and idolaters, and every one who loves and practices falsehood.

In this final chapter of the New Testament, John the Revelator is describing the new earth and its inhabitants. He reminds them of the types of people who will be received into the new earth and the holy city and of those rejected, who remain outside.

"Outside" does not mean that evil doers will be forever clamoring at the gates of the city, vainly seeking admission, but is akin to the "outer darkness" Matthew 24, implying eternal destruction. This thesis is strengthened in Revelation 21:8 where five of the six character traits men-

---

99 See Moulton and Milligan, pp. 219, 229, who cite usage of the word for "incubation," i.e., dreams received while sleeping in a temple. The word as used in our text is perhaps a vague allusion to the groping blindness of the men of Sodom, who could not find the door.
100 H. Balz, "*Hupnos,* etc." in *TDNT* 8 (1977): 553-54.
101 R. C. Trench, *Synonyms of the New Testament* (Grand Rapids: Wm. B. Eerdmans Publishing Co., 1963), p. 110.
102 Coleman, p. 111.

tioned are consigned to the lake of fire ("dog" is the only additional epithet in 22:15). "Outside" involves eternal destruction in the lake of fire.[103]

Among those outside is a group described as "dogs" (lit. "the dogs"), *hoi kunes*. The word is sometimes regarded as an exclusive reference to homosexuals, or sodomites. This has been discussed from an OT perspective, where we suggested that the word refers to a male cult functionary who may have been involved in heterosexual and/or homosexual acts.

But it is unlikely that this is a reference to a cult functionary; neither is it a special reference to Sodomites.[104] The word is more general here than in Deuteronomy 23:17, 18 where it appears as a quasi-technical term for male cult prostitutes. In the Revelation text the general characteristics of the undomesticated pack-hound come more to mind. Such animals were pariahs and scavengers of almost anything. Such wild dogs ate the body of Jezebel (2 Kgs 10:33-37) and befouled the streets and walls of the city. They licked the sores of beggars (Luke 16:21) and even worse (1 Kgs 21:19; 22:38; Prov 26:11).

In the Jewish culture of first century A.D. Palestine, the term "dog" became an epithet for anyone morally and ethically disgusting. The word appears in Scripture for various kinds of impure and malicious persons. It was used by the Jews in reference to the heathen (Matt 15:22ff.), to the godless in general,[105] and expressed utmost contempt. Barclay quotes a rabbinic saying: "Whoever eats with an idolater is the same as he would eat with a dog."[106] Among the Jews "dog" was a symbol of all that was disgusting and unclean.

A comparison with Deuteronomy cannot be entirely ignored in connection with this text, however.[107] From a Jewish point of view, it refers to a thoroughly immoral, unethical person; and those who persisted in the practice of homosexual activity would fall within the prophet's purview. But John's vision is wider than that of Judaism. As Beasley-Murray comments,

> It is evident that for John the term relates not to the heathen over against the Jew, but to the godless of any nation in contrast to the men of all nations who have washed their robes and made them white in the blood of the Lamb (7:14 and 22:14).[108]

---

103 R. H. Mounce, *The Book of Revelation* (Grand Rapids: Wm. B. Eerdmans Publishing Co., 1977), p. 394; M. Rist and L. H. Hough, "The Revelation of St. John the Divine," in *IB* 12 (1957): 547.
104 F. Düsterdieck, *A Critical and Exegetical Handbook to the Revelation of John*, tr. H. E. Jacobs (New York: Funk & Wagnalls Co., 1887), p. 491.
105 Sotah, 9:15.
106 W. Barclay, *The Revelation of John* 2 (Philadelphia: Westminster Press, 1960): 290.
107 J. Moffatt, "The Revelation of St. John the Divine," in *The Expositor's Greek Testament* 5, ed. W. R. Nicoll (Grand Rapids: Wm. B. Eerdmans Publishing Co., 1967): 491.
108 G. R. Beasley-Murray, *Revelation*, New Century Bible Series (Greenwood, SC: Attic Press, 1974),

The New Testament and Homosexuality

It is not correct, therefore, to apply this text exclusively to homosexuals. Just as the word *porne* once meant a cult prostitute but was widened in the Hellenistic world to include all kinds of fornication, so the term "dog" assumed a much wider meaning than a (possibly homosexual) cult prostitute and refers to a generally immoral person. Anyone tempted to feel smug at the thought that those who practice homosexual acts or are immoral and outside the city should read on, because sorcerers, fornicators, murderers, idolaters, and everyone loving and practicing falsehood are also found outside. Impudent persistence in such activities confirms a rebellious attitude toward God.

We will not discuss numerous other texts quoted as evidence of gay lifestyle, sometimes to claim New Testament approval. Neither will we dignify with an answer the assertion that Jesus Himself was a homosexual who,

> went around kissing, embracing and living only with men, who loved a younger man in a very special way, even allowing him to lay on his lap in public, who advocated pacifism, never legally married, wore a dress and long hair, used expensive perfume, stayed up all night, was very close to his mother, advocated decriminalization of non-violent sex crimes, often had clashes with the law and the church, and even spoke up for all kinds of eunuchs, "Canaanite dogs" and gay rulers.[109]

Hebrews 13:4 is sometimes cited as further evidence for the approval of gay lifestyle: "Let marriage be held in honor among all." The emphasis is placed on "all" and interpreted to include homosexuals.

Matthew 5:23 is interpreted to mean, Anyone who calls his brother a "queer" is in danger of hell. The man who assisted Jesus in the preparation of the last supper was a homosexual (Mark 14:13) for by custom only women carried water jars. Jesus approved of the homosexual centurion's relationship by healing his young male companion (Matt 8:5-13). The Greek word *pais* used in the text is used to describe a same-sex relationship. It is claimed that any Greek male in that culture would use the word to refer to his young lover.

Some theologians suggest that Jesus had a sinful human nature just like ours (Heb 2:14, RSV), that he was tempted in every respect as we are (Heb

---

p. 341.
109 Quoted from *The Gay Home,* p. 2, in P. R. Johnson and T. F. Eaves, *Gays and the New Right* (Los Angeles: P. R. Johnson, 1982), p. 93. H. Montefiore claimed that Jesus may have been a homosexual, *Newsweek* (August 7, 1967), p. 83. Jesus did not marry, he says, because He may not have been the marrying kind. He may have been tempted, but He never sinned. (H. Montefiore, *For God's Sake: Sermons from Great St. Mary's* [Philadelphia: Fortress Press, 1969], p. 182.)

4:15, RSV). If Jesus is to understand us in our sinful condition and if we can overcome as he did, then Jesus must have been tempted homosexually. That is to say, he must have had a genuine homosexual inclination.

We conclude that the secondary references to homosexuality in the New Testament do not refer specifically to homosexuality at all. The three references examined are general, vague, and diffuse, and none of them is a genuine reference solely to homosexual activity. Therefore any attempt to isolate homosexuality as *the* sin condemned in these verses is an inaccurate and misleading use of Scripture. Though homosexuality may be included within the context suggested by these writers, so are many other sins, both sexual and nonsexual.

Chapter 7
Conclusions

Now we gather the salient facts and reach conclusions. This book has looked at homosexuality from a specific point of view, taking into account seriously the historical, ethical, and moral pronouncements of the Scriptures. A high view of Scripture is assumed; approached from a conservative Protestant exegesis and hermeneutic.

Regarding homosexuality itself, it is clear that no one really understands its causes, whether it is a physical, mental, or psychosocial phenomenon. Indeed, it may be a combination of all three.[1] From an ethical, moral standpoint conservative theologians see it either as an aberration or a condition that fits into one of three categories:

First, the group that agrees that such a thing as a homosexual "condition" exists. This condition is accepted as a part of the general evil which exists since the Fall of man. It falls in the same category as chronic diseases such as diabetes or arthritis. A person is not responsible for a chronic disease, and often its causes are unknown. Only when a person deliberately aggravates the disease can he/she be held responsible for the consequences. If the disease is itself or provokes some kind of mental impairment, even this responsibility may be disqualified. Many theologians, therefore, separate the so-called "homosexual condition," sometimes called inversion or constitutional homosexuality, from the homosexual acts themselves. The condition, possibly multifactorial in origin and of unknown cause, must not to be considered the direct responsibility of the individual. Consequently, the homosexual who has the condition but who does not act out his/her impulses is not to be condemned in any way.

For these theologians, then, not only should the person not be condemned, the non-practicing primary homosexual should be welcomed into the church as a Christian brother enjoying all the rights and privileges with the other members. Such an individual struggles against sinful desires as do other church members and is not to be treated as a second-class citizen.[2]

---

[1] J. Marmor, "Homosexuality: Nature vs. Nurture," *Harvard Medical School Mental Health Letter* (October 1985), pp. 5-6.
[2] K. S. Kantzer, "Homosexuals in the Church," *Christianity Today* (April 22, 1983): 8-9.

Conclusions

Nor is such a person considered sick in the radical sense of the word, at least no more than a controlled epileptic, diabetic, or hemophiliac. Such a person struggles with a special problem with which he/she learns to live, work, and give a Christian witness. Naturally the analogy between the chronically ill and homosexuals is not complete. Most of the chronically ill can be diagnosed and receive therapeutic care to control a definite pathological condition. The homosexual generally has no recognized pathology or treatment. He/she must control desires for the same sex by choice and with the help of God. Apart from this attraction to the same sex, the homosexual may be as healthy or healthier than the next person.

Because the homosexual does not seem to be "ill," and because the question seems a matter of choice, homosexuals usually do not receive much sympathy. What we can say at this point is that the attraction and desire may stem from a very early age. Once the person reaches the age of accountability, however, he/she is responsible for how he/she expresses or controls those desires.

Second is a group holding that homosexuals are sick. Possibly it stems from psychological factors or some early psychosocial maladaptation. Many theories are propounded about the exact mechanism or mechanisms. But these theories are not mutually exclusive, for there is a core of consensus.

Many modern homosexuals object to this estimate of their condition. They claim that such findings are based on visits of disturbed homosexuals to psychiatrists. In general, the population of homosexuals, they say, is no sicker than the general population of heterosexuals. If all heterosexuals were judged by those who visit psychiatrists, the heterosexual population would be deemed sick too.

The main difference between this position and the first is that here the sickness or deviance is thought to be treatable. For the most part, the treatment consists of various kinds of psychotherapy.

Third, another group denies that homosexuality is a psychological or pathological condition at all. To them, what predisposes a person to samesex attraction is only the persistence of a sinful habit stemming from uninhibited sexual fantasies, both of which need to be repented of and abandoned.

This group sees great danger in confusing sin with pathology, especially if the pathology becomes an excuse for sin. For them, to postulate a pathology behind kleptomania, nymphomania, or inveterate adultery as excuse for those and other evils opens the field to a wide range of evils justified under the guise of illness or diminished capacity.

Again, these remarks are aimed at homosexual acts. The proponents of this view make it quite clear that temptation to adultery does not make an adulterer; the act does so. Likewise, temptation to homosexuality does not define a homosexual, rather the act. This view utterly rejects the idea of a homosexual condition or that it is an illness.

It is quite clear that two of these views, the first and third, consider same-sex acts on the part of adults to be sin.[3] As a result, both of these views require a Christian homosexual, namely, one having the condition, to live a lifestyle without same-sex genital acts. For the primary homosexual who is not at all attracted to the opposite sex, this is tantamount to requiring a celibate lifestyle. To date Adventist writers have favored the first view. They accept the idea that there may be a mechanism—as yet unknown—which predisposes some individuals to homosexual attraction. The individual must not be held responsible for the condition or for early psychosocial factors that may strengthen the tendency. The individual *is* responsible, however, for same-sex acts after the age of accountability. The condition may lie outside the individual's choice but the acts do not.

To argue that the acts are likewise determined and inevitable is to reduce the homosexual to the instinctive reflexive mating behavior of animals, which is unacceptable. Homosexually oriented individuals are human beings with the power of choice over their drives and desires. Since on biblical grounds homosexuality is not a part of God's plan and intention for the sexes, the power of the will and the power of choice must be exerted to inhibit such desires, not to enhance them.

Although the causes of homosexuality are ill-defined, the argument that homosexuality is due to some genetic or chromosomal defect has little support. The existence of identical twins, one homosexual the other not, keeps this thesis from gaining much credence.[4] Postnatal hormone changes likewise have not shown much promise. The quantity of hormone in the bloodstream seems not to affect choice of sex partner, although it may strengthen sex drive.

At present the most promising research lies in the study of prenatal hormonal influence in the sexual differentiation of brain development. Experiments on rats have shown that female rats subjected to stress during certain periods of gestation give birth to demasculinized male offspring. The offspring of the stressed mothers exhibit fewer mounts and no copulation in the presence of estrous females. Although physically male, when mounted by other males they also exhibit the stance and receptivity of female rats. These experiments have been reproduced with mice. The

---

3   Others argue that homosexuality is normal and therefore partially acceptable if done in a responsible manner, or fully acceptable in the context of "love."
4   However a higher degree of concordance (that is the appearance of homosexuality in both twins) has been found in identical twins than in nonidentical twins. (See Marmor, p. 5.)

Conclusions

effects of the prenatal stress syndrome on male rats, however, may be alleviated by socialization with sexually vigorous male rats.

These experiments seem not to work on primates, however, which raises questions about homology between rat experiments and any clinical deduction concerning human homosexuality. The doubt is reinforced by the fact that human males with diminished masculine characteristics are not all homosexuals, but tend to have the sex of assignment and rearing. Therefore the suggestion of a strong psychosocial element enters here. No studies have been carried out on human mothers unduly stressed during pregnancy. Some suggest that the increased ingestion of drugs during pregnancy, however, may produce the same effects as stress. Whatever the exact biological mechanism, it appears to be minor—only a contributing factor and not the sole cause of the homosexual orientation.

It is not surprising therefore to find so many experts supporting a predominantly psychosocial etiology for homosexual inversion. Numerous theories of origin conform to various schools of psychological theory. Most of these theories allow for a predisposing biological factor, but they also suggest that homosexuality is in some way a learned behavior, in some cases perhaps a subconscious one.

All that can be said at the moment about the cause or causes of homosexual inversion is that in some homosexuals there may be an elemental and subtle biological factor predisposing to homosexual orientation. In itself, however, this apparently is not the sole cause of homosexuality. Subsequent social environment may enhance or discourage the tendency, but again the relevant psychosocial factors are not known.

It is unlikely that a single mechanism underlies all forms of homosexuality. The biological rationale applies at best to a subgroup of homosexuals; and even if valid for this subgroup it is likely to be multifactorial. Homosexual inversion then appears to arise from multiple etiology—some homosexuals having more of one factor than another and vice-versa.

Not all who practice homosexual activity have an overwhelming predisposition for the same sex. Some heterosexuals turn to homosexual practice for a "safe" sexual outlet. For other heterosexuals it provides thrills and variety. Others have homosexual predispositions that vary in intensity and length of homosexual experience, who feel they are meeting deep personality needs. Consequently, homosexuals (inverts and non-inverts) pursue a variety of activities for various reasons. Cruising and gay bars cater to the tastes of some while others prefer bathhouses and bathrooms. Many homosexuals circulate largely in discreet circles of friends and prefer more stable relationships with one or a few companions. Homosexuals may participate in mutual masturbation, sex acts with children, and anal or other

Conclusions

forms of intercourse with adults. Fellatio is practiced in the bathroom or tearoom trade, as we have seen. All these sexual behaviors can and have been practiced by heterosexuals with heterosexuals as well. Homosexuals by no means have a monopoly on unusual sexual practices.

Homosexual practices were well-known in antiquity. In nations contiguous to Israel, they were known and practiced with few restrictions, as was bestiality. Extant literature provides evidence that homosexual acts played a part in some religious cults in the ancient Near East. Female dress, eunuchism, and the accoutrements of women often were employed as well. For these reasons Israelite warnings and restrictions about male and female dress, homosexual acts, and bestiality were not a figment of national imagination but addressed the situation at hand.

The Old Testament presents the male/female relationship as reflecting the full image of God in man. Marriage and sexual relationships take place within this male/female bonding as described in Genesis. For Jesus and Paul Genesis constitutes the normative, natural, and God-intended pattern for sexual relations. The Old Testament's negative judgment on homosexual acts is consistent with this position. Both Genesis 19 and Judges 19 condemn more than homosexual acts, however. Other sins with violence also led to the judgments described in these passages. Homosexual acts cannot be isolated as the sole cause. But we disagree with any conclusion that dismisses homosexual acts from the sins of Sodom and Gibeah.

The prohibition in Leviticus clearly opposes same-sex acts. Arguments that try to connect it exclusively with idolatrous homosexuality are not convincing. Neither are arguments that limit the texts to demands for ritual purity rather than moral purity. We cannot relegate these prohibitions to Levitical purity laws disregarded by early Christians as not morally binding.

Translation of to^cebah with the Greek *bdelugma* ("abomination") in the Septuagint supports placing homosexuality in the ethical moral category, not merely the cultic. And the claim that $yada^c$ ("know") means "get acquainted with" rather than "sexual intercourse" in the Genesis 19 account of Sodom does not stand. On the basis of the historical background, "cult prostitutes" and "dog" in the Old Testament are seen as having a probable homosexual connotation. The possibility of cultic homosexual elements cannot be completely eliminated from these words in their Old Testament context and historical setting.

Other texts that purportedly represent homosexual relationships in the Old Testament are less clear upon close examination. The David-and-Jonathan and Ruth-and-Naomi experiences, when studied in context, do not really support a homosexual interpretation, as is claimed by some. A

Conclusions

brief exegesis of these passages shows that not only is a homosexual interpretation not required, it is not the one most compatible with the context. The one story in the Old Testament where a homosexual interpretation may be correct is the case of Ham and Noah. But this is scarcely cast in a good light by the biblical narrative.

In moving from East to West we find that in ancient Greece homosexual activity was a convention regulated by certain laws and tradition. Probably it came to the Greek mainland from Crete via Sparta, where it was connected with military training and comrades in arms. In later Greek and Hellenistic times military training of the young took place in the gymnasium and pederasty became the inheritance of the gymnasium.

In some of these academic relationships the erotic element may have been sublimated and the improvement of the youth by the elder male purely an intellectual and spiritual exercise. At its best the relationship may have been "platonic" in the modern sense of the word.

However the tradition in which another man educated one's sons and was repaid by sexual submission of the son to him if he so desired carried the potential for much mischief. For those not guided by the philosophical-theological ideals of Plato, it degenerated into preoccupation with physical beauty and sexual excitement.

In the Hellenistic world, both the manly pederastic ideal of the West and the effeminate cultic homosexuality of the East existed side by side. The Romans tended to identify homosexuality predominantly with the latter, and the worst forms of homosexual violence and exploitation are documented for this period. The pagan moralists themselves entered into a debate about its good or evil aspects.

A great many Hellenistic writers, especially Stoics, considered all such acts unnatural. Others defended the more refined forms of homosexual activity. Hellenistic Judaism and Christianity both condemned homosexual acts, also speaking of them as unnatural, but from a biblical, theocentric creation rather than from the logos-based ethical doctrines of the Stoics.

The core of Paul's condemnation of homosexual acts in Romans is that they are unnatural. They cannot be understood as a part of God's providential ordering of nature in Creation. Elsewhere Paul refers to homosexual acts as sin, and as we have pointed out, it is significant that the context of homosexual acts in the New Testament is the vice list. Such lists consist of qualities and activities not to be found in Christians. Although people cite numerous texts to condone or condemn homosexual acts, most of them do not apply. Although homosexual acts may be included within some of the references, their limitation to homosexual acts alone is unwarranted.

J. B. Nelson has characterized approaches to homosexuality in four theological categories:[5] (1) the rejecting punitive stance; (2) the rejecting non-punitive stance, which in essence is the approach of Karl Barth; (3) the qualified acceptance position, basically the approach of Thielicke in approving what is called "responsible" homosexual activity; and (4) full acceptance, the position of Quakers, J. McNeill, and Norman Pittenger.

In dealing with Barth's position, Nelson suggests that Barth has forgotten human historicity, assuming that human nature is an "unchangeable, once-and-for-all essence given by Christ." For Nelson human nature essence is shaped in the historical environment. The question here is, How does this apparently existential self-discovery square with biblical theology? In an evolutionary existentialist context, existence precedes essence; whereas in a biblical theological context, essence precedes existence.

This book has made a historical and biblical survey of the question. Numerous questions remain to be answered. As homosexuals of Christian heritage relate to the church and its individual members, more ethical and moral questions arise. Although some Christians argue that responsible homosexual acts may be allowed to church members,[6] others think that any homosexual act is a sin, and a change of lifestyle is the only means of full acceptance.[7]

At the moment the most confusing aspect of the homosexual scene deals with claims and counterclaims concerning the possibility of change in lifestyle and the reversal of homosexual inversion. People on both sides are equally convinced, earnest, and zealous for their positions, either that change can take place—some testifying to changes in their own lives—or that change is all but impossible. Those who claim to be changed, they say, were never inverts in the first place. Clinical evidence indicates that older homosexuals with long experience are not good prospects for change.

The more liberal view, arguing that change is impossible, has been in the ascendancy for some time now. For example, in a lecture before the Royal Society of Health Dr. Elizabeth R. Moberly suggested three reasons for the development.[8]

First is the growth of modern knowledge; second, the civil rights issue; and third, "the relatively limited success of traditional attempts to cure or change homosexuals." For her, the third argument favors the liberal case

---

[5] J. B. Nelson, *Embodiment: An Approach to Sexuality and Christian Theology* (Minneapolis: Augsburg Publishing House, 1979).

[6] C. M. Berry, "The Christian Homosexual," *Journal of Psychology and Christianity* 1 (1982): 33-38; J. F. Alexander, "What Harm Does it Do? Do Permanent Homosexual Relationships Hurt Anybody?" *Other Side* (April 1984), pp. 30-31.

[7] J.R.W. Stott, "Homosexual Marriage: Why Same-sex Partnerships Are Not a Christian Option," *Christianity Today* (November 22, 1985): 21-27.

[8] E. R. Moberly, "New Perspectives on Homosexuality," *Journal of the Royal Society of Health* (December 1985): 206-210.

Conclusions

and is entirely valid. She is convinced that there are genuine grounds for therapeutic pessimism with respect to homosexuality. She attributes this pessimism to a fundamental misunderstanding of the nature of homosexuality. She defines the homosexual condition as one of same-sex ambivalence; a disruption in attachment to the parent of the same sex. For her the classic "mother fixation" of many homosexuals is an effect rather than a cause. Therefore increased contact with the opposite sex is seen as irrelevant to solving the condition.

What is needed, she maintains, is remedying of same-sex developmental deficits. Because the deficits stem from preadult development, the drive should be fulfilled non-sexually. "Same-sex relationships are valid and legitimate, on a developmental perspective. But it is not appropriate to express them sexually, again precisely because of their developmental character."[9] She asserts that in the homosexual condition preadult psychological needs are being confused with adult physiological desires. The answer is not, therefore, merely abstinence from sexual activity; for the sexual activity is only an inappropriate way of meeting a legitimate need for same-sex love.

Dr. Moberly continues, "It is misleading to assume that the homosexual condition is essentially sexual, and to evaluate it as such. The homosexual condition—although often an occasion for sexual expression—is in itself a state of unfulfilled developmental needs."[10] Therefore the conservative demand that the developmental needs of the homosexual should not be fulfilled sexually should never be mistaken for a denial of the legitimacy of the developmental needs themselves.

Pessimism about a change of orientation on the part of homosexuals, Dr. Moberly maintains, is due to a totally wrong approach to the condition. A different therapeutic approach might produce quite different results. Total pessimism is not warranted, especially for younger and relatively inexperienced homosexuals whose prospects for change are much more encouraging, even with current methods of therapy.

We must distinguish also between change of orientation and change of lifestyle. The homosexual should not be led to believe that all desire for and temptation toward same-sex acts will be quickly removed. Just as heterosexuals are subject to lustful thoughts and inordinate desires, so the homosexual may be also.

As Christians however, we believe that the Lord can change what the world cannot, both for the homosexual and the heterosexual. This change will not take place until there is a reformation in both camps.

---

9   Ibid., p.208.
10 Ibid., p. 209.

Homosexuals who insist on and even glorify an active homosexual lifestyle need to rethink that position with respect to Christianity. The idea that all can be forgiven while the practice willfully continues is a cheap grace the church cannot accept. It becomes "the grace which amounts to the justification of sin without the justification of the repentant sinner who departs from sin and from whom sin departs."[11] Cheap grace is in this case powerless grace. It accepts justification, acceptance by God on the basis of Christ's perfect righteousness. But it totally severs forgiveness from sanctification, the working out of righteousness in the actual behavior of the believer through the power of the Word and Spirit. Such a dichotomy creates a situation ethic that is inevitably antinomian. It is not surprising, therefore, to find some Christian-oriented homosexuals accepting an open-ended existentialist ethic in which the real nature of man is unknown and yet to be discovered.

If the church accepts the idea of powerless grace it nullifies its evangelistic mission in the world. The gospel is no longer the "power of God for salvation to everyone who believes," and as Lovelace points out about such a church,

> it should logically be prepared to tolerate many other forms of sin within the church which might cause neuroses if repressed: compulsive adultery and fornication, compulsive racism and other forms of hatred acted out in physical hostility, compulsive disobedience to authority, compulsive theft, and so on. The argument that sexual control is impossible for most homosexuals because they do not have the gift of continence leads necessarily to the church's encouraging premarital and extramarital sex among single persons, the divorced and the widowed. Neither the Bible nor the common convictions of Christians support this implication, and we must conclude that where there is responsibility to be continent God will supply the gift.[12]

The prohomophile literature written in a Christian context overemphasizes love and the Spirit at the expense of the Word. It is true that without these the church is a dry, lifeless husk. But it is equally true that the church without the objective Word of God is a ship without a rudder. It simply rides out the swells of world events, fads, and opinions with all the other flotsam and jetsam until it is beached or smashed on the rocks. Uncontrolled and drifting, it has no means of directing its course.

---

11 D. Bonhoeffer, *The Cost of Discipleship* (New York: Macmillan Publishing Co., 1959), p. 36.
12 R. F. Lovelace, *Homosexuality and the Church* (Old Tappan, NJ: Fleming H. Revell Co., 1978), p. 75.

For the church to try to function ethically without objective information from God concerning His will means that it is dead in the water without chart, compass, or any real way of steering itself or anyone else. With both Spirit and the Word, the church has power, a means of direction, and can safely find a passage between subjective antinomianism and the rocks of legalism.

Homosexuals need to reconsider the scriptural passages in both Old and New Testaments that relate to homosexual behavior. Exegetical and hermeneutical attempts to displace the plain meaning of these passages and a too simple reliance on the exegesis and arguments of scholars who support their opinions will not help. Rather than make other human beings masters of their consciences, homosexuals in the Christian context need to study the Scriptures for themselves. Then they will recognize that many prohomophile arguments are "strained, speculative and implausible, the product of wishful thinking and special pleading."[13]

Not all reforms, however, need to be made in the Christian-oriented homosexual community. Straight or heterosexual members of the church need to take a good look at their attitudes as well.

The heterosexual church needs to set its own house in order as far as sexual mores are concerned. The dizzying pace of remarriage, divorce and remarriage, the increase of one-parent families due to premarital sexual activity and other liberalizing tendencies in the sexual lifestyle of heterosexuals place the church in a poor position to preach to gays.

Many homosexuals are convinced that increasingly permissive sexual attitudes in the church will in time lead to acceptance of their sexual behavior. Consequently, it is difficult for many Christian gays to understand why they are scapegoats for sexual sins in the church. Are adultery or fornication less culpable than homosexuality? The church must become serious about all sexual immorality or it has little case against the homosexual and stands accused of rank hypocrisy. On the other hand homosexuals need to realize that two wrongs never make a right.

Secondly, the church needs to come to terms with homophobia and some of its ultra-conservative knee-jerk reactions even to the mention of homosexuality. Homophobia is a fear and hatred of homosexuals and homosexuality. As with most phobias, usually it is unreasoned and unreasoning. As with race prejudice, homophobia is often a transferred hostility. The homosexual becomes a convenient whipping boy on whom old fears, hurts and angers may be safely focused. Hatred of homosexuals may mask insecurity about one's own sexual identity. Christian concern is missing.

---

13 Ibid., p. 133.

Conclusions

Whatever its cause, church members need to rise above it and to foster an attitude of compassionate concern for homosexuals while at the same time they strongly disapprove of the active homosexual lifestyle. Many who lack a conviction of sin in their own lives and their need of the grace of Christ for daily strength will find it difficult to do this.

Christians who understand human frailty and know the power of sin will be able to empathize with the pain, hopelessness, and guilt, the loneliness and rejection felt by many exclusive homosexuals. They will understand also that for many homosexuals the condition is not the result of voluntary choice and will begin to appreciate why numerous homosexuals from a religious background sink in despair to the verge of suicide and sometimes complete the act.

All of this does not suggest that biblical and theological arguments put forward by homophile advocates should persuade the church to change its position on the subject. On the contrary, how the church relates to homosexuality may determine how it relates to all other questions of morality. As a prominent Jewish author put it,

> When religion begins to adapt its norms to current practice, it succeeds in becoming "popular religion" of the kind the Bible fought against through all antiquity. It then surrenders its right to speak in the name of a higher calling. Moral law must apply even—especially!—in the face of popular neglect. Religion must teach society; it must hold up for it moral ideals for which to strive, ethical and spiritual norms the neglect of which will give men a bad conscience. The direction some churches are taking today threatens to leave the majority religion in our country shorn of its ideals, its challenge, its role as conscience—and its courage. I fear that, in some measure, contemporary Christianity is reverting to its pre-Judaic roots by institutionalizing the sanction of popular immorality.[14]

This statement also is a challenge to the Seventh-day Adventist Church. The church cannot condone homosexual activity without betraying its biblical, historical, and spiritual heritage. Its conscious acceptance of the authority and inspiration of Scripture would need to undergo such a radical, liberalizing change that the fundamental teachings of the church would be left without foundation.

The consequences of such change with its ramifications for theological, ethical, and moral teaching might be labeled by some as progressive, cal-

---

14 N. Lamm, "The New Dispensation on Homosexuality: A Jewish Reaction to a Developing Attitude," *Jewish Currents* (January-February 1968): 15-16.

culated to enlighten the church and produce a more compassionate laity accommodated to the modern society in which it lives. But in reality such a move would be a giant step toward repaganization of the church. The resulting religion would not be a Bible religion or that of the prophets, the Lord, or the apostles, not Christianity except in name.

The church must accept the individual of homosexual orientation who needs help and support and struggles against same-sex tendencies. But those who insist on and promote the active homosexual lifestyle as normal, natural, or even superior to heterosexual relations by that very act disregard and undermine the sole authority upon which the church's very existence and mission is based, namely, the Scriptures.

Index of References

Genesis	
1:27	52
2:18, 24	53
6:1-4	145, 146, 147
6:14	146
9:20-24	74
9:21-17	69
9:22	77
13:13	57
18:20	57
18:23-33	143
19	67, 68, 81, 110, 112
19:4-10	55, 56
19:19-30	145
21:9	69
24:67	72
25:28	72
39	68, 69

Exodus	
20-40	59
20:14	68
21:5	72
22:19	48

Leviticus	
18:1	58
18:1-3, 24-30	33
18:7	75
18:14	75
18:21	68, 62
18:22	58, 60, 62, 63, 111, 135
18:23	48
19:18	59
19:19	59
20:13	58, 60, 63, 111, 135
20:17	76
20:23-25	33

Deuteronomy	
5:18	68
22:5	48, 65
23:17	40, 64, 65
23:17-18	63, 111
23:18	110
25:16	61
27:20	75
27:21	48
28:13	41
29:23	145

Judges	
19	68
19-21	66
19:22	41
19:22-25	65

Ruth	
1:16, 18	69, 78-80
4:14, 15	78
4:15	72

1 Samuel	
16:21	72
17:38, 39	72
18:1	69, 71
18:1-3	70
18:8	72
18:16	22, 72
18:22	73
18:28	73
18:3	71
18:4	72
19:1	69
19:2	72
20:13-16	72
20:17	72
20:30	69, 70
20:41	70
20:41b	73

2 Samuel	
1:23	71
1:26	69, 70
11	68

1 Kings	
5:1	72
14:23-24	63-64
14:24	40
15:12	40, 64
21:19	149
22:38	149
22:46	40, 64
23:7	40

2 Kings	
10:33-37	149
23:7	64

Proverbs	
8:7	61
9:8	72
16:12	61
26:11	149

Reference	Page
29:27	61

Ecclesiastes
16:8	57

Isaiah
1:9	47
13:19	57

Jeremiah
6:15	61
23:14	57
49:18	57
50:40	57

Ezekiel
16:49	50, 57

Hosea
3:1	72

Amos
4:11	57

Zechariah
2:9	57

Malachi
2:14	71

Matthew
5:23	150
8:5-13	150
11:8	134
15:22ff.	149
19:7-10	52
22:30	147
24	148

Mark
10:2-9	52
14:13	150

Luke
7:25	134
16:21	149
22:34	143

John
9:2	125

Acts
2:23	143

Romans
1	58
1:16-17	123
1:18-23	132
1:18-25	52
1:18-32	129
1:24	124
1:24-28	120, 144
1:24-32	120
1:26	124
1:26, 27	131
1:26-28	120, 131
1:26-31	119
1:27	147
1:28	124
1:28, 32	125
1:29-31	119
1:29-32	120
1:32	131
3:21—5:21	124
6:1-23	124
7:1—8:39	124
7:16	138
9:10	136
13:13	136

1 Corinthians
1:2	117
1:4	117
1:10—4:21	132
5:1—6:20	132
5:9-13	117
6:1-11	111, 132
6:9	134
6:11	137
8	117
9:21	143
10	117
11:14	122
11:17-34	132

Galatians
5:6	123
5:22-23	141

Ephesians
4:17	117

Colossians
3:12ff.	117
4:5	117

1 Timothy
1:7	138
1:8-10	137
1:8-11	140
1:9b	141
1:10	134
4:1, 5	138

2 Timothy
2:18	138
3:2-4	119
3:4-7	138
3:8	138

Hebrews
2:14	150
4:15	150
13:4	150
13:14	136

2 Peter
2:6-10	142-143

1 John			21:8	148	1 Enoch	
1:6-10		137	22:14, 15	148-149	Book of 1 Enoch	146
2:4		137			1:9	146
3:6-9		137	Wisdom		6	146
			113	118	6:1, 2	146
Jude			10:8	57	7:1, 2	146
7, 8		144	2-14	125		
9		46	14:25-26	118	Jubilees	
			29:8	57	16:5	111
Revelation			19:13, 14	57		
7:14		149	19:14	57		

Index

A
abomination, 46, 60
Adams, J. E., 10, 11
adolescent experimentation, 31
adultery, 60
Aeschylus, 100
'ahab, 72
AIDS, 28
Aischines, 89
Albright, W. F., 38, 43
Alford, H., 144
Almanac of Incantations, 45, 46
ambisexuals, 30
anal intercourse, 30
Anat, 37
andrapodistes, 140
androgens, 15-17
androgynous myth, 97, 101
anomia, 60
antinomianism, 162
Aphrodite, 96, 97
apocryphal literature, 122
Apuleius, 106
Aristobulus, 105
Aristophanes, 100, 101
arsen, 111
arsenokoitai, 134, 139
arsenokoites, 111, 136, 140, 142
Artemidorus, 107
assinnu, 41, 44
Assyria, 45
Assyrian Laws, 41
Astarte, 37
Athens, 110
Attic Comedy, 98
Atum, 37
authority and inspiration of Scripture, 163

B
Babylonia, 45
Bailey, D. S., 3, 33, 55, 56, 65, 66, 68, 69, 121
Barnhouse, R. S., 9
Bartlett, D. L., 68, 123
bdelugma, 60, 61, , 157
Beasley-Murray, G. R., 149
Bell, A., 1
Bergler, E., 8, 9
berith, 73
bestiality, 34, 46, 47, 59, 62, 112, 157
Bible religion, 164
Bieber, I., 9, 13, 23
Boaz, 78
Book of the Dead, 35, 39
Boswell, Dr. John, 60 , 134
Bottero, J., 43, 45
Bruns, J. Edgar, 74, 75
Bryant, A. A., 91
Buckley, M. J., 24
Buzzard, L. R., 7, 10

C
Caligula, 106
Callimachus, 104
Campbell, E. F., Jr., 80
Canaan, 33, 77
Canaanite, 46
Canaanite myth, 38
Canaanite ritual, 47, 48
castrati, 44
catamite, 40, 41
chesed, 79, 80
Chevins, P.F.D., 17

child sacrifice, 47, 59
choice, 10
Churchill, W., 106
Cicero, 107, 127
cinaedus, 38
clinical homosexual, 9
Closet Queens, 30, 31
Clouds, The, 101
Cole, W. G., 47
Collins, R., 67
comedy, 99, 100
conditional, 11
constitutional homosexual, 3, 11, 16, 71, 121, 130, 137, 153
contingent homosexuals, 2
convention, 121
Conzelmann, H., 136
Corinth, 110
Cory, D. W., 6, 7
covenant (berith), 71
culpable, 3
cult prostitutes, 65, 157
Cundall, A. E., 67
Currie, S. D., 67
Cybele, 65, 106

D

Daphnaeus, 108
David, 69, 70, 71, 72, 73, 99
Decalogue, 139, 140, 141, 142
Demosthenes, 89
Devereux, G., 92, 93
Diaspora Judaism, 104
Diodorus Siculus, 126
dog, 63, 64, 65, 149, 157
Dorian invasion, 83
Dörner, G., 16, 19, 20
Dover, K. J., 83
Driver, G. R., 41

E

Eastern religious cults, 106
Easton, B. S., 118, 119
effeminatus, 106, 107
effeminate, 134

Egypt, 34, 43
Egyptians, 57
Ehrenburg, V., 98
endocrine influences, 13
Ennead, 36
ephebes, 104
Epistle of Aristeas, The, 125
Epstein, L. M., 63
erastes, 87, 88, 90, 93, 95, 98, 104, 109
eromenos, 88, 90, 93, 98, 104
eromenos-erastes, 91
eros, 88
eroticization, 10
Erra IV 58, 45
essential, 11
estrogen feedback, 19
etiology of homosexuality, 13, 20
eunuchism, 106, 109, 110
eunuchs, 44

F

Feldman, M. P., 15
fellatio, 29, 30, 98, 107, 112, 157
female prostitution, 33
Field, D. H., 129
Fluck, E. J., 94
Foster, J., 78

G

gadabout (wasi), 40
gadal, 71, 73
galah, 75, 76
Galba (A.D. 68-69, 130
Galli, 106
Gardiner, A. H., 36
gay bar, 28, 29
Gay Guys, 30
genetic abnormality, 24
genetic basis, 15
genetic factors, 13
genetic thesis, 13
ger, 66
Gesenius, W., 73

Gibeah, 65-69
Gnosticism, 138
Goliath, 71
Gomorrah, 145, 147
Greek Anthology, The, 104
Griffiths, G. W., 35
gymnasium, 88, 103, 104, 110

H

Ham, 77, 158
Ham and Noah, 69, 74
Hampson, John and Jean, 21
harimtu, 41
Harrison, R. K., 33
Harvey, J. F., 2, 22
Harvey, P. W., 17
Hatterer, L. J., 4, 13, 23
Haustafeln, 117
Henry, G. W., 70
Herodotus, 34, 42, 87
hetaira, 104
heterosexual, 18, 22, 121, 129, 130, 160, 162
heterosexual rape, 69
heterosexuality, 6, 23, 108
heterosexuals, 11, 45, 156, 160
hierodule, 41, 45, 47, 64
Hillers, D. R., 47
Hittite law, 46
Hoffner, H. A., Jr., 48
Holladay, W. L., 73
Homer, T. M., 70, 79, 83
homology, 17, 18
homophobia, 162
homosexual "marriage", 31
homosexual behavior defined, 18
homosexual condition, 153
homosexual disposition, 105
homosexual inversion, 156, 159
homosexual love, 104
homosexual promiscuity, 31
homosexual rape, 69
homosexual subculture, 30
Hooker, E., 28, 29
hormones, 14, 15

Horus and Seth, 35-40
host at Gibeah, 67
household, 116
Humphrey, L., 29
hurkel, 46, 47
hyperandrogenized females, males, 18
hypothalamic, 16

I

idolatry, 62
image of God, 52, 54
incest, 59, 60
inversion, 3, 4, 153
invert, 3, 27, 31, 46, 50, 93, 130
Ishtar, 43, 44
Isis, 36, 37
Israel, 61
istaritu, 41

J

Japheth, 77
Johnson, P. R., 71, 78
Jonathan, 69, 70, 71, 72
Josephus, 111, 127
Judge, E. A., 116, 118

K

Kahun, 35, 36
Kallmann, F. J., 13
Karlen, A., 90, 106
keleb, 65
kinaidia, 89
King David, 79
Kinsey, A. C., 14, 22, 26, 27, 31
Klinefelters syndrome, 13
Knights, The, 100
"know," 56, 66, 157
koite, 111
Kramer, S. N., 43
Kubo, S., 4, 7, 52
kulmasitu, 41

L

lack of hypothalamic exposure, 15

laeuach, 71
Lang, T., 13
law of Solon, 90
Laws, 98
Laws I, 636, 126
Laws of Hammurabi, 40
Laws VIII, 126
legalism, 162
Lesbianism, 4, 7, 83, 84
Lesbos, 84, 86
Letter of Aristeas, 112
Levite, 66
love *('ahab),* 71
Lovelace, R. F., 131, 161
Lucian, 42, 109
Lucian of Samosata, 108

M

Macculloch, M. J., 15
makrothymia, 119
maladaptation, 22
Maat, 37
malakos, malakoi, 134, 108, 134, 136, 142
Malherbe, A. J., 117
Malloy, E. A., 1, 2, 3, 9, 28
Marcus Aurelius, 127
Mark Anthony, 107
Marmor, J., 9
Mary Douglas' *Purity and Danger,* 59
Masoretic text, 111
masturbation, 31, 98
McEleney, N. J., 119
McNeill, J., 6, 56, 58
Mesopotamians, 43
Metamorphoses, 106
Meyer-Bahlberg, H.F.L., 17, 18, 19
Middle Assyrian Laws 19, 20, 40
Miles, J. C., 41
mishkav zakur, 111
Mishnah, 110
misogyny, 99, 108, 109
misozenia, 57
Moberly, Elizabeth R., 10., 159, 160
Moffatt, J., 134

Molech, 62
mollis, 107
Money, J., 20
monozygotic homosexual twins, 13
Musonius Rufus, 126
Mycenaean civilization, 83

N

Naomi, 69, 78, 80
Near East, 33
nebalah, 67
necrophilia, 34
Nelson, J. B., 7, 158, 159
Neofiti text, 110
Nephelim, 145
Nero, 106
neutral, 3, 4
Noah, 74-78, 158
Noahides, 63
Noth, M., 62, 67
nymphomaniac, 130

O

Oberholtzer, W. D., 21
Old Attic Comedy, 99, 100
Orpah, 78
Ovid's perverse epistle, 85
Oxyrynchus, P., 86

P

P. Chester Beatty VII, 37
paedagogos, 91
paederastia, 91
Page, D., 85, 86
Palatine Anthology (IX, 686), 135
Palestinian Judaism, 110
Palestinian literature, 111
Papyrus Chester Beatty I, 35
papyrus fragment, 35
papyrus Hibeh 54, 134
passive homosexuality, 44
pathic, 106, 107
Pausanius, 103
pederastic rape, 111

pederasty, 87, 90, 94, 95, 99, 100, 101, 102, 103, 104, 108, 109, 110, 112, 127, 140, 158
Pentateuchal law, 110
Perloff, W. H., 14
Perry, T.D., 5
perversion, 4
pervert, 3, 23, 31, 93, 130
Petronius, 107
Petschow, H., 43, 45
phallic worship, 43
philanthropia, 119
philia, 88
Philistines, 70
Philo, 111, 108, 118
philogenetic scale, 20
Pittenger, N., 5
Plato, 90, 94, 95, 96, 97, 98, 101, 102, 126, 158
Plato's Lysis 222, 95
Platonic friendship, 94
Plutarch, 108, 109, 127
Plutarch of Chaeronea, 87, 108
Plutarch's *Erotikos,* 108
porne, 150
pornos, 89, 139, 140
postnatal endocrine studies, 15
pre-Platonic homosexuality, 92
preferential, 10
prenatal hormones, condition theory, 20
Presbyterian *Blue Book,* 15, 59
Pritchard, J. B., 34
Protogenes, 108, 109
pseudepigraphal literature, 111
psycho-endocrine, 15
psychodynamic definition, 9
psychosexuality, 17
psychosocial, 13, 24, 25
psychosocial maladaptation, 8, 10, 12
psychosocial origin, 22

Q

qadesh, 65

qashar, 71
Quinn, J. D., 141

R

rabbinic literature, 111
Radin, M., 57
Ramsey, W. M., 115
rape of Anat by Baal, 38
Republic, 90, 98

Rhianus, 104
ritual intercourse, 40, 42
Robinson, D. M., 84, 94
Ruth, 78
Ryle, H. E., 77

S

sacro-homosexual practices, 33
sadomasochism, 30, 106, 110
Sapp, 62
Sappho, 83-87
Saul, 70, 71, 72, 73
Scroggs, R., 50, 51, 111, 108, 129, 136, 140
Secor, N. A., 20
self-mutilation, 47
Septuagint, 61, 64, 74, 111, 112
Seth, 35, 36, 37
Seven Against Thebes, 100
Shem, 77
Sibylline Oracles, 73, 112, 135
sin of Sodom, 57
sinnisanu, 44
slave prostitution, 104
Smedes, L. B., 52, 53
Sodom, 57, 66, 69, 81, 111, 112, 145-148, 157
Sodom and Gibeah, 33
Sodomites, 69, 107, 111, 134, 139, 146, 149
sodomy, 63, 64, 74, 98, 127
Solon, 87
sons of Belial, 66
Sparta, 93
Spartan lifestyle, 83

Sporus, 106
Stadelmann, R., 38
Stoics (Stoicism), 119, 120, 126, 127, 158
Strabo, 42
Suetonius, 130
Summa alu, 44
Symposium, 90, 95, 103

T

Talmud, 34, 63
tappau, 41, 44
Targum Jonathan, 110
Te Velde, H., 37
tearoom(s), 29-31
telete, 64
Testament of Naphtali, 113
Testaments of the Twelve Patriarchs, 112
testosterone, 14
thelus, 125
thiasos, 85
Thielicke, H., 4, 7, 54
Thompson, J. A., 72
Timarchos, 89
Timarchus, 136
to^{c}ebah, 60, 61

Trade, 30, 31
transvestite behavior, 47

V

Veyne, P., 106
von Rad, G., 52, 67
von Wilamowitz-Moellendorf, Ulrich, 85
Vulgate, 64

W

Ward, I. L., 17, 20
Weltge, R. W., 21, 22
West, D. J., 13
Westendorf, W., 36
Wolfenden Report, 14, 23, 31, 55
Wood, L. R., 76
Woods, R., 5, 10
Wright, D. F., 135

Y

yada^c, 56, 61, 66, 72, 157
Young, W. C., 17

Z

Zeus, 97